AMERICA'S
WAR
MACHINE

AMERICA'S WAR MACHINE

VESTED INTERESTS, ENDLESS CONFLICTS

JAMES McCARTNEY

WITH MOLLY SINCLAIR McCARTNEY

Thomas Dunne Books
St. Martin's Press New York

THOMAS DUNNE BOOKS.
An imprint of St. Martin's Press.

AMERICA'S WAR MACHINE. Copyright © 2015 by Molly Sinclair McCartney.
All rights reserved. Printed in the United States of America. For information,
address St. Martin's Press, 175 Fifth Avenue, New York, N.Y. 10010.

www.thomasdunnebooks.com
www.stmartins.com

Designed by Meryl Sussman Levavi

The Library of Congress Cataloging-in-Publication Data is available upon request.

ISBN 978-1-250-06977-1 (hardcover)
ISBN 978-1-4668-7876-1 (e-book)

Our books may be purchased in bulk for promotional, educational, or business use.
Please contact your local bookseller or the Macmillan Corporate and Premium Sales
Department at (800) 221-7945, extension 5442, or by e-mail at MacmillanSpecial
Markets@macmillan.com.

First Edition: October 2015

10 9 8 7 6 5 4 3 2 1

Love forever

to Becky, Dan, Maggie,
Jessica, Kristen, Liam,
and all those who will shape the future

CONTENTS

OPENING NOTE

James Harold McCartney met the military world as a teenage soldier from East Lansing, Michigan, living in foxholes on the front lines in France and Germany in World War II. In late March 1945, he was walking along a road in the suburbs of Worms, Germany, near the Rhine River when he and his group of GIs heard incoming artillery fire from the Germans' deadly eighty-eight-millimeter guns. The GIs dived into a ditch. Jim landed facedown to protect himself. It didn't work. He was hit by shrapnel that sliced into the seat of his pants, tearing a gaping hole and leaving him a bloody mess. He passed out from the injury and was airlifted to a military hospital for treatment. He was recovering there on April 12, 1945, when a nurse came through his ward announcing that President Franklin Roosevelt had died.

Home from the war and finished with college, Jim went to work as a reporter for the *Chicago Daily News*. In 1961, as a new member of the newspaper's Washington bureau, he was assigned to cover Dwight Eisenhower's final speech as president. Deep into the text, Ike said, "We must guard against the acquisition of unwarranted influence, whether sought or unsought, by the military-industrial complex. The potential for the disastrous rise of misplaced power exists and will persist."

Newspaper stories about the speech were mixed, to say the least.

Editors at the *Chicago Daily News,* where Jim worked, saw the president's warnings about the military-industrial complex as the vague musings of the "old soldier" and buried them inside a story on page 14. The part of Ike's speech that made the front page was Jim's story on the economy; the headline was "Economic Outlook Bright, Ike Insists." *The Wall Street Journal* published a brief front-page item that quoted the president's forecast of "a pickup in business shortly" but did not mention the military-industrial complex. *The Evening Star* newspaper in Washington, D.C., had a similar spin with a headline that read: "Eisenhower Predicts Early Economic Upturn."

The *Chicago Tribune* lead story headline was "President Warns Red Struggle Will Go On." The *Washington Post* report began this way: "In a farewell to the Nation, President Eisenhower said last night that the Communist danger promises to be of 'indefinite duration.'"

The *Los Angeles Times* published a banner headline—"Ike Warns of Danger in Massive Defenses"—and a story about the "unwarranted" influence of a military-industrial complex. *The New York Times* summed up the story with this headline: "Eisenhower's Farewell Sees Threat to Liberties in Vast Defense Machine."

But, as Jim often said to me and to others, none of the stories published about Ike's speech at the time explained the military-industrial complex or the danger it represented in terms that would matter to the average reader. He said that he personally was baffled by the president's language. "I didn't know what Eisenhower was talking about." But he was curious and began researching the issue. Ten months later, in November 1961, his five-part series on the military-industrial complex was splashed across the front page of his newspaper. It was a focus that Jim would never relinquish.

As a Nieman Fellow at Harvard University in 1963–64, Jim studied national security issues. His classes included one taught by Henry Kissinger, a faculty member who became secretary of state under President Richard Nixon.

In 1968, Jim joined the Knight newspaper chain as its Washington-based national security correspondent. He reported from more than thirty countries, writing about the U.S. war in Vietnam, the Cold War with the Soviet Union, the confrontations in the Middle East over oil and arms, and American military interventions in Grenada, Panama, Haiti, and elsewhere.

From those experiences, Jim saw the growing military-industrial nexus as a war machine that imperils our country. It erodes our democracy, leads us into endless conflicts, and adds billions to our debt.

In his news stories and in columns, Jim sought to explain this complicated issue to readers by translating the jargon and double-talk of policymakers into stories that made sense. He saw his readers as people who work hard to support their families, who care what Washington does with their money, but who may not always have time to read and digest the decisions of Big Government.

But he also sought to reach policymakers and academics by asking tough questions and using their answers—and nonanswers—in the articles he wrote to reveal the truth.

In his retirement years, Jim taught at Georgetown University. One of his most popular courses was War and Peace and the Media, which focused in part on the war machine. Students gave him outstanding evaluations.

Jim's passion on this issue flared anew on February 5, 2003, when Secretary of State Colin Powell addressed the United Nations Security Council in a speech intended to justify the U.S. invasion of Iraq over its alleged possession of or quest for nuclear, biological, or chemical weapons. After watching the speech on television, Jim declared that the allegations were bogus and that the United States had no evidence that Saddam Hussein had such weapons.

"We have no business going into Iraq," he said. "We don't know what we are getting into, except that it means a lot of people are going to be killed."

This became the theme of the classes Jim taught, the newspaper columns he wrote, and the speeches he gave to veterans, civic groups, and political clubs. He argued that the U.S. invasion of Iraq was the latest example of pro-war constituencies out of control. People would listen and then say that they had no idea that this was how our defense system works. They urged Jim to write a book explaining America's war machine.

He had finished more than half of this manuscript and written an outline for the rest when he died May 6, 2011, after a brief battle with cancer. As his wife, I listened to his speeches, prepared the graphics for his talks, and read his newspaper reports about this during more than twenty-six years of marriage, and I am convinced he was right. He was an independent thinker who had the credentials and the intellect to prove his point of view. As a journalist myself with more than thirty years of reporting experience at five newspapers, including fourteen years at *The Washington Post,* I admired his ability to ferret out the truth in these life-and-death issues and explain it in understandable terms. I found his views consistent with those I developed in my studies at Georgetown University, where I earned my bachelor's degree, and at Harvard University, where I was a Nieman Fellow in 1977–78. I have also had the benefit of travel to many countries in Asia, Europe, and the Middle East, including a trip to Syria in 2010, just months before its civil war broke out.

Most recently, I had the opportunity as a 2012 Public Policy Scholar at the Woodrow Wilson International Center for Scholars in Washington, D.C., to update, edit, and expand Jim's manuscript. With Wilson Center resources, I have added information on defense spending and national security policy. The twelve chapters provide readers with a guide to what has become America's war machine, how it works, and why it is everybody's business.

—MOLLY SINCLAIR MCCARTNEY

AMERICA'S
WAR
MACHINE

PROLOGUE

Along with five thousand other soldiers, I crossed the Atlantic Ocean in the Army troop ship *George Washington,* landed in southern France, and rode a truck five hundred miles north into the Vosges Mountains to fight in the front lines against Nazi Germany. It was October 1944 and I was nineteen years old. The weather was bitterly cold. We forged ahead in summer uniforms because winter clothing had not caught up with us.

As we ascended single file up a mountain trail toward the Germans, we met American soldiers coming down carrying stretchers of the wounded victims of what we came to call "shoe mines," which the Germans planted to cover their retreat. A shoe mine typically was a small container about the size of a cigar box, buried just below the surface of the path. The box lid was propped up by a matchstick, which would collapse if you stepped on it, setting off the charge—about a quarter pound of TNT.

It was just enough to blow off a man's foot.

The guys on the stretchers had lost their feet to the shoe mines. We could see their bloody stumps as they passed. Even worse was what happened in my company about ten days after we got into the mountains. A patrol of six GIs was leading the way up the trail, trying to avoid the shoe mines. As night began to fall, the Germans unleashed an eighty-eight-millimeter artillery barrage, and the guys in the patrol sought to take cover off the trail. The sergeant in charge fell on a shoe mine, losing his right hand. When he tried to crawl for help, he set off another shoe mine, blowing off one of his legs. I don't know if he lived, but all of the others on that patrol were wounded either by shoe mines or by incoming eighty-eights.

I was in combat from the first of November 1944 until the end of March 1945. We did not receive warm winter clothing until sometime in December. We did not receive winter footwear until January. We pushed forward past dead Germans and the rotting corpses of cows, horses, and sheep. We dug foxholes in frozen ground and chopped down trees to provide cover over our foxholes. Many times in the snow and rain, you would get six inches of water in your foxhole during the night, but you dared not get out of the foxhole because of incoming artillery.

My mind has blissfully blanked out many details of that winter in the mountains with the 100th Infantry Division, 398th Regiment, and then with the 45th Infantry Division, 179th Regiment. What I will never forget is the horror. Looking back, I believe that my combat experience was the beginning of a lifelong journey to understand war and the American War Machine that has evolved since World War II.

As a Washington-based correspondent, starting in the 1960s, it was my job to report on national security and defense. In the years since, I have studied these issues and written about their consequences. Now I am putting what I have learned into this book as a way to help people understand how America has come to have vested interests in war, a concept apparently alien to many Americans, who think of their country as a force for peace and stability. Yet the facts show that a vast complex of political and economic forces has developed in America over the last half century that pushes us into wars and interventions. These forces now dominate American foreign policy.

And I would go further. I believe that these forces now threaten the very foundation of a democratic society.

These forces have led us into interminable military interventions, with no indication that even a relatively enlightened administration—as we have under President Barack Obama—understands them well enough to mount an effort to bring them under control.

When President Dwight D. Eisenhower used his farewell address to warn Americans of the dangers of the military-industrial complex, he foresaw its potential to undermine democracy. "We must not fail to comprehend its grave implications," he said. "Our toil, resources, and livelihood are all involved; so is the very structure of our society."

Tragically, Eisenhower's warning has not been heeded, and the problems he feared have exploded.

These forces and their interconnections are poorly understood. They are rarely examined publicly. There has never been a congressional investigation of anything resembling a military-industrial complex. I know of no effort by any of the most influential newspapers or television networks to try to analyze and explain, in ways that are clear to the average person, these forces and how they work. There has been no Ken Burns documentary.

There are reasons for this. It is easy to understand why Congress has avoided the questions, because Congress is a major part of the problem. Jobs created by defense spending create vested interests in military action, and few members of Congress are willing to oppose defense spending in their states or districts.

In the academic world, much has been written about growing American militarism and the building of the so-called American Empire. But little explanation of the forces at play has been provided for the people of Main Street or for students in the classroom, who believe in a good America and who may be reluctant to question the president, the Congress, or other top decision makers for fear they will be seen as unpatriotic.

The development and growth of these forces is a direct result of the Cold War and the building of what is best described as our national security state over the course of more than half a century.

This process began in the late 1940s and expanded dramatically with the Korean War, which began in 1950. Even though that war ended in 1953, defense spending remained at historic levels as fear of communist expansion dominated American politics. Defense spending soared in the mid-1960s as the Vietnam War intensified. With President Ronald Reagan's military buildup in the 1980s, Cold War defense spending hit a new peak of $552 billion.

Times changed with the collapse of the Soviet Union. In a 1992 program sponsored by the liberal Center for Defense Information, the narrator made this observation: "During the 1980s, the military spent more than two trillion dollars to wage the Cold War against the Soviet Union. Now the Soviet Union no longer exists. The Cold War is over. Common sense dictates spending less money on defense."

A modest reduction in defense spending occurred in the 1990s, under President Bill Clinton.

But with the September 2001 attacks, defense spending skyrocketed. We launched two wars and churned out more Cold War weapons even though some of them were useless against our new enemies—the terrorists living in caves and among the people of Afghanistan, Pakistan, and other Middle Eastern countries. Our invasions of Afghanistan and then Iraq killed more than 350,000 people and added billions to the defense bill. The fiscal year 2013 budget for the new Department of Homeland Security was $59 billion. With 240,000 employees, DHS is the third-largest cabinet department after the Department of Defense and the Department of Veterans Affairs.

Today the United States spends about as much on its military as the next nine countries with the largest military spending combined.

The questions raised in this book are simple: Why does the American military budget continue at near-record levels—even under President Obama—when the Cold War ended in 1991? Why does the United States continue to act as the world policeman, with bases and ships all over the globe? Why has the role of the military continued to expand, including a new tilt to Asia, even as U.S. combat troops have been pulled from Iraq and Afghanistan?

A review of the federal budget tells the story. Defense spending nearly doubled in the decade after 2000 as the United States focused on the terrorist threat. The United States now spends nearly $1 trillion annually on defense, including the Pentagon budget, the wars, Homeland Security, nuclear weapons, veterans benefits, and various other defense-related expenses. U.S. defense spending today averages 20 to 30 percent more than during the Cold War.

Our two most recent wars—Iraq and Afghanistan—cost more than $1 trillion, and that price could reach $4 trillion to $6 trillion in future years due to interest on our war debt and benefits for our veterans, including the thousands disabled and damaged in those wars, many of them grievously. If the war costs soar to $6 trillion as predicted, that would be the equivalent of about $75,000 for every American household, according to the calculations of Linda J. Bilmes of the Harvard University Kennedy School of Government.

The growing power of our national security state and its negative effects raises many questions. As part of its campaign to make us safer, the federal government has created or reconfigured an estimated 260 organizations as a response to the attacks in September 2001. Republicans, who normally stand for smaller government, have endorsed this expansion, along with Democrats, afraid of being smeared as soft on defense. In the name of security, we are subject to ridiculous screenings at airports and public buildings. Our communication via telephones and other devices is subject to monitoring. And drones seem to be everywhere, from Pakistan to the Mexican border.

Meantime, we have continued our historic record of wars and interventions that are difficult to defend in retrospect.

Why did President George W. Bush insist on invading Iraq—staging a preemptive strike that relied on flawed intelligence and think-tank advocacy? Why did we stay there when allegations of Iraq's possession of weapons of mass destruction were proved false?

Why did we escalate the war in Afghanistan in a supposed effort to confront Al Qaeda when government officials estimated that Al Qaeda had no more than a few hundred members in Afghanistan? Why have we remained in Afghanistan long after many Afghans called for us to leave—especially in the wake of the mistakes that American troops made in the 2012 burning of Korans and the tragic slaughter of unarmed children and families?

Why did the United States remain in Vietnam for more than a decade after Defense Secretary Robert McNamara privately concluded the war could not be won?

Why did Ronald Reagan invade Grenada in 1983?

Why did George H. W. Bush invade Panama in 1989?

Was Operation Desert Storm, the 1991 Gulf War under George H. W. Bush, necessary to extricate Iraq from Kuwait? What exactly did this war accomplish?

After the 2011 Arab uprisings, which began in Tunisia and Egypt and spread to Libya, there was a wave of calls for American military intervention. Some called for U.S. forces to establish a no-fly zone to stop Libyan leader Mu'ammar al-Gaddhafi from using his air force to attack Libyans who were seeking to overthrow his decades-long tyrannical rule.

Defense Secretary Robert Gates, a Republican originally appointed by President George W. Bush but kept on by President Obama, tried to discourage such speculation by pointing out that establishing a no-fly zone would require eliminating ground-based antiaircraft systems—which would be an act of war.

But his warning did little to stop the clamor for a no-fly zone. Even Senator John Kerry, a Democrat from Massachusetts, then chairman of the Senate Foreign Relations Committee, joined the pack along with an established liberal columnist, Nicholas Kristof of *The New York Times*, and a chorus of conservative Republicans and fearful Democrats.

Ultimately, we did get involved in Libya as part of a NATO military action aimed at protecting civilians. The result was a campaign that lasted for eight months—much longer than had originally been predicted—and ended with the killing of Libyan dictator Gaddhafi and the collapse of his government.

But it isn't clear yet how the winners in control of Libya will be better than the losers. Certainly the new Libyan government was unable to protect the U.S. consulate or the CIA listening post in Benghazi, both of which were attacked by anti-American terrorists in 2012, resulting in the deaths of the popular U.S. ambassador to Libya, Christopher Stevens, and three other Americans.

America, almost blindly, continues to attempt to dominate the world with military forces, even though the rationale for its massive military buildup has long since disappeared. We continue to build Cold War weapons long after the Cold War is over.

In countless documented examples, Congress and the executive branch have approved the building of weapons that the Pentagon did not consider necessary, costing untold billions—dangerous and unstable helicopters, submarines with no definable military role, cargo planes in numbers far beyond what the Pentagon requested.

We are building weapons to fight enemies that do not exist.

Gates, the former secretary of defense, has shown that he understands the problem far better than most of his predecessors. In office, he raised questions about unnecessary spending and made efforts to end a number of Cold War weapons systems, undoubtedly saving the taxpayers billions. He clearly saw that those with vested interests in defense spending in Congress contribute to the problem. His efforts should be applauded. But like other defense secretaries who contemplated an assault on this complex of interests, he failed to bring it under control.

Some on the left and on the right believe that the United States should be the world cop, and they are willing to foment exaggerated fears of what might happen if America pulled back or spent one penny less on defense. They testify before Congress about their fears. They write opinion pieces and appear as experts on television. They make headlines and try to scare others into believing that anyone who disagrees with them is unpatriotic and that we are only safe if we continue defense spending at record levels.

President Obama knows that America's worldwide superpower role must change. He spoke of economic constraints on American foreign policy when he announced in December of 2009 that he was sending an additional thirty thousand troops to Afghanistan rather than the forty thousand to eighty thousand originally recommended by the military. In going with the smaller number, Obama cited the need "to rebuild our strength here at home." He even made reference to Eisenhower's speech on the military-industrial complex, saying, "I'm mindful of the words of President Eisenhower, who—in discussing our national security—said, 'Each proposal must be weighed in the light of a broader consideration: the need to maintain balance in and among national programs.'"

More recently, in his January 28, 2014, speech before Congress, Obama pledged to get the United States off a "permanent war footing."

But don't expect change to come quickly—if ever. As debate has heated up over federal spending, including defense spending, there have been some reductions. U.S. defense spending is down slightly from its peak, mostly because of U.S. troop reductions in Iraq and Afghanistan. The 2011 spending cuts known as sequestration required a reduction in defense spending—with spending on wars exempt. It isn't clear that Congress has the political will to make significant defense cuts because of its own vested interest in defense jobs and the pressure from those who believe the United States should continue to be the world's protector, ready to send in boots, bombers, and Special Forces.

This book will identify and explain the powerful pressures, political and economic, aimed at justifying our defense policies and our defense spending. These forces are alive and well today in our politics and our economy, no matter what any president promises.

Describing all these forces as a war machine is an unsettling and upsetting concept to some people. But it is the best way to characterize the groups that dominate defense spending and play such an important and influential role in our national political system. It is not a pretty picture because it suggests a degree of greed and venality at the higher reaches of influence and power in our country. But the proof is rooted in our history, and it needs only a thoughtful review of that history to see how we have gotten to where we are today.

—JAMES McCARTNEY

1

MILITARY MIGHT AND MONEY:
THE PENTAGON RULES

*U.S. foreign policy is still too dominated by the military, too
dependent upon the generals and admirals who lead our
major overseas commands.*

—Admiral Mike Mullen, former chairman of the Joint Chiefs of Staff

If you think the State Department runs American foreign policy,
think again.

The primary force that controls U.S. foreign policy in most recent
administrations—including the administration of Barack Obama—
has been the Pentagon. In the simplest sense, the Pentagon is where
the money is, and in Washington, as elsewhere, money talks.

Even Admiral Mike Mullen, the former chairman of the Joint Chiefs
of Staff, has expressed concern about the Pentagon's overwhelming
influence on foreign policy. In a March 3, 2010, speech, Mullen declared, "U.S. foreign policy is still too dominated by the military, too
dependent upon the generals and admirals who lead our major overseas commands."

Former secretary of defense Robert Gates has made the same point, noting that it seems to be much easier for Congress to vote for money for the Pentagon than for the State Department.

The September 11 terrorists understood the sources of influence that drive the American government. In targeting Washington, they crashed their hijacked airplane into the Pentagon. They ignored the State Department.

No part of the American power structure has a deeper vested interest in war than the Pentagon.

The United States emerged as a superpower in the years of the Cold War, beginning in the late 1940s, with a vast structure of sophisticated military forces, thousands of nuclear weapons, and a worldwide network of military bases. An American empire was constructed, far stronger and more extensive than any of the great empires of history.

Because of the competition with the Soviet Union, few questioned the necessity of a substantial military budget. It was inherent in America's role as a leader of the so-called Free World. But the Cold War ended with the collapse of the Soviet Union in 1991, and elemental logic would seem to dictate a substantial change in military posture. That has not happened.

For at least the last three decades—ever since Ronald Reagan became president in 1981—and on many occasions before that, American foreign policy has had a distinct militaristic flavor that is well described by historian and former military officer Andrew Bacevich:

> Today as never before in their history, Americans are enthralled with military power. The global military supremacy that the United States presently enjoys—and is bent on perpetuating—has become central to our national identity. More than America's matchless material abundance or even the effusions of its pop culture, the nation's arsenal of high tech weaponry and the soldiers who employ that arsenal have come to signify who we are and what we stand for.

One measure of America's bent toward a militarized foreign policy is its defense budget. According to an analysis by the International Institute for Strategic Studies, a London-based authority on military spending, the United States outspends the rest of the world on defense. The IISS reported that the United States spent $739.3 billion in 2011, compared to a total of $486.7 billion for the next nine countries, including $89.8 billion for China, $62.7 billion for the United Kingdom, and $52.7 billion for Russia.

Money talks, and in the U.S. budget it screams military.

UNITED STATES OUTSPENDS THE REST OF THE WORLD ON DEFENSE

Top Defense Budgets for 2011 (in Billions of Dollars)

United States	739.3
China	89.8
United Kingdom	62.7
France	58.8
Japan	58.4
Russia	52.7
Saudi Arabia	46.2
Germany	44.2
India	37.3
Brazil	36.6

Information from 2012 report by International Institute for Strategic Studies.

Note: U.S. totals shown are for basic defense spending and do not include nuclear, veterans affairs, military retirement, retiree health care, or Homeland Security.

As of 2013, the U.S. Defense Department employed more than 2 million people, including 1.4 million uniformed personnel and more than seven hundred thousand civilians, plus another 1.1 million part-time members of the National Guard and Reserves. The State Department employed about sixty-nine thousand people, including its Foreign Service, Civil Service, and overseas staff. Depending on whether you count the military's part-timers, the Department of Defense is thirty to forty-six times larger than the Department of State.

American foreign policy is meant to be run by the State Department, with its diplomatic officers on the front lines researching international affairs, negotiating with foreign governments, promoting

America as a partner, and protecting U.S. citizens. But a sad clue to the real balance of power is that the U.S. government in recent years has employed more musicians in military bands than it has diplomats. As ridiculous as that may seem, it's not a joke. In 2008, a typical year, the score was seventy-five hundred military musicians versus fifty-five hundred diplomats.

Among the officials who have decried this imbalance are military leaders such as former defense secretary Robert Gates. In a lecture at Kansas State University, Gates said, "What is clear to me is that there is a need for a dramatic increase in spending on the civilian instruments of national security—diplomacy, strategic communications, foreign assistance, civic action, and economic reconstruction and development. . . . We must focus our energies beyond the guns and steel of the military, beyond just our brave soldiers, sailors, marines, and airmen."

For much of the past decade, the United States has struggled to help Afghanistan build a government that will meet its people's needs well enough to stabilize that country. The U.S. military established Provincial Reconstruction Teams to lead that work at the ground level. But when it needed U.S. diplomats to play key roles in working with local Afghan community leaders and officials, those jobs went unfilled because the State Department was too short on money to hire a thousand diplomats to fill vacant posts worldwide. As *New York Times* columnist Nicholas Kristof said in reporting that story, the State Department could have filled all those positions for the cost of just one military C-17 cargo plane.

That is one example of the dramatic imbalance between the resources the United States devotes to diplomacy and the resources it devotes to the military. In short, America channels far more money into war than into peace.

The irony is that diplomacy and negotiations are more likely to end terrorism than is war. Of 648 terrorist organizations that operated worldwide between 1968 and 2006, only 7 percent were defeated by military force, according to a 2008 study by the RAND Corporation, a U.S.-government-funded think tank. Fully 43 percent of terrorist campaigns came to an end when members of the terrorist groups decided "to adopt nonviolent tactics and join the political process," according to the RAND study. One example of a political settlement between a government and terrorist groups, RAND said, is the Belfast (Good Friday) Agreement, announced April 10, 1998, in which the Irish Republican Army "ended its terrorist activity following negotiations with the United Kingdom and the Republic of Ireland." The other major group (40 percent) of terrorists in the study were defeated by police and intelligence work—not military force—that saw their leaders killed or arrested.

In the first half of the Obama administration, the most reliable voice in articulating foreign policy was Defense Secretary Gates—not Secretary of State Hillary Rodham Clinton. Chuck Hagel, who replaced Gates, appeared to have more clout than John Kerry, who succeeded Clinton.

Like most of her predecessors in recent years, Clinton's role as secretary of state was largely verbal. She publicly defended policies developed in the Pentagon or by the White House national security apparatus, where the military mind-set is well represented. There is little evidence that Kerry has had any more success in setting policy than Clinton.

The record is clear on this imbalance. The Pentagon's top generals in the Middle East orchestrated the escalation of the war in Afghanistan; so far as we know, Clinton was barely involved.

The Pentagon's domination of American foreign policy is not new. As secretary of defense from 1961 to 1968, Robert McNamara was the principal architect of the war in Vietnam, acting as the agent of President Lyndon Johnson. Secretary of State Dean Rusk was little more than a salesman for the Vietnam War, a public defender of McNamara's decisions.

The most authoritative history of the Vietnam War is detailed in the *Pentagon Papers,* a study of U.S.-Vietnamese relations from 1945 to 1967 that McNamara had prepared within the Defense Department. McNamara didn't even bother to inform President Johnson or Secretary Rusk about the *Pentagon Papers,* which were leaked to *The New York Times* in 1971. While Rusk served as secretary of state from 1961 to 1969, he is not a major figure in the seven thousand pages of this record. There is no comparable State Department record of the war that dominated U.S. foreign policy for more than a decade.

A similar pattern played out in the decisions in the administration of President George W. Bush to invade Afghanistan in 2001 and Iraq in 2003. In his book *Rise of the Vulcans,* James Mann, of the Center for Strategic and International Studies, wrote that the Pentagon, under Defense Secretary Donald Rumsfeld, was "the driving force in American foreign policy." The invasion plans were also strongly supported by Vice President Cheney.

In the beginning, Secretary of State Colin Powell did argue against the 2003 Iraq invasion. Powell believed that sanctions against Iraq were working adequately to keep Saddam Hussein in check. In a meeting with President Bush, Powell warned that if the United States invaded Iraq and took down Saddam, "You are going to be the owner of twenty-five million people. You will own all their hopes, aspirations, and problems. You'll own it all." The president chose to ignore Powell's argument. The Pentagon won.

When President Bush felt he needed someone credible to make the case for war to the United Nations Security Council, he called upon Powell—and Powell accepted the assignment. In his infamous speech, he declared, to his everlasting shame, that the United States had proof that Iraq possessed weapons of mass destruction—which was not true. Powell, the secretary of state, like his predecessor Dean Rusk, was little more than a puppet.

An earlier sign of the Pentagon's foreign-policy dominance followed Saddam Hussein's invasion of Kuwait in August 1990. In response, President George H. W. Bush—Bush the elder—sent a team to Saudi Arabia to meet with King Fahd. Bush did not dispatch his secretary of state, James Baker, for that mission. Rather, the team was full of Pentagon officials, headed by Secretary of Defense Dick Cheney and including Defense Department aide Paul Wolfowitz; General Norman Schwarzkopf, the commander of U.S. forces in the Persian Gulf; and Pentagon spokesman Pete Williams, who left the Defense Department in 1993 to become a correspondent for NBC News.

Cheney had two objectives: first, persuade the king that Saddam Hussein intended to invade Saudi Arabia, and second, offer American troops for Saudi defense.

In his book *The Commanders,* Bob Woodward says that the Cheney group showed the king "satellite pictures of Iraqi tanks on the way to the Saudi border" and "SCUD launchers pointing menacingly south." After hearing the Cheney presentation in early August 1990, the king agreed to invite U.S. troops into his country, which has a quarter of the world's oil reserves.

But were Iraqi troops really massing on the Saudi border? Or was the government claim of an Iraqi troop buildup part of a U.S. disinformation campaign to build support for the U.S.-led invasion?

In a front-page story published January 6, 1991, *The St. Petersburg Times* said that it had obtained commercial satellite photographs showing "no evidence of a massive Iraqi presence in Kuwait in September" 1990. Reporter Jean Heller said that Peter Zimmerman, a George Washington University satellite-imagery expert, had examined the photos of the border between southern Kuwait and Saudi Arabia and found no Iraqi troops visible near the Saudi border.

If there had been Iraqi troops on the way to the Saudi border in August, as the Cheney group claimed, why didn't those troops appear in the September photos?

Others had the same photos and the same questions, but "cautiousness overcame curiosity," according to John R. MacArthur in his book *Second Front: Censorship and Propaganda in the Gulf War.* The result, he wrote, was that "nothing was reported" in the media besides Heller's story. MacArthur also says that Pentagon spokesman Pete Williams admitted to the *Washington Journalism Review* that he discouraged ABC, CBS, and the *Chicago Tribune* from pursuing the story.

There have been powerful secretaries of state: George Marshall in the Truman administration, John Foster Dulles in the Eisenhower administration, and Henry Kissinger when he held that title in the Nixon administration. Marshall, although a retired general, proved to be one of the great secretaries of state. Dulles and Kissinger were hard-line conservatives, each contributing to the militarization of American policy.

After the Soviet Union collapsed in 1991, signaling the end of the Cold War, efforts were made to revamp U.S. defense policy and cut back on military spending, but they did not last. In the immediate aftermath, cuts were made in military personnel. The armed forces shrank from 2.1 million personnel in 1989 to 1.3 million in 1999. The defense budget declined from $439.6 billion in 1992 to $391.1 billion in 2000.

But that pattern changed sharply with the election of George W. Bush as president and the terrorist attacks on September 11, 2001. In the eight years of Bush's administration, from 2001 to 2008, the defense budget nearly doubled.

The numbers tell the story of the tilt to war spending. The Department of Defense base budget by 2010 was $579 billion, not counting the supplemental war budget or other defense-related expenses. The State Department budget stood at about $50 billion.

Even if the United States cut its military budget in half, it would still be far bigger than that of any conceivable rival. According to a comparison of ten countries by the International Institute for Strategic Studies, the U.S. base defense and supplemental war budget for 2011 was $739.3 billion—about fourteen times as much as Russia's, twelve and a half times as much as France's, and eight times as much as China's.

Wall Street Journal economics editor David Wessel provided an even more impressive comparison. In his 2012 book *Red Ink*, Wessel notes that the U.S. defense budget is more than the combined military budgets of the next seventeen countries: China, the United Kingdom, France, Russia, Japan, Saudi Arabia, Germany, India, Italy, Brazil, South Korea, Australia, Canada, Turkey, the United Arab Emirates, Spain, and Israel.

Wessel estimates that $1 of every $5 the federal government spent in 2011 went for defense.

U.S. defense spending soars to nearly $1 trillion annually when all defense expenditures are counted, such as veterans benefits, Homeland Security, and other defense-related activities.

WE SPEND ABOUT $1 TRILLION ANNUALLY FOR NATIONAL SECURITY
(Figures in Billions of Dollars)

	2014 as Enacted	2015 as Requested
DOD base budget discretionary	496.0	495.6
DOD base budget mandatory	5.7	6.2
DOD base budget total	501.7	501.8
Overseas Contingency Operations	85.2	79.4
DOD Subtotal	**586.9**	**581.2**
Department of Energy, Nuclear	18.6	19.4
Defense-related	8.2	36.0
National Defense Total	**613.7**	**636.6**
Military retirement costs	35.8	37.8
DOD retiree health care	1.1	0.1
Veterans Affairs	151.3	161.2
International affairs	38.5	39.0
Homeland security	51.0	52.1
Share of interest on debt	76.3	82.7
Grand Total	**967.9***	**1,009.5**

Source: Winslow Wheeler, Director, Straus Military Reform Project, Project on Government Oversight
*Total is the result of rounding.

The size of the Pentagon budget alarmed even Secretary of Defense Gates, who described spending after the September 11 attacks as the opening of a "gusher." By Gates's own admission, he was unable to bring it under control. But he did try, triggering alarm in the neoconservative community, where the mere suggestion of defense spending cuts is anathema.

Max Boot, one of America's most prominent advocates of a militarily aggressive foreign policy, exemplifies neoconservative thinking about America's military budget. Boot has in recent years argued that America must avoid cutting military spending as U.S. troops are pulled out of Iraq and Afghanistan. In a 2010 column for *The Washington Post,* Boot said America has excessively—and wrongly—demobilized its army after every major war all the way back to the Revolution. By sending its troops home after the defeat of Lord Cornwallis, Boot wrote, "we were ill-prepared to fight the Whiskey Rebellion, the quasi-war with France, the Barbary wars and the War of 1812—all of which might have been averted if the new republic had had an army and a navy that commanded the respect of prospective enemies, foreign and domestic."

The rule of the right wing as exemplified by Boot's arguments is that you cannot spend too much for defense. America is always too weak.

The nation's generals know how to play the Washington game and to advance their agendas. War is the name of their game. A dramatic illustration was provided by the successful campaign waged by the Pentagon and top officers in the Middle East to force President Obama's hand and obtain a substantial increase in the number of troops for the war in Afghanistan.

Obama had made clear in his 2008 election campaign that he intended to escalate the war in Afghanistan while getting out of Iraq, but had not said what troop levels he had in mind. Within weeks after assuming office, he paid off on his campaign pledge by ordering an additional twenty-one thousand troops to Afghanistan.

In the following months, he launched a broad review of the war, asking his military advisers to give him a range of options. As he did, the Pentagon and the generals waged a public campaign for a major new escalation that effectively boxed in an inexperienced Obama.

Their campaign was not subtle. General David Petraeus, who headed all U.S. forces in the Afghan region as chief of the U.S. Central Command, called *Washington Post* columnist Michael Gerson in September 2009. According to Bob Woodward, Petraeus told Gerson "that the war would be unsuccessful if the president held back on troops." Later that month Admiral Mike Mullen, chairman of the Joint Chiefs of Staff, said much the same thing in Senate testimony.

General Stanley McChrystal, the U.S. commander in Afghanistan, was even more blatant, leaking his sixty-six-page assessment of the war—a supposedly secret document written for Obama's review process—to none other than Bob Woodward, *The Washington Post's* master of inside dope.

McChrystal's report called for forty thousand more troops within a year. If he didn't get them, he wrote, the war "would likely result in failure."

This trapped Obama, for the president had sacked McChrystal's predecessor, General David McKiernan, only four months earlier. If Obama rejected McChrystal's now-public advice, Obama would have to fire his new commander—a step that would leave the new president looking indecisive in his wartime leadership. He would have risked a political firestorm. Obama understood he had been sandbagged, leaving him in a cold fury.

A month later, in October, McChrystal went further in a public speech in London. He publicly shot down an alternative approach to the Afghan problem supported by Vice President Joe Biden, a prominent voice in Obama's foreign policy deliberations. Biden, having served as chairman of the Senate Foreign Relations Committee, opposed sending more troops to Afghanistan and sought instead to focus on fighting Al Qaeda militants in Pakistan.

Asked if he supported that approach, McChrystal said, "The short answer is no."

Both President Obama and Defense Secretary Gates clearly sensed they had been outfoxed. Both issued public statements deploring leaks of highly confidential information. But it was too late. McChrystal and the Pentagon had won.

Under pressure from the leaked assessment, Obama made a complex and somewhat contradictory decision. He agreed to add thirty thousand more troops to Afghanistan but said he would begin withdrawals after eighteen months.

Obama had learned a lesson. He did not intend to get trapped again. In late November 2009, as he prepared to formally announce his plans, he summoned his top national security team to the Oval Office. Those attending included Gates, Mullen, Petraeus, Joint Chiefs vice chairman General James Cartwright, and National Security Adviser James Jones. Here is how the conversation went, according to journalist and bestselling author Jonathan Alter:

> Obama asked Petraeus, "David, tell me now. I want you to be honest with me. You can do this in eighteen months?"
>
> "Sir, I'm confident we can train and hand over to the ANA [Afghan National Army] in that time frame," Petraeus replied.

"Good. No problem," the president said. "If you can't do the things you say you can in eighteen months, then no one is going to suggest we stay, right?"

"Yes, sir, in agreement," Petraeus said.

"Yes, sir," Mullen said.

Gates said he agreed as well.

The president clearly wanted to nail down the military agreement to accept troop withdrawals without complaint. The transcript of the discussion was then leaked to Alter so that the record was clear.

Bob Woodward gave a similar account of the meeting in his book *Obama's Wars*. The president is quoted as telling the assembled group, "I need you to tell me now whether you can accept this [decision to send thirty thousand more troops]. And if you can't, tell me now. If you can, then I expect your wholehearted support. And that includes what you say in public, to Congress, and internally to your own organizations."

Obama then handed all the officials a six-page, single-spaced "terms sheet" specifically outlining his decision. There would be no doubt about his intentions in making the decision.

But as Woodward put it starkly in his book, "The military was getting almost everything."

But McChrystal eventually went too far, and it cost him his job. In 2010, he agreed to allow a reporter for *Rolling Stone* magazine to travel extensively with him and sit in on conversations with him and with his staff, in which they criticized and belittled the president and high officials of the national security team. Obama had little choice but to fire him.

To control its message, maximize its impact on policy—and avoid the kind of media maelstrom that led to McChrystal's downfall—the Pentagon operates a vast propaganda machine, which has served Republicans and Democrats. The Defense Department doesn't say how much it spends to influence public opinion abroad and in the United States. But the Associated Press revealed at least a glimpse of it in 2009, finding in a yearlong investigation that the department spent at least $4.7 billion that year on a mix of public relations and propaganda campaigns.

The biggest chunk of funds (about $1.6 billion) goes into recruitment and advertising, AP found. Another $547 million goes into public affairs, which reaches American audiences. About $489 million more goes into what is known as psychological operations, which target foreign audiences.

"This year," the AP reported "the Pentagon will employ 27,000 people just for recruitment, advertising and public relations—almost as many as the total 30,000-person workforce in the State Department."

While the assistant secretary of defense for public affairs deploys thirty-eight hundred military and civilian personnel in the United States and worldwide to promote its information programs, the number of newspaper, news agency, and broadcast reporters assigned full-time to cover the Pentagon in 2010 was exactly ten, down from twenty-three in 2003, according to the *American Journalism Review*. Because of the financial crises faced by American newspapers and TV networks, the number was cut by more than half.

Pentagon propaganda programs take many forms. One that worked exceptionally well was the Pentagon's recruitment, during the Iraq and Afghanistan Wars, of seventy-five retired military officers who worked as supposedly independent "analysts" for U.S. television and radio networks. In reality, they were working to help promote the war—at taxpayer expense. They appeared on NBC, CBS, ABC, CNN, Fox, and MSNBC.

The program, first revealed in 2008 by *New York Times* reporter David Barstow, gave the officers special access to top government officials in exchange for pro-Pentagon commentary in their broadcasts.

The retired officers had a special incentive to hawk Pentagon assertions in their broadcasts. They were working collectively for more than 150 companies selling to the Pentagon. The special access to policymakers that they received by parroting the Pentagon's talking points about the wars gave them lucrative opportunities to pitch their companies' offers of everything from armored vehicles to Arabic-language translators. In a sign of the analysts' importance to the Pentagon's information war, Secretary of Defense Rumsfeld required that he personally approve each retired officer for inclusion in the program.

When Barstow's stories first appeared, the Pentagon denied the existence of such a program. Months later, however, an inspector general's investigation concluded that Barstow had it right. A statement was quietly issued withdrawing the denials.

In 2009, Barstow won the Pulitzer Prize for investigative reporting. The selection committee cited his "tenacious reporting that revealed how some retired generals, working as radio and television analysts, had been co-opted by the Pentagon to make its case for the war in Iraq and how many of them had undisclosed ties to companies that benefited from policies they defended."

One of the most prominent participants in the Pentagon program was Army general Barry McCaffrey, a retired four-star Army general who has continued as a defense analyst for NBC and MSNBC television. McCaffrey also worked for a company called Defense Solutions, which produced armored vehicles and wanted to sell them to the Pentagon for use in both Iraq and Afghanistan. While on the NBC payroll McCaffrey wrote a fifteen-page briefing packet recommending the use of five thousand of these armored vehicles to General David Petraeus, then the commanding U.S. general in Iraq. McCaffrey did not tell Petraeus he was working for Defense Solutions, nor did he tell NBC, where he often appeared. In testimony to Congress he once criticized a Pentagon plan to supply Iraq with armored vehicles made by one of Defense Solutions' competitors. McCaffrey said he had no difficulty separating his on-air analyses from his business interests. Really?

Commenting on McCaffrey's double life, reporter and press critic Charles Kaiser asked in an article for the *Columbia Journalism Review,* "Is there any limit to the shamelessness of NBC News?" As Kaiser explained, "That is one of several questions sparked by David Barstow's 5,000-word assault against the military-industrial complex in general and 'One Man's Military-Industrial-Media Complex' in particular—the one owned and operated by retired General Barry McCaffrey."

Kaiser concluded, "It turns out that McCaffrey is the living embodiment of all the worst aspects of entrenched Washington corruption—a man who shares with scores of other retired officers a huge financial interest in having America conduct its wars for as long as possible."

There could hardly be a better example of America's vested interests in war.

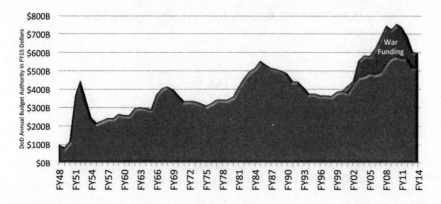

Source: Todd Harrison, Center for Strategic and Budgetary Assessments

This illustrates the base Department of Defense budget from 1948 to 2014 and the additional war funding from 2002 to 2014. These numbers do not include nuclear or other defense-related activities.

DEPARTMENT OF DEFENSE BUDGETS FOR 1948 TO 2015

Below are the Department of Defense base budgets in constant dollars, adjusted for inflation, from 1948 to 2015, from the DOD Green Book. War spending was included in base DOD budgets until 2001. The third column from 2001 to 2015 includes the base and war supplemental budgets. Omitted from these totals is the cost for veterans, nuclear, and other defense-related expenses.

Year	DOD Base (in billions of dollars)
1948	97,219
1949	83,206
1950	113,990
1951	365,027
1952	444,518 (Korean War peak)
1953	352,508
1954	245,975
1955	216,369
1956	227,298
1957	240,002
1958	239,754
1959	264,417
1960	257,660
1961	257,133
1962	295,301

(continues)

DEPARTMENT OF DEFENSE BUDGETS FOR 1948 TO 2015

(continued)

1963	301,100
1964	297,871
1965	289,387
1966	367,006
1967	404,436
1968	413,316 (Vietnam War peak)
1969	398,371
1970	364,144
1971	332,905
1972	334,901
1973	331,955
1974	323,665
1975	310,327
1976	323,553
1977	342,373
1978	341,420
1979	342,616
1980	359,541
1981	409,621
1982	459,336
1983	492,881
1984	513,211
1985	551,864 (Reagan buildup peak)
1986	529,372
1987	514,290
1988	505,877
1989	498,641
1990	484,767
1991	441,336
1992	439,643
1993	407,383
1994	374,772
1995	373,361
1996	364,868
1997	363,381
1998	359,759
1999	382,745
2000	391,065

(continues)

DEPARTMENT OF DEFENSE BUDGETS FOR 1948 TO 2015

(continued)

After the 2001 terrorist attacks in New York and Washington, the Bush administration began pumping additional money into defense in the form of supplementary defense spending. The third column includes base plus supplementary war spending in billions of dollars.

2001	381,988	419,804
2002	425,242	447,063
2003	463,598	555,661
2004	470,546	583,363
2005	486,422	581,097
2006	479,795	623,909
2007	490,136	681,972
2008	539,844	747,212
2009	568,952	728,717
2010	579,043	756,296 (war peak for Iraq and Afghanistan)
2011	567,271	736,589
2012	566,228	686,831
2013	519,537	604,192
2014	510,308	596,970
2015	501,851	501,851

Source: Todd Harrison, Center for Strategic and Budgetary Assessments

2
INDUSTRY AT THE WHEEL

Until the latest of our world conflicts, the United States had no armaments industry. American makers of plowshares could, with time and as required, make swords as well. But now we can no longer risk emergency improvisation of national defense; we have been compelled to create a permanent armaments industry of vast proportions. Added to this, three and a half million men and women are directly engaged in the defense establishment. We annually spend on military security more than the net income of all United States corporations.

This conjunction of an immense military establishment and a large arms industry is new in the American experience. The total influence—economic, political, even spiritual—is felt in every city, every statehouse, every office of the federal government. We recognize the imperative need for this development. Yet we must not fail to comprehend its grave implications. Our toil, resources, and livelihood are all involved; so is the very structure of our society.

In the councils of government, we must guard against the acquisition of unwarranted influence, whether sought or un-

sought, by the military-industrial complex. The potential for the
disastrous rise of misplaced power exists and will persist.

—President Dwight D. Eisenhower

A grim-looking President Eisenhower was sitting behind his desk in
the Oval Office on January 17, 1961, when he made his historic
televised speech warning the nation about the dangers of the military-
industrial complex. Today in black-and-white images on YouTube you
can see excerpts of him delivering the speech. But at the time, as I
watched him on TV and followed his words in a White House press
release containing the text of the speech, I was baffled.

What was he talking about? What was this military-industrial complex and why was it dangerous? As a Washington-based correspondent,
I had the opportunity to get answers to those questions, and to report
what I found in a five-part series that was published in November 1961
by my newspaper, the *Chicago Daily News.*

Those articles could be reprinted today because the story is essentially the same. The difference is that the complex has dramatically
expanded and defense spending has soared.

One of my articles, headlined "Pressure's on for Profits," focused on
how defense contractors wooed congressmen to win a share of the
money that the nation was spending on weapons and supplies at the
height of the Cold War. Here's the pattern described by one of my
sources, a former public relations man for a firm that held more than
$1 billion in defense contracts:

We staged huge selling campaigns at the Pentagon, setting up
dozens of interviews in a single week with procurement supply
officials. The campaign would be outlined in a book two inches
thick, organized to the finest detail, right down to selecting the
'psychologically right' colors for charts and graphs for maximum
selling impact. Our excuse for the meetings would be that we
wanted to bring the military up-to-date on our capabilities.

Really, we were selling.

The 1961 tactics that the man described have been replaced by PowerPoint presentations, e-mail, texting, cell phones, and other sophisticated forms of communication. But the pressure for defense contractors to land lucrative government contracts is as powerful—if not more so—than ever.

Access to contract deciders is key to the process. One way that contractors can get that is to hire former military officers, especially those who were part of or close to contract decision making in the active-duty services: Army, Navy, Marine Corps, Air Force, and Coast Guard.

Consider Gregory "Speedy" Martin, a four-star general in charge of Air Force weapons programs, including the B-2 stealth bomber. When Martin retired in 2005 after thirty-five years in the Air Force, he was offered two positions. Northrop Grumman wanted him to work as a paid consultant on the B-2. The Pentagon invited him to participate in a secret panel looking at stealth aircraft technology. He took both jobs.

In reporting the Martin story, *The Boston Globe* found "such apparent conflicts are a routine fact of life at the lucrative nexus between the defense procurement system, which spends hundreds of billions of dollars a year, and the industry that feasts on those riches. And almost nothing is done about it."

The *Globe*'s 2010 report and its conclusions were based on an analysis of the career paths of the highest-ranking generals and admirals who had retired during the last two decades. "For most, moving into what many in Washington call the 'rent-a-general' business is all but irresistible," the *Globe* said.

It is fair to say that the rent-a-general pattern is evidence that defense contractors now find these officers turned salesmen one of the best tools for winning contracts. This practice also suggests that the weapons or services purchased with taxpayers' dollars may be selected less on the basis of merit and more on who wins the race to hire the right three- or four-star insider.

From what I have learned in reporting and writing about this during my thirty-five years in Washington, the interconnections between military and industry help power America's war machine. Politics provides the fuel.

The revolving-door system between the Pentagon and the defense industry has been under attack for decades. In 1969, Senator William Proxmire, a Democrat from Wisconsin, declared, "The easy movement of high-ranking military officers into jobs with major defense contractors and the reverse movement of top executives in major defense contractors into high Pentagon jobs is solid evidence of the military-industrial complex in operation. It is a real threat to the public interest because it increases the chance of abuse. . . . How hard a bargain will officers involved in procurement planning or specifications drive when they are one or two years from retirement and have the example to look at of over two thousand fellow officers doing well on the outside after retirement?"

Proxmire said that 2,072 retired, high-ranking military officers were on the payroll of the nation's one hundred leading defense contractors. He called it a "most dangerous and shocking condition" that threatens the public interest by increasing the chances of abuse of the military procurement system.

In November 2009, *USA Today* published the first in a series of stories about a military mentor program in which dozens of retired officers working as consultants to defense contractors were hired to advise active-duty officers. In response to those articles, the Pentagon ordered a review of the program. Defense Secretary Robert Gates tightened the rules in 2010 to require mentors to file financial disclosures, but he did not eliminate the program. *USA Today* continued to publish articles raising questions about the mentors.

In a 2011 letter to Defense Secretary Leon Panetta, who succeeded Gates, Senator John McCain blasted the Pentagon mentor program for allowing a retired general turned Boeing executive to participate in a war game for a $51 billion aerial-tanker contract Boeing was competing to win. The general, Charles Robertson, was invited to take part in the exercise as an adviser to the Pentagon under its senior mentor program. In reporting the story, *USA Today* said that e-mails requested under the Freedom of Information Act showed that the Air Force was concerned about the potential conflict of interest and altered the war game to let him participate.

McCain, a Republican from Arizona and a member of the Senate

Armed Services Committee, criticized the Pentagon for taking two years to fulfill the FOIA requests and urged a "serious inquiry" into the mentor program.

Panetta eventually responded to McCain with a letter saying Robertson did not have a conflict of interest. Meantime, Boeing won the $51 billion contract to build the tanker for the Air Force.

In addition to defense contractors who build weapons, the military depends on service contractors who peel potatoes, serve meals, and do laundry for U.S. troops. This shadow army of contractors was intended to save money while making it possible for soldiers to concentrate on their main duties and for the armed services to stretch the capabilities of an all-volunteer military.

By 2008, the Department of Defense employed more contractors in Iraq than troops—155,826 private contractors and 152,275 troops. As of 2013, DOD had 108,000 contract workers in Afghanistan, compared to 65,700 troops—1.6 contractors for each soldier.

"This degree of privatization is unprecedented in modern warfare," according to a *Christian Science Monitor* opinion piece by Molly Dunigan, and has had deadly consequences. As of June 2012, for example, 1,569 American contractors had died in Iraq and 1,173 in Afghanistan.

One of the most sensational cases took place on March 31, 2004, when four security guards employed by Blackwater Worldwide were assigned to protect a convoy of three empty trucks going to pick up kitchen equipment in Fallujah, a city west of Baghdad. The Blackwater men were ambushed, killed, and set on fire before being dragged through the streets. As a jubilant crowd watched, two of their blackened, charred corpses were hung from a bridge.

Sadly, civilian contractors have been perpetrators of violence as well as victims.

On September 16, 2007, a group of Blackwater employees engaged in a firefight in a busy Baghdad square. Seventeen civilians were killed and more than twenty others wounded, including women and children. "It was a horror movie," according to an Iraqi policeman at the scene.

The FBI concluded that at least fourteen of the seventeen shooting deaths were unjustified. Five Blackwater guards were charged with manslaughter. The case was dismissed by a federal district judge in 2009 but reinstated by an appellate court in 2011. Four of the guards were convicted in a federal district court in October 2014. The fifth guard pleaded guilty to manslaughter and cooperated with prosecutors.

Blackwater founder Erik Prince, a former Navy SEAL, renamed the company Xe before selling it in 2010. The new owners changed the name to Academi and created a new Web site, but the company continues as an "elite services provider."

The heavy involvement of U.S. contractors was a defining feature of the American presence in Iraq. One of the biggest contractors was the Halliburton Company, whose CEO was Dick Cheney from 1995 until 2000, when he resigned to run for vice president of the United States. He was vice president, under President George W. Bush, from 2001 until 2009. There couldn't be a better example of the interconnections in the forces that make up America's war machine than the Halliburton-Cheney relationship.

For many years, Halliburton had exclusive rights to provide the military with a wide range of work that included "keeping soldiers around the world fed, sheltered and in communication with friends and family back home," according to a July 2006 report in *The Washington Post.* The deal represented billions of dollars for Halliburton.

But in mid-2006, at the height of the U.S. wars in Iraq and Afghanistan, the Army decided to discontinue its expensive, exclusive deal with Halliburton. In reporting the story, the *Post* said the military's decision came after years of complaints from people who saw the contract as a "symbol of politically connected corporations profiteering on the war."

Government audits had also turned up more than $1 billion in questionable costs. Whistle-blowers claimed that "Halliburton charged $45 per case of soda, double-billed on meals and allowed troops to bathe in contaminated water." Halliburton denied the allegations after pocketing more money, according to the *Post,* than any other contractor as a result of the invasion of Iraq.

The many billions of dollars sloshing around in the defense budget provide ample opportunity for corruption, greed, and other forms of avarice.

Contractor scandals are not new. As long ago as October 1975, I wrote stories about how Senate investigators had turned up evidence that at least eleven major defense contractors, including Northrop, had operated lush facilities to entertain Pentagon brass, including those for quail and pheasant hunting, yachting, and recreation. Northrop acknowledged use of a Maryland goose-hunting lodge to court Pentagon and congressional VIPs.

In responding to the scandal, Defense Secretary James Schlesinger said that defense contractors had apparently found a loophole in Defense Department regulations. A few weeks later, in November 1975, the Pentagon announced it was closing "potential loopholes" in its reporting rules that allowed some officials to receive free hunting trips and other favors from defense contractors.

Another memorable defense scandal was the $600 toilet seat, which made headlines in February 1985. Political cartoonist Herblock drew Defense Secretary Caspar Weinberger with a toilet seat hanging like an albatross around his neck. Asked about the $600 price, Lockheed Corporation president Lawrence Kitchen said his company had made only a 13.4 percent profit on the units, which were a special plastic case for the Navy's P-3C Orion antisubmarine planes. Even so, Kitchen reduced the price to $100 each and gave the Department of Defense a $29,165 refund.

The mideighties also saw reports of $660 ashtrays, $7,600 coffee-makers, and $74,000 ladders. President Reagan, who was pushing to build up America's defenses with increased spending, responded to these stories by declaring that "our attack on waste and fraud in procurement—like discovering that $436 hammer—is going to continue, but we must have adequate military appropriations."

As defense budgets have increased, so has the size of the spending scandals. In 2011, Boeing charged the Army $1,678 apiece for rubber cargo-loading rollers that actually cost $7 each. In 2012, Senator Tom Coburn, a Republican from Oklahoma, who puts out an annual report on government waste, said the Department of Defense could save $69 billion over the next ten years without cutting vital defense priorities. "Using defense dollars to run microbreweries, study Twitter slang, create beef jerky, or examine *Star Trek* does nothing to defend our nation," he declared.

In 2013, the Navy was hit with its biggest corruption scandal since the 1991 Tailhook incident in which more than one hundred U.S. Navy and Marine Corps aviation officers were alleged to have sexually assaulted eighty-three women and seven men at a Las Vegas symposium. In this latest case, a Malaysian defense contractor and the chief executive of Glenn Defense Marine, Leonard Glenn Francis, known as Fat Leonard because of his size, was alleged to have routinely overbilled the Navy for everything from tugboats to fuel. He was accused of bilking the U.S. Navy of more than $10 million. Helping him execute the scheme over several years were two Navy commanders, who were charged with providing him with classified information about ship and submarine movements. A Naval Criminal Investigative Service agent was also arrested. Fat Leonard paid his Navy informants with cash, prostitutes, and various other favors, including tickets to a Lady Gaga concert in Thailand.

The September 11 attacks unleashed a new flood of defense spending authorized by a nervous Congress eager to finance President Bush's war on terror. Contractors were awash with riches. *Time* magazine reported that U.S. military spending was $2,700 per capita in 2008, up from $1,500 per capita in 1998. The article, by Mark Thompson, said that our NATO allies spent only about $500 per capita over the same period. The U.S. willingness to spend big on defense, Thompson reported, allowed our allies "to skimp on theirs and instead pour their savings into infrastructure and healthcare."

Among the beneficiaries of government defense spending are the thousands of defense industry workers. Jennifer Rizzo reported for CNN in 2011 that about 3 million people are employed by the defense industry, "both directly, making things like weapons, and indirectly, such as working in local businesses supported by a contractor's location in a town." Rizzo explained, "It's these big money and job figures that make lawmakers fight for defense contracts in their districts and defense contractors lobby for their contracts."

Because of the high demand for technologically advanced

equipment in the military, a good proportion of defense industry jobs are well paying. The Aerospace Industries Association reported in 2012 that the average annual salary paid to aerospace and defense workers is $80,175, or about 80 percent more than the $44,410 that the average American worker earned at the time.

The sequestration that took effect in 2013 forced cuts in defense spending, at least temporarily. But defense contractors see cybersecurity as the next cash cow that could bring them billions of dollars. A market research report has estimated that the U.S. federal cybersecurity market could total $65.5 billion for 2013 to 2018. Senator Tom Carper, a Democrat from Delaware, said federal agencies had spent more on cybersecurity as of 2013 than the entire GDP of North Korea, a country that some have speculated is involved with some recent cyberattacks. "The issue du jour is cyber warfare. It isn't science fiction. It's reality," he said.

How close are the cyberspace contractors to the government contract deciders?

One answer is James R. Clapper, Jr., Obama's chief intelligence official since 2010 and a former executive with Booz Allen Hamilton, a $1.3 billion national security consulting company. Clapper is a retired Air Force general and his career path demonstrates how a military man can move to a defense contractor and then to the top of a federal spy agency. Talk about the revolving door.

Other famous Booz Allen employees include Edward Snowden, the young computer wizard earning $200,000 a year before he walked off with a computer full of national security secrets. Snowden leaked his material to the news media, embarrassing the Obama government and even Clapper, who told Congress in March 2013 that the National Security Agency was not collecting data on millions of Americans. Clapper later apologized for misstating the level of government monitoring.

Snowden, who fled the country, has been charged with espionage. His revelations, however, have provided an unprecedented look inside the global intelligence dragnet created by the NSA to capture an estimated 1.7 billion communication intercepts daily. To help with analyzing the information pouring into the NSA, the agency relies on more than 480 private companies including Booz Allen Hamilton, Boeing, SAIC, Northrop Grumman, Raytheon, and CACI International, to mention a few.

"Contractors have become essential to the spying and surveillance operations of the NSA," according to Tim Shorrock. In a 2013 *Salon* posting, he said 70 percent of national intelligence budgets are spent on the private sector. The largest concentration of these cyber contractors work in a business park about a mile from the NSA's headquarters in Fort Meade, Maryland.

Many defense contractors also have Washington offices near the Interstate 495 loop that is known as the Beltway and that passes near the enormous Pentagon complex in Arlington County, Virginia. Because these contractors feed on federal government contracts, they are known as Beltway Bandits.

In 1961, when I first wrote about the military-industrial complex, the headline described the political and economic forces at play in defense contracts as "our $25 billion tug of war." That's how much money the Department of Defense was spending a half century ago to buy everything from milk to missiles. But as big as that number seemed at the time, it is only a fraction of the $536.8 billion in defense contracts that the government awarded to 170,000 contractors in 2011. Much of the money ended up in the hands of a small group of big contractors who emerged in the consolidation of the arms industry that occurred after the Cold War ended.

With the September 11 attacks, hopes evaporated for a smaller defense budget that might produce a peace dividend. A Polaris Institute report put it this way: "The ongoing war on terror is providing greater protection for corporations through a war economy." Polaris, a Canadian think tank, explains, "The defense industry is now comprised of a few very large and powerful corporations who have the ability to dictate market prices and who possess enough power to play an influential role in the formation of defense policy. The giant military contractors are thriving in the present climate of heightened militarization and are being fostered by preferential treatment [subsidies] by the U.S. government and international bodies [World Trade Organization]."

Here's a look at the ten biggest defense contractors, based on a CNBC study of data from USAspending.gov, a Web site established by the U.S. Office of Management and Budget to make federal awards publicly available:

- Lockheed Martin. $40 billion in 2011 contracts. $46 billion in 2011 revenue. "Headquartered in Bethesda," a Maryland suburb of Washington, D.C. Lockheed "researches, designs, develops and manufactures satellites, space vehicles, combat aircraft, missile defense systems" and other products and services. "Lockheed's biggest contract 2012 was for $3.48 billion with the Department of Defense for a fixed-wing aircraft. In Lockheed's 2011 annual report, the company notes that it derives 82% of sales from U.S. Government customers, including 61% from the Department of Defense and 17% of sales to foreign governments."

- Boeing. $21.5 billion in 2011 contracts. $69 billion in 2011 revenue. "Boeing's main sources of revenue are commercial airlines," but its "Chicago-based company's Defense, Space & Security segment deals primarily with the U.S. government."

- General Dynamics. $19.5 billion in 2011 contracts. $33 billion in 2011 revenue. Based in Fairfield, Connecticut. Most of the company's contracts were with "the Navy ($12.9 billion) and the Army ($4.6 billion). Many of its large contracts include the manufacturing of submarines and destroyers, with its largest contract for a submarine worth over $2 billion."

- Raytheon. $15 billion in 2011 contracts. $25 billion in 2011 revenues. "Headquartered in Waltham, Massachusetts, Raytheon's . . . most recognizable product . . . is its Tomahawk cruise missiles, which are supplied to the U.S. Navy." The company's "major contracts" include "air defense systems, marine combat systems, missile systems and other military products."

- United Technologies. $8 billion in 2011 contracts. $58 billion in 2011 revenues. "Headquartered in Hartford, Connecticut," the company makes "a wide range of products, from aircraft engines and helicopters to fuel cells, elevators and building systems." Its largest contract in 2011 "was for $910 million to manufacture a gas turbine and jet engine aircraft."

- SAIC (Science Applications International Corporation). $7.4 billion in 2011 contracts. $11.1 billion in 2011 revenues. "Headquartered in McLean, Virginia." The firm's forty-one thousand workers are involved in robotics, information technology services, and intelligence analysis. (In 2012, *The Washington Post* reported that SAIC faced a scandal with a New York City contract. This news broke as SAIC sales and profits were slumping and the company was wrestling with several lawsuits. SAIC agreed to pay a $500 million fine to settle the case, removed three company executives, and hired a new CEO, who happened to be a four-star, retired Air Force general, John P. Jumper, sixty-seven. Jumper had been on the SAIC board since 2007 but had little corporate experience. *Forbes* reported his annual compensation in his new position was $2.75 million.)

- L-3 Communications (LLL). $7.38 billion in 2011 contracts. $15.17 billion in 2011 revenue. Headquartered in New York City, "L-3 describes itself as a 'prime contractor in command, control, communications, intelligence surveillance and reconnaissance systems; aircraft modernization; and maintenance and government services.'" Nearly half of the company's 2011 contracts were with the Air Force.

- BAE Systems. $6.9 billion in 2011 contracts. $30.1 billion in 2011 revenue. BAE "is a British multinational defense, security and aerospace company headquartered in Farnborough, UK. . . . Its largest contract was for a combat assault and tactical vehicle."

- Oshkosh Corporation. $4.94 billion in contracts. $7.6 billion in 2011 revenue. "Oshkosh, headquartered in Oshkosh, Wisconsin . . . has been a contractor [for] the U.S. Department of Defense for over 80 years, becoming its leading supplier of heavy- and medium-payload tactical trucks."

- McKesson Corporation. $4.7 billion in 2011 contracts. $112 billion in 2011 revenue. "Headquartered in San Francisco, California," McKesson "describes itself as a pharmaceutical distributor and health-care information technology company. A majority of the government contracts ($3.8 billion) with the company arose from the Department of Veterans Affairs."

Defense contractors have learned that the surest way to get Congress to approve defense projects is to locate the manufacturing of weapons and other products and services in as many states and congressional districts as possible. Thus defense work may be done in your very own hometown—whether it is needed, whether it is flawed, whether it is misguided—because it provides jobs. What member of Congress is going to vote against a deal that promises to bring jobs to his district and enhance the local economy?

The answer is hardly anyone.

The defense contractors will also probably want to build on their relationships with your representatives to Congress—and your president— by contributing to their election campaigns as well as their favorite charities and projects.

AMERICA'S ARMS MERCHANTS SELL TO THE WORLD

The business of selling conventional arms—including missiles, rockets, and torpedoes—to other countries is booming in peace-loving America.

U.S. commercial arms sales to the global community reached $44.28 billion in the fiscal year 2011—a $10 billion increase over the previous year, according to a report by the Center for Public Integrity, a nonpartisan investigative news organization. The report was based on a State Department review of commercial arms sales.

The center said these sales, along with government-to-government arms exports, make the United States the world's top provider of major conventional weapons. "Much of the recent increase came from vastly expanded sales to Saudi Arabia, Brazil and India," the center said.

Is this hypocrisy? You bet. Consider the record.

U.S. arms shipments approved by the State Department go to some countries that the very same State Department has criticized for abuse of human rights. The State Department has defended the shipment of arms to less than democratic countries by emphasizing that the arms are for external defense, not internal suppression.

The U.S. arms sales in 2011 of $44.28 billion went to 173 countries, including three with recent records of suppressing democratic dissent: Algeria, Egypt, and Peru.

The center reported that $877 million in weapons was authorized for Saudi Arabia, including firearms, toxicological agents that may have included tear gas and riot-control agents, heavy guns, explosives, missiles, rockets, and torpedoes as well as armored vehicles, aircraft, and guided-missile systems. Human rights problems with Saudi Arabia, the State Department said, included restrictions on freedom of expression and a lack of equal rights for women, children, and workers.

Israel was authorized to receive $1.5 billion in weapons similar to those going to Saudi Arabia. The State Department human rights review cited Israel for "terrorist attacks against civilians and discrimination against Arab citizens" in housing and employment as well as detention practices.

Bottom line: America, while professing to want peace in the world, has a vested interest in war.

3

CONGRESS AND THE WHITE HOUSE:
A VITAL PART OF THE PROBLEM

The military-industrial complex has become much worse than President Eisenhower originally envisioned: it's evolved to capture Congress. So, the phenomenon should now rightly be called the "military-industrial-congressional" complex.

—Senator John McCain, 2011

As the U.S. vice president in 2003, Dick Cheney pushed the George W. Bush administration into invading Iraq to overthrow Saddam Hussein. That policy victory confirmed Cheney's status as both America's most powerful neoconservative policymaker and its most accomplished political infighter.

But even Cheney's formidable skills proved unequal to an earlier battle he waged, as secretary of defense under Bush's father, President George H. W. Bush. In 1990 Cheney wanted Congress to fund the purchase of 120 C-17 cargo jets, built by McDonnell Douglas. That was as many of the giant planes as the military needed, Cheney said, and once they were built, the program should be terminated.

Congress disagreed and voted to provide more C-17s than the Pentagon wanted. And for twenty-plus years, under presidents of both political parties, Congress has continued to fund even more of the planes.

Robert Gates, who served as defense secretary under Presidents George W. Bush and Barack Obama, told Congress in April 2009 that the 205 C-17s then planned for the Air Force were enough and that the program should be halted. Congress ignored Gates, as it had ignored Cheney, and added another eighteen planes. The expansion of the fleet to 223 has come as the cost of each jet has spiraled from an initial $200 million to about $250 million.

Why? The answer is simple. The C-17 program supports 650 suppliers and more than thirty thousand jobs in forty-four states, according to Boeing, which inherited the program when it merged with McDonnell Douglas in 1997. The C-17 is not merely a defense program. It is also a welfare program, offering profits for companies, jobs for workers and unions, and political support for cooperative lawmakers. Planes the Pentagon has not thought necessary have been built to promote the reelection of congressmen and senators.

In 2009, *Bloomberg Business* summed up its story of the C-17 in the headline: "It's a Bird, It's a Plane, It's Pork!"

The C-17 is a dramatic example of the economic and political forces that have vested interests in a huge defense budget, in militarism, and even in war. If there is a safe vote for almost any congressman or senator in our militarized society, it is a vote for "strong" defense. A candidate for Congress who fails to support military spending in his or her district or state will be attacked by opponents as weak on defense.

When I wrote my Tug of War series for the *Chicago Daily News* in November 1961, I quoted Representative Jamie L. Whitten, a Democrat from Mississippi and a member of the House appropriations defense subcommittee, who made this point in testifying before a congressional committee: "I am convinced defense is only one of the factors that enter into our determination for defense spending. The others are pump priming, spreading the immediate benefits of defense spending, taking care of all the services, giving all defense contractors a fair share, spreading the military bases to include all sections." In comments on the

House floor, Whitten added that special interests involved in military spending are "probably the biggest factor in American domestic policy and politics."

David Packard, the multimillionaire who built the Hewlett-Packard Company and then joined the Pentagon as the number two man under Defense Secretary Melvin Laird in the early 1970s, estimated that "we could save a billion dollars a year" in defense spending "if we could act without constraints."

What kind of constraints?

"Political constraints," Packard said, making clear at a December 1971 press conference that he meant congressmen who didn't want to close military bases because they pour money into their districts. Packard's blunt assessment came as he was resigning his Pentagon job.

Secretary Laird was clearly sorry to see him go. "Dave Packard," he said, "is the best thing that has happened to the Department of Defense since it was established."

Traditionally, both America's conservative and liberal movements have found reason to critically examine and oppose proposed increases in military spending. The best example would be President Eisenhower, a Republican who used the White House to warn against the military in which he had served as a five-star general and as a leader of the Allied forces that won World War II. In his eight years as president, the former general sought to force the military to justify its programs. In a March 1956 meeting at the White House, he complained that it had taken the Army fifty years to get rid of horses, and he questioned why new Navy missiles cost so much more than the weapons they replaced. The meeting notes show Eisenhower becoming exasperated that "no one ever comes up to him and says 'let's get rid of something.'"

Liberals traditionally have favored spending on butter rather than guns. But those historical patterns have been upended to a large degree by the electoral power of the defense industries.

In 2006, Senator Barbara Boxer, a Democrat from California who is widely considered a liberal, was one of a group of eighteen senators who urged continued funding of the C-17 in spite of the Pentagon's arguments.

Boeing, which has been the plane's primary contractor since 1997, has a plant employing five thousand workers in Long Beach, California.

Similarly, Kit Bond, a Republican who represented Missouri in the Senate from 1987 until 2011, was an enthusiastic supporter. Boeing's defense business is headquartered in St. Louis, Missouri. "We need these planes," Bond said. "It is a defense industrial-base issue, too. It produces jobs in forty-three states. But that is secondary. We wouldn't push that unless there is a real need."

President John F. Kennedy held a press conference in the State Department auditorium on January 15, 1962—almost precisely a year after Eisenhower's farewell speech warning about the dangers of the military-industrial complex. I managed to get a seat near the front so that I could ask Kennedy if he had similar concerns.

Kennedy said that Eisenhower's point deserved "continuing attention." The problem, Kennedy said, is that "there gets to be a great vested interest in expenditures because of the employment that is involved, and all the rest, and that's one of the struggles which he had and which we have."

In other words, defense spending provides jobs.

Weapons makers are well aware of the desire by senators and congressional representatives—and presidents—to preserve jobs for their constituencies. But to insure their influence in Washington, contractors routinely donate millions of dollars in campaign contributions to support their favorites in both houses of Congress.

And those contributions pay off. According to a study by the non-profit, nonpartisan Center for Responsive Politics, the defense community donated $27 million to political candidates and committees during the 2012 campaign cycle. The biggest contributors included Lockheed Martin, Northrop Grumman, Boeing, Raytheon, United Technologies, and General Dynamics.

The study found that $16.4 million went to Republicans and $11 million to Democrats. Contributions were tilted toward House and Senate members who sit on the armed forces and appropriations committees that oversee military and defense spending and who are strong on defense. Representative Buck McKeon, a Republican from California, a hawk on defense, and chairman of the powerful House Armed Services Committee in 2013, had received more than $1.4 million in defense contributions since he first ran for the House in 1992, including $567,000 during the 2012 campaign. Senator Carl Levin, a Democrat from Michigan, who ran the Senate Armed Services panel and was viewed as far less friendly to defense, received only $495,000 from defense since his first Senate campaign in 1978.

Sometimes the dealings between eager defense contractors and hungry members of Congress go too far and break the law. Randy "Duke" Cunningham is a Vietnam war hero who became a powerful congressman, able to push multimillion-dollar defense deals through Congress. For fifteen years, beginning in 1991, he represented a district in San Diego with the nation's largest concentration of defense assets and the home port for more than half of the U.S. Navy's Pacific Fleet. Defense contractors courted Cunningham, helping him buy a $2.5 million California mansion and giving him the use of a luxury yacht and a Rolls-Royce. They gave him antiques and Persian rugs.

In 2005, Cunningham pleaded guilty to accepting $2.4 million in bribes in exchange for steering more than $200 million in federal deals to two defense contractors. He served seven years in federal prison.

The symbiotic relationship between defense industries and members of Congress is a root element of the military-industrial complex that President Eisenhower warned against half a century ago.

In his 1961 speech, Eisenhower didn't mention the role that Congress plays, but some sources have said that an early draft warned of the "growing influence of the military-industrial-congressional complex." This idea has been disputed, and an archivist at the Eisenhower Library said recently that none of the twenty or so drafts of the speech in their files include Congress as an element of the complex of forces that concerned Eisenhower.

But Melvin A. Goodman, a senior fellow at the Center for International Policy, reported in January 2011 that he was part of a small group of Johns Hopkins University students who heard from Ike's brother Milton that the president had considered saying "military-industrial-congressional complex." Milton Eisenhower was president of Johns Hopkins University and played an important role in the drafting and editing of that 1961 speech. According to Goodman's account, Milton Eisenhower told the students that "one of the drafts of the speech referred to the military-industrial-congressional complex" and that President Eisenhower had inserted that phrase himself.

According to Goodman, Milton Eisenhower asked his brother about the dropped reference to Congress in the delivered speech, and the president replied, "It was more than enough to take on the military and private industry. I couldn't take on the Congress as well."

In terms of public understanding, it was a tragic omission.

Senator John McCain, a Republican from Arizona, underscored this point in 2011 when he said on the Senate floor, "The fiftieth anniversary of President Eisenhower's address presents us with a valuable opportunity today to carefully consider, have we heeded President Eisenhower's admonition? Regrettably and categorically, the answer is no. In fact, the military-industrial complex has become much worse than President Eisenhower originally envisioned: it's evolved to capture Congress. So, the phenomenon should now rightly be called the 'military-industrial-congressional' complex."

And Congress is not the only branch of government in love with the defense industry. The executive branch is also guilty of pushing its favorite defense programs even when the professional military doesn't want them.

There is a history of this, says economist and defense policy expert Gordon Adams, who served as the senior White House official for national security from 1993 to 1997. The best example is President Ronald Reagan's 1983 proposal for the Strategic Defense Initiative—a vast high-tech network of laser-armed satellites and other weapons to be fired in case of a Soviet nuclear attack. The idea was to destroy the Soviet Union's incoming nuclear missiles and warheads before they could strike the United States. Critics derided Reagan's program, labeling it Star Wars. Mainstream scientific organizations such as the Union of Concerned Scientists and the American Physical Society declared the project impractical as a defensive shield.

"Everyone knew it was loony," says Adams. But Reagan was determined to go forward with the project, which he said would render nuclear weapons "impotent and obsolete." Sitting in his book-filled office at American University, where he is a professor of foreign policy, Adams said that none of the uniformed branches—Army, Air Force, Navy, Marines—wanted Reagan's Star Wars program included in their budgets because it "didn't fit with their core missions." To satisfy Reagan, the Defense Department created a new agency to fund the program.

A decade after Reagan launched Star Wars, the Soviet Union was history and President Bill Clinton scrapped the notion of building a national defense shield against attacks by intercontinental ballistic missiles. But Clinton kept the Star Wars initiative alive by shrinking it into a program to build smaller, regional missile defense systems. Its mission today is to defend against a future ability by rogue states such as North Korea to fire intercontinental missiles. Every president—Democrat and Republican—has continued to support some form of a Star Wars program, including Barack Obama.

In its 2011 budget request, the Pentagon asked Congress for $9.9 billion for missile defense. A House Armed Services subcommittee added nearly $400 million, which included $50 million for an airborne laser that many experts say doesn't work and that Defense Secretary Gates had largely canceled a year earlier.

Altogether, the United States has spent more than $200 billion since 1983 on missile defense and has yet to produce a reliable weapon. So why does it continue? Frances FitzGerald, in her acclaimed book *Way Out There in the Blue: Reagan, Star Wars and the End of the Cold War*, describes how the Star Wars program survived: "Every time the program seemed ready to expire, or collapse of its own weight, something would happen to bring it to life." In his 2000 review of FitzGerald's book, Stephen M. Walt summarized her conclusion: FitzGerald "suggests that the support is largely a matter of ideological conviction, but several other factors are at work as well. To begin with, the missile-defense program is now well entrenched within the defense establishment, and government programs rarely go out of business without a fight."

But let's return to Congress and its shocking defense-spending tradition.

The C-17—as explained earlier—is not the only cargo plane that has been vastly oversupplied beyond the Pentagon's official requests. The story of Lockheed Martin's C-130, dubbed the Hercules, is almost unbelievable. Produced in Georgia, it was shepherded through Congress by powerful southerners, including Georgia's Sam Nunn, the former chairman of the Senate Armed Services Committee, and former Speaker of the House Newt Gingrich, also of Georgia.

According to a 1998 report by the General Accounting Office (now the Government Accountability Office), from 1978 to 1998 the Air Force requested a total of 5 C-130s. Congress voted funds for 256—which led Senator John McCain, a conservative and strong supporter of the Pentagon, to complain, "We're purchasing equipment that the military neither wants nor needs." He said the pressure to keep building the planes was so great that "we're going to have a C-130 in every school yard in America."

Here is how the game is played: Defense industries seeking to sell a particular weapons system to the Pentagon and to Congress make an effort to develop a subcontracting pattern with manufacturing plants in as many states and congressional districts as possible. This virtually guarantees support for their weapons system, regardless of its merit or its need. Typically, for a major system—an airplane, a missile, a ship, a tank—contracts will be spread to forty or more states and as many congressional districts as possible.

Another way to support a favored member of Congress is to give money for a special event in his honor. At the Republican National Convention in 2000 a group of major corporations and industry groups bankrolled a lavish 1950s-style party and fund-raiser for Senate majority leader Trent Lott of Mississippi. Pop singer Bobby Vee and the Four Tops performed, and Dick Clark emceed the event, called the "Lott Hop," which attracted about fifteen hundred supporters for Lott, then one of the most powerful members of Congress.

Lockheed Martin, the top U.S. defense contractor, donated $60,000 toward the "Lott Hop," according to a 2000 report by William D.

Hartung and Frida Berrigan for the World Policy Institute. Lockheed Martin has—predictably—denied it was seeking to influence Lott, who was the Senate majority leader from 1996 to 2001.

As defense secretary in 1992, Cheney upbraided legislators in testimony before the Senate Armed Services Committee. "Congress has let me cancel a few programs, but you've squabbled and sometimes bickered and horse-traded and ended up forcing me to spend money on weapons that don't fill a vital need in these times of tight budgets and new requirements," he fumed. "You've directed me to buy the V-22 [Osprey helicopter], a program I don't need."

Cheney also testified, "You've directed me to buy more M1s, F-14s, and F-16s—all great systems, but we have enough of them." What was more, Cheney testified, "Congress has directed me to spend money on all kinds of things that are not related to defense, but mostly related to politics back home in the district."

Cheney tried to kill the V-22 Osprey program on four separate occasions, arguing that technical problems with the plane were irremediable, but Congress overruled him every time.

Inspired by the U.S. failure to rescue hostages in Iran in 1980, the V-22 Osprey is a hybrid plane designed to take off and land as a helicopter, but to fly like a plane. The Marine Corps has pitched the Osprey as its top priority for years. The Osprey was designed to transport combat troops, supplies, and equipment for the Marines and to support other armed services. But its development has been dogged by fatal crashes, including one in 1992 that killed seven. Efforts by the Pentagon— initially by Cheney—to halt the program have failed, largely because of congressional support in key manufacturing states: Texas, with Bell Helicopter, and Pennsylvania, with Boeing. More than two thousand smaller companies in forty states serve as suppliers for the V-22.

In October 2007, *Time* magazine devoted its cover story to the Osprey. The words on *Time's* cover neatly summed up the problem: "It's unsafe. It can't shoot straight. It's already cost 30 lives and $20 billion. And now it's headed for Iraq."

As *Time* reported, the Osprey was indeed put into service in Iraq. But the plane was so unreliable it could only be used as a troop carrier, not in combat. In Iraq it was used primarily to ferry visiting VIPs—presidential candidate Barack Obama flew in Ospreys during his 2008 tour of Iraq.

A Government Accountability Office report in 2009 said the Osprey had "not performed" as expected in Iraq and was capable of conducting missions only two-thirds of the time. The report cited unreliable component parts and said the Osprey had not achieved the "required level of versatility."

A few members of Congress have opposed the V-22. At a House hearing in 2009, after receiving the GAO report, Representative Edolphus Towns, a New York Democrat, said the program should be killed. "It can't be used in hot weather. It can't be used in cold weather. It can't be used in sand," Towns said. "The list of what the Osprey can't do is longer than what it can do." Towns, who served in the House until 2013, represented the Tenth Congressional District, which is entirely in Brooklyn. No defense contractors were in his district. The Osprey survived.

In April 2010, less than a year after the GAO report, an Osprey crashed in southern Afghanistan, killing three American military personnel and one civilian and injuring several others. Each Osprey cost about $100 million. At last count, the Osprey program had cost more than $20 billion, and its ultimate cost is expected to run to at least $39 billion, a 43 percent increase over original estimates.

Campaign contributions have clearly played a role in the votes cast by members of Congress. Studies by the Center for Responsive Politics have shown that defense contractors give millions of dollars to members of Congress who vote for defense weapons that include the Osprey, manufactured by Bell Helicopter and Boeing; Tomahawk missiles, made by Raytheon; high-tech aircraft, made by Lockheed Martin; the M1 Abrams tank, made by General Dynamics; and a host of other weapons systems.

Between 1990 and 2012, the defense sector contributed nearly $200 million to candidates, the center said, noting that it "also has a formidable federal lobbying presence, having spent $132 million in 2012."

Congress, often acting with shameful cynicism, routinely votes for elaborate and expensive weapons systems that the Pentagon has said the nation does not need. Take the case of the Navy's initial plan to modernize its destroyer fleet with a new ship called the DDG-1000. Here's what happened, according to *The Washington Post:*

In July 2008 intelligence reports led the Navy to change its mind about the DDG-1000. Fifteen separate reports concluded that the fourteen-thousand-ton vessel was vulnerable to a range of foreign missiles, including an advanced missile being developed by China and simple ones already possessed by Hezbollah. The top Navy brass agreed to end production of the ship, capping the program at two ships rather than seven.

Not so fast, said a group of senators and congressmen, including seven Democrats and four Republicans. They fired off a letter demanding that the Defense Department stick with the original production plan. Otherwise, they said, Congress would cut off funding for surface combat ships in the next budget. The pressure was too much for Secretary of Defense Gates. He and the Navy reversed course and endorsed production of a third DDG-1000—a ship they had not wanted. The price: $2.7 billion.

A Navy spokesman told *The Washington Post* after the reversal was announced that the service still considered the DDG-1000 "a ship you don't need."

Two Democratic senators from Massachusetts signed the letter demanding continued ship production: Edward Kennedy and John Kerry. A Kennedy aide confirmed that Raytheon, which makes the destroyer's electronic components in Massachusetts, had contacted Kennedy's office about keeping the ship in production.

Another example of congresspersons' eagerness to fund defense programs in their home districts was the proposal to develop an alternative engine for the controversial F-35 fighter plane, the so-called Joint Strike Fighter jet, which has been described as the centerpiece of U.S. airpower for the coming years. Secretary Gates has called the second engine "costly and unnecessary." He added, "Every dollar additional to the budget that we have to put into the F-35 is a dollar taken from something else that the troops may need." The defense secretary repeatedly recommended that President Obama veto a defense-spending bill if it included the engine funding. Obama himself has said, "Think about it: hundreds of millions of dollars for an alternative second engine for the Joint Strike Fighter when one reliable engine will do just fine."

The fight over the second engine raged for five years as both the Bush and Obama administrations sought to kill funding for the second engine. Squaring off in a heated media campaign were Pratt & Whitney, which makes the primary engine for the F-35 and argued that one engine was enough, and the team of General Electric and London-based Rolls-Royce, manufacturers of the second engine. The two sides ran full-page ads in major newspapers and presented their different perspectives in blogs and social media.

In 2010 the battle reached fever pitch. One Pratt & Whitney ad said, "This is the year for Congress to stop funding an extra engine for the F-35. For all those Republicans and Democrats who have talked about cutting government waste, here's your chance."

To counter his competition, Dennis Jarvi, then president of Rolls-Royce U.S. operations, appeared at a National Press Club briefing in Washington, D.C., and declared, "It is important to the war fighter, the industrial base, and the taxpayer that this [second-engine] program continues to exist." He and other Rolls-Royce officials emphasized how deeply they are involved in the United States, with sixty-five hundred employees at eighteen facilities in a dozen states.

The second engine got strong support from lawmakers in both political parties whose constituencies included major workshops for the project. House minority leader John Boehner, a Republican from Ohio, had been one of the most vociferous critics of wasteful spending and government deficits, but he backed the second-engine project. General Electric has a plant right outside Boehner's home district. The House, under Boehner's leadership, voted in May 2010 to approve the second engine at a cost of $485 million.

A year later, in February 2011, the House reversed its approval in a bipartisan vote that included the votes of some new Tea Party members eager to reduce government spending and willing to go against the GOP leadership on defense issues. The vote was a rare victory for good government-spending decisions over pork-barrel politics.

The Center for Responsive Politics, which monitors campaign spending, has noted that Democratic lawmakers, including many prominent liberals, have been as active as Republicans in force-feeding unwanted weapons systems to the Pentagon. In a study of two committees that control military spending in the House, Democrats collected 63 and 66 percent, respectively, of all defense industry funds given to members of the two committees in the 2008 election cycle. *The Washington Post* reported that the champion was John Murtha, a Democrat from Pennsylvania, who was chairman of the House Appropriations subcommittee for defense. Murtha collected $743,275 of industry money. Second was the House Armed Services Committee chairman, Representative Ike Skelton, of Missouri, who collected $268,799.

Defense contractors regularly filter money to election campaigns of key figures in Congress with jurisdiction over the Pentagon budget. After the GOP gained control of the House of Representatives in the 2010 midterm elections, defense contributions to members of the House Subcommittee on Defense shifted from the Democrats, who had lost control, to the newly empowered Republicans. For the 2014 election campaign, Republican defense subcommittee members received twice as much in defense contributions as Democratic members. On its Web site at opensecrets.org, in a chart showing the top twenty contributors, the nonpartisan Center for Responsive Politics lists contributions posted as of March 31, 2015, totaling $885,050 from the defense industry to Republican defense subcommittee members for the 2014 campaign, compared to $402,799 for Democrats. Representative Rodney Frelinghuysen of New Jersey, chairman of the subcommittee, received the most defense money—a total of $228,350 from individuals and political action committees on behalf of eight defense contractors. That was slightly more than the $217,400 that House Appropriations Committee chair Mac Thornberry of Texas received from seven defense sources. Frelinghuysen's biggest donor was Lockheed Martin, which sent him $83,350. The ranking Democrat, Representative Pete Visclosky of Indiana, also got Lockheed Martin money—but only $20,000. All in all, Lockheed Martin gave $261,200 to Republican subcommittee members and $50,000 to Democratic members. The Center for Responsive Politics bases its analyses on Federal Election Commission data. In explaining its methodology, the CRP notes that the organizations listed as contributors, such as Lockheed Martin, did not themselves give money to campaigns. "Rather the money came from the organizations' PACs, their individual members or employees or owners and those individuals' immediate families. Organization totals include subsidiaries and affiliates."

As these many cases illustrate, Congress is very much a part of a complex system with deep vested interests in militarism and even in war. Votes against weapons systems are politically hazardous because no politician of either party in America today can risk being portrayed by his or her foes as weak on military defense.

Members of Congress also have a "backyard" incentive to vote for weapons and bases in their districts, according to American University professor Gordon Adams. "It's not like foreign aid. It's about contracts in my district, contributors to my election campaign, things that directly affect my prospects of staying in office and my ability to say to my constituents, 'I got one for you!' That's the heart of a weapons decision."

Federal spending on defense does create jobs—but not as many jobs as spending on clean energy, health care, or education. That's the finding of a University of Massachusetts study, updated in 2011, on the economics of federal spending. The study found that spending $1 billion would create 11,200 military jobs—or 16,800 clean-energy jobs, 17,200 health-care jobs, or 26,700 education jobs. In their report, researchers Robert Pollin and Heidi Garrett-Peltier said, "As we show, in comparison to these alternative uses of funds, spending on the military is a relatively poor source of jobs creation."

One reason that America gets more "bang for the buck" with nondefense federal spending is that "more of the military dollar goes to capital, as opposed to labor," according to the defense expert William D. Hartung at the nonprofit Center for International Policy. For example, he said, "only 1.5 percent of the price of each F-35 Joint Strike Fighter pays for the labor costs involved in 'manufacturing, fabrication, and assembly.'" At least 85 percent goes for overhead.

Hartung said another reason why defense dollars create fewer jobs than other forms of expenditure is that a "large share of that money is either spent overseas or on imported goods. By contrast, most of the money generated by spending in areas like education is spent in the United States."

Former GOP congressional staffer Mike Lofgren has blogged that the defense budget creates comparatively few jobs: "The days of Rosie the Riveter are long gone; most weapons projects now require very little touch labor. Instead, a disproportionate share is siphoned off into high-cost research and development (from which the civilian economy benefits little); exorbitant management expenditures, overhead and out-and-out padding; and, of course, the money that flows back into the coffers of political campaigns. A million dollars appropriated for highway construction would create two to three times as many jobs as a million dollars appropriated for Pentagon weapons procurement, so the jobs argument is ultimately specious."

In the same blog post, his departing one, Lofgren attacked the congressional embrace of the military. He said the problem is bigger than jobs and campaign contributions: "Take away the cash nexus and there still remains a psychological predisposition toward war and militarism on the part of the GOP. This undoubtedly arises from a neurotic need to demonstrate toughness and dovetails perfectly with the belligerent tough-guy pose one constantly hears on right-wing talk radio. Militarism springs from the same psychological deficit that requires an endless series of enemies, both foreign and domestic."

Few would question that the nation needs its military and its contractors, but if Eisenhower were alive today, more than a half century after his most celebrated speech, he would probably want to deliver it again.

TANK TROUBLE

The funding fight over the future of the armored tank—a symbol of American military might for the past century—is a classic example of the struggle between those who want to trim defense spending and those who want to protect industry and the jobs that produce the tanks.

Army officials say they have more than enough combat tanks in the field to meet the nation's defense needs and could save $3 billion by holding off repairing, refurbishing, or making new tanks for three years. As Army chief of staff Raymond T. Odierno told Congress in 2012, "We don't need the tanks. . . . We're in good shape."

Congress promptly objected. In a letter to Defense Secretary Leon Panetta, 173 House members—Democrats and Republicans—urged him to support the production of more tanks. They said that a pause in tank production and refurbishment will hurt the nation's industrial economy. The tanks create sixteen thousand jobs and involve 882 suppliers, according to defense contractor General Dynamics, which has a tank-manufacturing plant in the northwestern Ohio city of Lima.

In reporting the story, CNN asked Representative Buck McKeon, a Republican from California, about the $56,000 in campaign contributions he had received from General Dynamics since 2009 and whether that might influence congressional action. McKeon, chairman of the House Armed Services Committee, said he didn't know he had received that amount from General Dynamics. He said he was thinking about the long-term implications: "If someone could guarantee us that we'll never need tanks in the future, that would be good. I don't see that guarantee."

Representative Silvestre Reyes, a Democrat on the Armed Services Committee, received $64,000 from General Dynamics. He said he was worried about the workforce if the Lima plant was closed. What's more, he said, "we don't want to play Russian roulette with the national security of this country."

Congress prevailed, allocating well more than the Army requested—an extra $181 million for Abrams tanks in fiscal 2013 and about $140 million more for Bradleys.

4
THINK-TANK HAWKS
AND INTERVENTIONISTS

The term think tank *is a misnomer because "they don't think, they justify."*

—Jonathan Rowe

In 1998, a small organization of American conservatives called the Project for the New American Century (PNAC) sent President Clinton a letter urging him to use the American military to topple Saddam Hussein from power as a way to "secure the interests of the U.S. and our friends and allies around the world." Clinton ignored the letter, which was signed by Donald Rumsfeld, Paul Wolfowitz, Richard Perle, and fifteen others.

Four years later, PNAC saw its chance to try again. On September 20, 2001—just nine days after Osama bin Laden's Al Qaeda slammed hijacked airliners into New York and Washington—PNAC wrote to President George W. Bush repeating its call for regime change in Iraq. "It may be that the Iraqi government provided assistance in some form to the recent attack on the United States," the new letter said. "But even if evidence does not link Iraq directly to the attack," Saddam, PNAC contended, should be removed because he was a leading terrorist.

This time, ten of the signers of the first letter were in high-level posts as Bush's own appointees. Donald Rumsfeld was the new secretary of defense. Paul Wolfowitz was deputy secretary of defense. Richard Perle was chairman of the Defense Policy Board, an agency that advises the Defense Department.

The hawks were inside the government and positioned to drive decisions.

Within weeks of the September 11 attacks—and that second PNAC letter—the Bush administration was actively planning an Iraq invasion, which it launched in March 2003, overthrowing Saddam's government and eventually capturing Hussein.

But the war was a disaster. It was launched on the false premise that Iraq was prepared to use weapons of mass destruction. While the Bush administration had said the war would end in weeks and cost little, it lasted for nearly nine years, killing 4,488 U.S. soldiers and wounding 32,000 more. At least 100,000 Iraqis died. The war cost more than $1 trillion and helped trigger the worst U.S. economic collapse since the Great Depression.

PNAC's wrongheaded push for the Iraqi invasion shows how a web of hawkish conservative think tanks—with support from liberal interventionists—can provide the rationale for the use of American military force and help take our country to war.

When President Eisenhower expressed his concerns about America's military-industrial complex in 1961, he didn't mention the think-tank community, which then consisted of a few staid institutions, conceived as "universities without students." The Council on Foreign Relations, the Brookings Institution, and others ponderously churned out policy papers for officials and fellow scholars.

But since Eisenhower's speech think tanks have changed and proliferated. America now is a beehive of 1,828 think tanks, according to a 2014 University of Pennsylvania report. More than four hundred of them crowd in and around Washington. While the old, university-style institutions survive and flourish—the Washington-based Brookings Institution has been rated tops in the world—many newer ones don't just recommend policy ideas but fight for them politically, going straight to the public with combative rhetoric, TV news analysts, and Twitter feeds.

The conservative think tanks typically are hawks on defense. They are financed by corporate money, much of it from defense industries or right-wing billionaires. They hire conservative academics and policy experts to write papers, letters, and opinion articles that advocate a robust defense policy, and they often argue for war. The think-tank hawks are an integral part of the American war machine and the forces that have come to dominate American foreign policy.

The group that built the rationale for the Iraq War—PNAC—was a small appendage of one of Washington's largest and best-known conservative think tanks, the American Enterprise Institute (AEI). Conservatives William Kristol and Robert Kagan cofounded PNAC in 1997 as a nonprofit educational organization. It was headquartered in the same thirteen-story, glass-and-concrete building as the AEI, across a downtown Washington street from the National Geographic Society.

When Al Qaeda terrorists struck on September 11, the PNAC players saw a golden opportunity to reintroduce their argument for war against Iraq. In its letter to President Bush, PNAC said, "Even if evidence does not link Iraq directly to the attack, any strategy aiming at the eradication of terrorism and its sponsors must include a determined effort to remove Saddam Hussein from power in Iraq. Failure to undertake such an effort will constitute an early and perhaps decisive surrender in the war on international terrorism."

The forty-one signatories of this letter represented a virtual who's who of American conservative thought, including William Kristol, William Bennett, Midge Decter, Frank Gaffney, Robert Kagan, Jeane Kirkpatrick, Charles Krauthammer, John Lehman, Richard Perle, and Kenneth Adelman.

Adelman wrote "Cakewalk in Iraq," an opinion column arguing that the U.S. invasion of Iraq would be simple to accomplish. The piece was published in *The Washington Post* in February 2002, five months after the 9/11 attacks and a year before the invasion of Iraq. Adelman's enthusiasm faded as the "cakewalk" turned into a fiasco. In an interview with *Post* reporter Peter Baker in November 2006, Adelman said President Bush was "responsible" for what Adelman called "the debacle that was Iraq." But many others, including Richard Perle, continue to stick by Bush.

PNAC's true significance in molding American policy is in the worldview that it advocated and sold to the Bush administration. In promoting war in Iraq, PNAC was advocating what it believes is America's proper role in the world after the demise of the Soviet Union and the end of the Cold War. PNAC envisioned a new Pax Americana—a label it did not reject. In its 2000 report *Rebuilding America's Defenses*, published a year before the 9/11 attacks, PNAC said, "America should seek to preserve and extend its position of global leadership by maintaining the preeminence of U.S. military forces."

Right here is the key to understanding the role of militaristic thinkers in the complex of forces dominating American policy. When the Cold War ended in 1991, the rationale for worldwide military forces to oppose and contain Soviet power should have collapsed. But in 1997—six years after the Soviet Union disintegrated—PNAC called for the United States to "increase defense spending significantly." Its "Statement of Principles" declared, "Of course, the United States must be prudent in how it exercises its power. But we cannot safely avoid the responsibilities of global leadership or the costs that are associated with its exercise. America has a vital role in maintaining peace and security in Europe, Asia, and the Middle East. If we shirk our responsibilities, we invite challenges to our fundamental interests. The history of the 20th century should have taught us that it is important to shape circumstances before crises emerge, and to meet threats before they become dire."

This last sentence was making a case for preventive war, a case that was to be adopted in the George W. Bush administration, a radical departure from the traditional notion that American military forces exist for defense. This was an argument for aggression.

Going beyond such statements of principle, PNAC proposed a detailed program of military spending, naming particular weapons systems to be developed. Specifically, it sought to do the following:

- Maintain nuclear strategic superiority.

- Increase the U.S. forces' active-duty strength from 1.4 million to 1.6 million.

- Shift permanently based forces to southeast Europe and Southeast Asia and change naval deployment patterns to reflect growing U.S. strategic concerns in East Asia.

We now know just how powerful these arguments were to become. For all practical purposes PNAC wrote the foreign policy script of the George W. Bush administration. That became clear in a speech delivered by President Bush on June 1, 2002, at West Point, in which he formally accepted PNAC's argument for preventive war. "We cannot defend America and our friends by hoping for the best," Bush said. "We cannot put our faith in the words of tyrants, who solemnly sign nonproliferation treaties and then systematically break them. If we wait for threats to fully materialize, we will have waited too long."

The West Point cadets applauded.

In that speech, Bush, in effect, adopted PNAC's worldview of a new Pax Americana: "America has, and intends to keep, military strengths beyond challenge, thereby making the destabilizing arms races of other eras pointless, and limiting rivalries to trade and other pursuits of peace."

Among those who gave life to the PNAC view were half a dozen men who served in high-level policy positions in the George W. Bush administration. In their new government jobs, they were able to help implement the PNAC recommendations. This group included Rumsfeld, the defense secretary; Paul Wolfowitz, deputy secretary of defense; Elliott Abrams, special assistant to the president; Zalmay Khalilzad, ambassador to Afghanistan and later ambassador to Iraq; John Bolton, ambassador to the United Nations; and Richard Perle, chairman of the Defense Policy Board Advisory Committee.

But those names are only part of the story. Other PNAC members who rose to top levels in the Bush administration were Dick Cheney, vice president; I. Lewis "Scooter" Libby, Cheney's chief of staff; Peter

Rodman, assistant secretary of defense for international security affairs; and Richard Armitage, deputy secretary of state. The membership of PNAC provided a cadre for running the foreign policy of the George W. Bush administration.

Wolfowitz and Rumsfeld were both present at the meeting President Bush convened at Camp David, the 148-acre presidential retreat in Maryland, a few days after the 9/11 attacks. More than a dozen cabinet members and military leaders attended. In his book *Days of Fire*, Peter Baker describes the scene and the discussion about how the United States should respond to the attacks. Here is a summary of what Baker reported:

Secretary of State Colin Powell began with a report on building a coalition for the war to come. CIA director George Tenet handed out a packet called "Going to War," with information about Al Qaeda. When it came Rumsfeld's turn to speak, he turned the table over to Wolfowitz, who argued for pursuing Saddam Hussein. Wolfowitz "declared that there was a 10 percent to 50 percent chance that Hussein had been involved in the attacks, although he presented no evidence."

Others in the meeting objected to the idea, and the discussion moved to Afghanistan and three military options there. The first was a cruise missile strike. The second was a cruise missile strike accompanied by manned bombers. But before the third option could be presented, Wolfowitz interrupted: "But we really need to think broader than that right now. That's not big enough. We've got to make sure we go ahead and get Saddam out at the same time—it's a perfect opportunity."

Bush became incensed. "How many times do I have to tell you we are *not* going after Iraq right this minute?" he snapped at Wolfowitz.

But only a short time later, Bush changed his mind and began planning for the U.S. invasion of Iraq.

Nothing is more revealing of the influential role that PNAC played in formulating the argument for war against Iraq than the explanation given when PNAC folded its tent and went out of business in 2006. Gary Schmitt, a former executive director of PNAC who is now a scholar at the AEI, explained, "When the project started it was not intended to go on forever. That is why we are shutting it down. It has already done its job . . . our view has been adopted."

The staunchest defenders of the war have never retreated from their position. In 2013—on the tenth anniversary of the Iraq invasion—Richard Perle, a PNAC-letter signatory and one of the most vociferous backers of the war, was interviewed by NPR's Renee Montagne, who put this question to Perle: Was the war worth it?

Perle said, "I've got to say, I think that is not a reasonable question. What we did at the time was done in the belief that it was necessary to protect this nation. You can't a decade later go back and say, well, we shouldn't have done that."

Wolfowitz, in a Fox News column, wrote that the problem was just a matter of strategy: "The principal reason why the war in Iraq proved so difficult and lasted so long is that it took so long to develop a counterinsurgency strategy."

Some liberal interventionists—such as Michael O'Hanlon of the Brookings Institution—also argued in favor of a war on Iraq. But the hawkish, conservative think tanks did the main advocacy work, contending that the Iraq War was essential to American security.

In another illustration of the role of think tanks influencing policy, PNAC's close ally, the American Enterprise Institute, has been widely credited with playing a critical role in promoting a "surge" of American troops in Iraq in 2007 in the latter stages of the Bush administration. Likewise, the Heritage Foundation, another powerful conservative think tank, "employed a variety of means over the past two decades to influence the policy process in Washington on the issue of missile defense," according to Heritage Foundation research fellow Baker Spring. In his article for *Foreign Policy*, Spring said the foundation advocated the deployment of an effective ballistic missile defense system in a 1982 study and has been working ever since to "educate policy-makers about the need to deploy such a system." Spring is referring to the Star Wars initiative proposed by President Ronald Reagan in 1983 to stop incoming nuclear missiles. The program has cost more than $200 billion but still isn't effective.

To fully grasp the prominent role of the hawkish, conservative think tanks in Washington's power game, it's important to see how the think-tank world has changed in the past half century. A think tank is an organization where people think about policies and write papers about them. But, as writer and civic activist Jonathan Rowe has observed, the term *think tank* is a misnomer because "they don't think, they justify." His remark was aimed at the conservative Heritage Foundation but applies to many others.

In their book *Trust Us, We're Experts,* Sheldon Rampton and John Stauber warn readers to be especially skeptical of think tanks, which they say have proliferated in recent years as a "way of generating self-serving scholarship to serve the advocacy goals of industry." Think tanks have a decided political leaning, they say. "There are twice as many conservative think tanks as liberal ones, and the conservative ones generally have more money. This is no accident, as one of the important functions of think tanks is to provide a backdoor for wealthy business interests to promote their ideas."

James McGann, a University of Pennsylvania professor who publishes annual surveys of the think-tank industry, summed up the unique nature of the think-tank community: "It's the noisiest political debating society in the world—a babble of voices airing contrary opinions on how this country should be run. For this democracy, where every view is permissible and each faction seeks to persuade, the Republicans, Democrats, left, right and centrist, lobbyists, journalists, scholars, religionists . . . are the yeast in the ever-fermenting discussion."

America's first think tanks developed in the early 1900s and grew out of a desire to improve government and to help government think, according to McGann. The first kind of think tank was the academic model, such as the Brookings Institution, founded in 1916 by reformers devoted to fact-based studies of national public-policy issues. Experts at Brookings played a role in shaping plans for the United Nations and the Marshall Plan to rebuild Europe after World War II. The next model, McGann says, was the RAND Corporation, established in 1920 as a consulting agency for the government.

The advocacy think tanks emerged in the 1960s. These new-style organizations, which campaigned actively for their policy preferences, tended to reflect that decade's swing to the political left. But the next two decades saw what McGann calls "a sort of conservative counter-revolution," leading to a "war of ideas," with openly ideological or partisan think tanks proliferating on both sides.

In 1963, during the period of the Vietnam War and the Great Society, the first advocacy institution was the left-leaning Institute for Policy Studies. The neoconservative Heritage Foundation was founded in 1973.

Conservative think tanks have more power and influence today in U.S. politics, McGann says, adding that there is "increasing criticism and worry over the domination of the right on policy." David Callahan wrote in the *Washington Monthly* in November 1999, "The big development of the 1990s is that conservative institutes have had spectacular new success in tapping business money to fund ideologically charged policy research." According to Callahan, "Corporate giving to right-wing groups has steadily increased as private sector leaders have seen the effectiveness with which conservative think tanks, and their armies of credentialed 'experts,' advance business interests in the political arena. Money, it turns out, can buy scholars as well as politicians."

Callahan wrote that the "current gusher of corporate funding for right-wing policy work has its roots in the 1970s, when leading conservative thinkers appealed to corporations to fund intellectuals who supported their economic interests." He pointed out that corporate leaders make up the overwhelming majority of board members at most conservative think tanks. "Even the American Enterprise Institute, among the most scholarly of conservative think tanks, has some two dozen corporate leaders on its board and only one academic, James Q. Wilson." Wilson, who taught at Harvard, died in 2012.

One of the most powerful underwriters of far-right-wing conservative causes is Koch Industries, the oil and chemicals conglomerate based in Wichita, Kansas, with annual revenues estimated to be $100 billion. The conglomerate operates oil refineries in Alaska, Texas, and Minnesota and controls some four thousand miles of pipeline.

Writer Jane Mayer described the political activities of Koch's owners, David and Charles Koch, in an August 30, 2010, issue of *The*

New Yorker magazine. Since the 1980s, the Koch brothers have provided more than $30 million to George Mason University, in Arlington, Virginia, much of it for a think tank called the Mercatus Center, which describes itself as "the world's premier university source for market-oriented ideas and real world problems."

Mayer quotes an environmental lawyer who has clashed with the Mercatus Center and who explained to her how corporate interests use think tanks to promote their private agendas. "You take corporate money and give it to a neutral-sounding think tank" that "hires people with pedigrees and academic degrees who put out credible-seeming studies. But they all coincide perfectly with the economic interests of their funders."

Among the largest and most influential of the conservative think tanks, in addition to the American Enterprise Institute, are the Heritage Foundation, based in Washington, D.C., and the Hoover Institution at Stanford University in California.

More than twenty AEI people wound up with top jobs in the George W. Bush administration. Paul Wolfowitz, the former deputy defense secretary and backer of the Iraq War, is now a visiting scholar at the AEI, which has an annual budget of about $20 million. It has about fifty so-called scholars and about 150 on the payroll. Its objective is to influence public policy. Christopher DeMuth, president of the AEI from 1986 through 2008, who worked in both the Nixon and Reagan administrations, put it this way: "We try to get in the newspaper op-ed pages and hawk our books and magazines much more aggressively than a university would feel comfortable with."

If you watch the op-ed pages in the newspapers carefully, you will find the AEI and other think tanks well represented, week after week, month after month. You will also see them on television presenting their point of view. When network-television talk shows and the Public Broadcasting Service (PBS) want "experts" on foreign policy, they often turn to the AEI or other prominent think tanks. But they don't always tell the public who is paying the salaries of the "experts." You can bet it is corporate America.

DeMuth, for example, has said that his board of trustees is composed of twenty-four business and financial executives. "They read our

work. They tell me what they like, and they tell me what they don't like."
In his 2005 interview, DeMuth said the AEI raised $20 million to $25
million a year with a third of the money coming from corporations, a
third from individuals, and a third from foundations. "We have over
three hundred corporate donors," he said.

Rob Stein, by profession a venture capitalist, but a former strategic
adviser to the Democratic National Committee, has spent years study-
ing conservative groups. From 2003 to 2005, by his estimate, conservative organizations spent about $295 million seeking to influence policy
while those of the left spent about $75 million.

More recently, bestselling author Thomas Frank wrote in a *New
York Times* column, "During the last three decades a cottage industry
of conservative institutions and foundations has grown into a powerful
quasi-academy with seven-figure budgets and phalanxes of 'senior fel-
lows' and 'distinguished chairs.' While real academics dither and fret
over bugbears like certainty and balance, the scholars of the American
Enterprise Institute, the Heritage Foundation and the Cato Institute
act boldly in the knowledge, to quote a seminal conservative text, that
ideas have consequences." The AEI "has long been the reliable source
of corporate money. Its principals effectively ran the Goldwater campaign in 1964 and it was deep thinkers from the institute who, after
moving into the Bush administration, dreamed up the war in Iraq."

A prominent opponent of the war was the libertarian Cato Institute, which is conservative on domestic issues but traditionally opposed
to foreign intervention. In California's *Orange County Register,* Cato
vice president Ted Galen Carpenter wrote—just days before the war
began—that the pro-war camp's justifications for invading Iraq were
faulty: "The United States is supposed to be a constitutional republic.
As such, the job of the U.S. military is to defend the vital security interests of the American people. U.S. troops are not armed crusaders with
a mission to right all wrongs and liberate oppressed populations. American dollars are too scarce and American lives too precious for such feck-
less ventures."

As for the idea that Saddam's overthrow would trigger a democratic
transformation in the Middle East, Carpenter said, "This is a fantasy.

The harsh reality is that the Middle East has no history of democratic rule, democratic institutions or serious democratic movements. To expect stable democracies to emerge from such an environment is naïve." He went on, "If free elections were held today in such countries as Egypt, Jordan and Saudi Arabia, they would produce virulently anti-American governments."

The libertarians were right. The hawks were wrong.

HAWKS IN AFGHANISTAN

Two of Washington's most successful think-tank hawks are Frederick and Kimberly Kagan, the husband-and-wife team who spent a year in Afghanistan working as unpaid volunteers for the U.S. general in charge of the war. Frederick Kagan is a scholar at the American Enterprise Institute, which has a history of supporting American military intervention around the world.

Having written papers that advocate an aggressive U.S. military policy, the Kagans moved to Afghanistan in 2010 and embedded themselves as "de facto senior advisors" to General David Petraeus. The Kagans were given top-level security clearance in Kabul, where they reviewed classified intelligence reports and participated in strategy sessions. The Kagans used their positions to advocate substantive changes in the U.S. war plan, "including a harder-edged approach," according to a *Washington Post* report about them, published December 18, 2012.

Think-tank hawks have always sought to impact defense policy. The Kagans found a way to go beyond traditional influence peddling and gain the ear of the military man in charge of a real war. The Kagans were not paid by the U.S. government for their work, but their proximity to Petraeus provided valuable benefits. The *Post* article reported that the arrangement with Petraeus "provided an incentive for defense contractors to contribute to Kim Kagan's think tank," the Institute for the Study of War, which advocates an aggressive U.S. foreign policy. At an August 2011 dinner, Kim Kagan thanked two contractors, DynCorp International and CACI International, for funding her institute and making it possible for her to spend a year in Afghanistan with Petraeus.

5

FLAWED INTELLIGENCE AND EXAGGERATED THREATS

Bush wanted to remove Saddam Hussein, through military action, justified by the conjunction of terrorism and WMD. . . . The intelligence and facts were being fixed around the policy.

—Note of secret July 2002 meeting recorded by British intelligence

On the morning of Wednesday, February 5, 2003, Secretary of State Colin Powell strode into the chambers of the United Nations Security Council to make the case for war against Iraq. With an American-flag pin in the lapel of his dark blue suit and a glass of water on his desk, Powell declared that the United States had incontrovertible evidence that Iraq had weapons of mass destruction, particularly biological and chemical, that threatened the United States and the world.

"My colleagues," he said, "every statement I make today is backed up by sources, solid sources. These are not assertions. What we're giving you are facts and conclusions based on solid intelligence." At Powell's right shoulder sat CIA director George Tenet, whose somber face on TV screens sent a message to the world that the U.S. intelligence community certified Powell's accusations.

As the world now knows—to its sorrow—Powell did not have solid sources, did not have facts, and did not have accurate intelligence. In his hour-long speech he made at least eighteen statements that were not true. But the speech sold the Congress, the media, and most Americans. Six weeks later, on March 20, the United States invaded Iraq, to ultimately find none of the elaborate weapons systems Powell had described in detail.

So how did the United States launch a war, killing or wounding more than thirty-six thousand Americans and tens of thousands of Iraqis, on the basis of "facts" that turned out to be fiction? Why were our government, and a man as experienced in statecraft and war making as Colin Powell, so wrong in a way so catastrophic to the long-term interests and reputation of both?

There is little doubt about the answer. On a politically sensitive issue, the Central Intelligence Agency faltered in its mission to provide the government with unflinchingly candid analysis. In a severe relapse of a chronic problem, America's preeminent intelligence organ buckled to White House pressure and tailored its intelligence reports to justify ideological preconceptions and policy decisions of the president and his aides.

The CIA describes itself as "an independent source of foreign intelligence information" for U.S. policymakers. But the agency and America's intelligence structure as a whole have often corrupted their analyses to conform to political pressures from their bosses. The CIA's record of understanding and accurately interpreting the most important foreign policy issues as they have occurred is frightening and abysmal. It was dead wrong on the most important assignment it faced and about the very reason it was created: the perceived threat by the Soviet Union. It vastly and repeatedly overestimated the military, economic, and political strength of the Soviets.

But the CIA has been only a part of the problem in the business of exaggerating threats facing the United States. A National Security Council study in 1950, which became known as NSC-68, chaired by the late Paul Nitze, deliberately and knowingly exaggerated threats facing the country and became the foundation of American foreign policy for more than two decades.

The record suggests that the nation's foreign policy establishment—of which the CIA is a part—has often been guilty of drumming up fear. That charge holds true to the present day. Two prime examples are Iraq and the Cold War, and in both cases the CIA played a crucial role.

Intelligence has been tailored to support policy emanating from the White House and top-level decisions driven by politics and ideological preconceptions. In short, the CIA has been an integral part of the complex of forces with vested interests in war. The role of the CIA has been crucial: to provide reasons to fear whether the reasons are true or not.

Iraq is an ideal case study. The campaign by right-wing ideologues for war in Iraq actually began in the later stages of the Clinton administration but gained traction in the Bush administration after the attacks on the New York World Trade Center and the Pentagon on September 11, 2001.

Vice President Cheney was determined to start a war on Iraq from the moment the Bush team took office, according to memoirs by several top policymakers. George Tenet, then the CIA director, says Cheney was pushing for war from the start. Paul O'Neill, who as treasury secretary was a member of the National Security Council, said the administration was fixed on this from the first NSC meeting, just ten days after Bush's inauguration and months before the September 11 attacks. "It was all about finding a way to do it. The president kept saying, 'Go find me a way to do this,'" O'Neill reported in *The Price of Loyalty*, a vivid account of how the Bush administration made policy.

Defense Secretary Rumsfeld and his deputy, Paul Wolfowitz, both pushed for the Iraq War. Cheney's support for the war was visible in his public appearances, such as an August 26, 2002, speech to the Veterans of Foreign Wars: "Simply stated, there is no doubt that Saddam Hussein now has weapons of mass destruction; there is no doubt he is amassing them to use against our friends, against our allies, and against us."

In retrospect, we know that this was not true. Saddam Hussein had no weapons of mass destruction and hadn't had any for years. He had abandoned any effort to obtain any shortly after the 1991 Persian Gulf War.

But the seeds for war against Iraq had been planted.

A wide array of Bush administration insiders have come forward in the past decade to describe on the record how Cheney, Rumsfeld, and others who had long been clamoring for war against Iraq saw the attacks of September 11 as an opportunity to achieve that objective. In his book *Plan of Attack,* Bob Woodward reports that Bush was determined to go after Saddam Hussein and made that clear to his defense secretary—but not the public—soon after the 9/11 attacks. Woodward says that the day before Thanksgiving 2001, Bush collared Rumsfeld and asked, "What have you got in terms of plans for Iraq? What is the status of the war plan? I want you to get on it. I want you to keep it secret."

What the Bush administration wanted was a reason to invade Iraq. When the head of the British Secret Intelligence Service visited Washington in July 2002 to discuss the buildup to the war, he reported in a secret memo that "Bush wanted to remove Saddam Hussein, through military action, justified by the conjunction of terrorism and WMD. . . . The intelligence and facts were being fixed around the policy."

In short, intelligence and facts were being manipulated to justify the invasion.

In early 2003 Bush decided he had to make his case for war to the United Nations but faced a difficult problem. His secretary of state, Colin Powell, had made clear to Bush that he opposed attacking Iraq. But as one of the most trusted figures in American politics at that time, Powell was the perfect choice to make the case to the UN. Loyal soldier that he was, Powell accepted the assignment. But he was deeply upset at a draft of the proposed speech prepared by administration officials. He decided to go to CIA headquarters in Langley, Virginia, to investigate personally the evidence that Iraq had weapons of mass destruction that posed an imminent threat.

By his own account, he spent three days at the CIA headquarters with Tenet as his guide. As Powell was asking questions, CIA officers such as the agency's European operations officer, Tyler Drumheller, were telling Tenet and deputy CIA director John McLaughlin that intelligence behind parts of the draft speech was not solid. Powell says he never got the message that key CIA analysts doubted that Saddam had WMD. "I was being as careful as I possibly could," Powell told the *Los Angeles Times* in a story published in November 2005.

Indeed, as Powell worked to clean the speech of unsupported allegations, he faced obstacles. Colonel Lawrence B. (Larry) Wilkerson, Powell's chief of staff, remembers that Powell ordered the speechwriters to remove several questionable parts of the draft. They were removed, Wilkerson said, but then reinserted. Eventually Powell agreed to keep those parts, despite his doubts about their truth.

Tenet had gotten the message from the White House. He did his job. Then he agreed to sit directly behind Powell in the UN Security Council, his presence backing up Powell's wild assertions. In his 2007 book, *Legacy of Ashes,* a history of the CIA, Tim Weiner seeks to explain George Tenet's behavior on Iraq: "Throughout his years in Washington, Tenet had been a fundamentally decent man. But under enormous pressures he faced after 9/11, his one flaw, his all-consuming desire to please his superiors, became a fault line. Tenet's character cracked and the CIA did too. Under his leadership, the agency produced the worst body of work in its long history."

Tenet was determined to give President Bush what he wanted. When Bush expressed disappointment in the evidence mustered by the CIA to prove Saddam's possession of chemical or biological weapons, Tenet told him that the CIA's ability to make a solid case was a "slam dunk." He later said, "Those were the two dumbest words I ever said." An obvious question remains unanswered: Why did he say them?

Twisted Intelligence

The tangled story of the beautiful blond spy Valerie Plame and her diplomat husband, Joseph Wilson, is rooted in the origins of the Iraq War but grew to include a larger cast of characters, including President Bush, Vice President Cheney, and Cheney's top assistant, Scooter Libby, who was convicted of perjury for his role in what happened. Hollywood made this account of twisted intelligence at the highest level of the American government into a 2010 movie called *Fair Game,* starring Naomi Watts and Sean Penn.

Here's the background: In early 2002, Bush and Cheney were making plans to invade Iraq but wanted evidence to justify the U.S. attack and remove Saddam Hussein from power. Cheney's office asked the CIA to investigate allegations that Saddam was seeking to purchase uranium yellowcake—which can be used to create weapons of mass destruction—from Niger. Plame's superiors at the CIA knew her husband, a former ambassador, had been posted in five African nations and that his first assignment had been in Niger. They asked Wilson to travel there to investigate the possibility that Saddam had tried to buy yellowcake.

Wilson went to Niger in February 2002 and met with officials in the U.S. embassy and in the Niger government. He concluded that it was "highly doubtful" that Niger had sold anything to Saddam.

One year later, in January 2003, President Bush said in his State of the Union address, "The British government has learned that Saddam Hussein recently sought significant quantities of uranium from Africa." The United States invaded Iraq a few weeks later, in March 2003.

In an opinion article published July 6, 2003, in *The New York Times,* Wilson challenged the White House uranium story. He said that on the basis of his experience with the administration in the months leading up to the war, he had "little choice but to conclude that some of the intelligence related to Iraq's nuclear weapons program was twisted to exaggerate the Iraqi threat." The headline on his article was "What I Didn't Find in Africa."

One week later, syndicated columnist Robert Novak disclosed in *The Washington Post* that Wilson's wife, Valerie Plame, worked for the CIA as an agency operative. Wilson and others believe that the disclosure, which effectively ended Plame's career with the CIA, was retaliation for his questioning the government's rationale for the Iraq War.

Federal investigators interviewed Novak and top government officials to try to find the source of the leak. Their investigation led to the conviction of Cheney's chief of staff, I. Lewis (Scooter) Libby. He was found guilty on four counts, including perjury and obstruction of justice, none of which related directly to the Plame disclosure. Instead, Libby was convicted of failure to cooperate with the probe into the disclosure. He was sentenced to thirty months in prison and a fine of $250,000.

President Bush commuted Libby's prison sentence but refused to pardon Libby, despite relentless lobbying by Cheney in their final weeks in office. In discussing the possibility of the Libby pardon with his lawyers, Bush asked, "So why do you think he did it?"—meaning, why did Libby lie?

Bush then answered his own question: "I think he still thinks he was protecting Cheney."

Bush "Sickened"

Although the Bush administration made the case for invading Iraq on the grounds that Saddam Hussein had weapons of mass destruction and might use them against the United States, President Bush has since said that his decision was not dependent on the WMD allegation. In a 2010 interview with NBC's Matt Lauer, Bush said he was "sickened" when he learned that Iraq did not have WMD. But he quickly added that he wouldn't have changed his decision because "the world is better off without Saddam Hussein."

Lauer asked Bush whether he had ever considered apologizing for the invasion. Bush said no. The former president explained, "Apologizing would basically say the decision was a wrong decision, and I don't believe it was the wrong decision."

Bush seems blissfully unaware that he had assembled a team of national security officials who had publicly advocated invading Iraq and toppling Saddam Hussein long before he became president. If Bush had really wanted clean, honest intelligence from the CIA, he destroyed any chance of getting it by failing to protect the agency from the pressures of his ideologically driven vice president and defense secretary. Bush may not be enough of a student of American history to understand the dangers of having an American president and his administration put pressure on the CIA to find evidence for a policy decision that has been made. The nearly seven decades of the agency's existence has shown that this is a recipe for disaster.

Here's how Weiner characterizes the CIA's problem: "To survive as an institution in Washington, the agency above all had to have the president's ear. But it soon learned that it was dangerous to tell him what he did not want to hear. The CIA's analysts learned to march in lockstep, conforming to conventional wisdom. They misapprehended the intentions and capabilities of our enemies, miscalculated the strength of communism, and misjudged the threat of terrorism."

The record of the CIA and the foreign policy establishment in the Cold War is more difficult to explain, but it is certainly clear now that they were wrong and Soviet specialist George F. Kennan was right.

Kennan, a political officer in the American embassy in Moscow in the late 1940s, was the father of what became known as America's "containment" policy toward the Soviet Union. For Kennan, the tools of containment were to be mainly political and economic pressures, rather than military force. Unlike more hard-line analysts, Kennan did not think the Soviet Union sought world domination or that it posed a risk of attack on the United States. In a famous *Foreign Affairs* magazine article in 1947 that he signed only as "X," Kennan stated, "Soviet society may well contain deficiencies which will eventually weaken its own total potential."

Historian Robert Dallek observed that Kennan "wisely described Soviet communism as a system of state management and controls that would eventually collapse when its inability to meet consumer demands for the sort of material well-being and freedoms enjoyed in the West became evident."

By 1950, more hard-line views of the Soviets, held by Secretary of State Dean Acheson, among others, left Kennan isolated. Acheson told him to take his Quaker views to a more hospitable setting than he could possibly find in Washington.

We now know that the Soviet Union rotted from within. Despite a series of economic, social, and political reforms in the 1980s, Soviet leader Mikhail Gorbachev failed to revitalize the economy. He resigned his post as president on December 25, 1991, a day before the Soviet Union officially dissolved. We will probably never know for sure the extent to which a contributing factor may have been spending on its military in an effort to keep up with the United States. We do know from Gorbachev's writings that he decided that he would have to cut military spending if he wanted to improve standards of living to rival those in the West.

Kennan did not envision America's policy of military expansionism and confrontation that evolved, beginning in the Truman administration and leading to the Korean War, the Vietnam War, and more than a dozen American invasions and incursions. Robert Dallek wrote, "As his life ended in 2005 at the age of 101, he [Kennan] was convinced more than ever that the tyranny of military containment had done little, if anything, to assure America's victory in that struggle. He saw the invasion of Iraq as another example of misplaced faith in a military solution to a political problem."

Exaggerated Threats

American officials, often led by the intelligence community, have exaggerated threats facing the nation for more than fifty years.

In examining this pattern, a good place to start is with the NSC-68 report to President Truman that deliberately overstated the threat from the Soviet Union and set the stage for the Cold War. The report was apocalyptic. It declared that the Soviet threat involved "the fulfillment or destruction not only of the Republic, but of civilization itself."

Richard Rhodes tells the story in his powerful book *Arsenals of Folly: The Making of the Nuclear Arms Race*. Rhodes describes how Secretary of State Dean Acheson and Paul Nitze, the State Department's chief policy planner and the principal author of the report, intentionally exaggerated the Soviet threat in order to "bludgeon the mass mind" of top government officials and thereby ensure a major expansion of U.S. military forces. Their threats worked.

World War II killed roughly 25 million of the Soviet Union's people—a casualty rate sixty times that of the United States—and obliterated half its industry. Where Kennan had recognized a USSR driven largely by its defensiveness and insecurity amid the destruction from this latest invasion by foreigners, Nitze's NSC-68 declared that the

USSR is "animated by a new fanatic faith, antithetical to our own, and seeks to impose its absolute authority over the rest of the world."

Nitze's exaggerations provide an early suggestion of how an influential foreign-policy hawk can help push the CIA to harden its own analyses of overseas threats. In NSC-68, Nitze used a just-completed CIA estimate that the Soviet Union might accumulate as many as two hundred nuclear bombs within four years. But according to a CIA-commissioned history by Soviet scholar and former diplomat Raymond Garthoff, Nitze ignored the CIA's "sensible judgment," issued secretly on April 6, 1950, that such a stockpile would not mean the Soviets were likely to attack. Instead, Nitze's State Department and military analysts pressured the CIA to accept their view of a higher danger of Soviet attack, and the CIA reversed its position in a document issued only sixty-four days after the first one.

Truman, in response to Nitze's alarmism, "quadrupled the defense budget and began a strategic program that would increase the U.S. nuclear arsenal to some 20,000 thermonuclear bombs by 1960 and 32,000 by 1966," according to nuclear arms specialist Joseph Cirincione, president of the Ploughshares Fund, a foundation devoted to ridding the world of nuclear weapons.

Nitze's idea that the Soviets were preparing to attack the United States was dramatically wrong, so far as we know. But it was perhaps a symptom of the dread of communism that goes back in American history to so-called Red Scares—fear of the rise of communism—shortly after World War I. The promotion of these fears is a favorite tool of anti-left groups and individuals.

In his history of the CIA, Weiner wrote that "Stalin never had a master plan for world domination, nor the means to pursue it." He notes that Stalin's longtime aide and successor, Nikita Khrushchev, recalled in a memoir that Stalin "trembled" and "quivered" at the prospect of a global combat with America. "He was afraid of war," Khrushchev said. "Stalin never did anything to provoke a war with the United States. He knew his weakness."

Khrushchev had a volatile temper and a taste for confrontation, but he understood the Soviet Union's limitations. President John F. Kennedy confessed to *New York Times* columnist James Reston that Khrushchev "savaged me" with threats of war in their first meeting. Khrushchev then stepped to the brink with his 1962 deployment of nuclear-armed missiles in Cuba. But the same Khrushchev backed down, making a secret deal with Kennedy to remove the weapons if the Americans would remove similar missiles from Turkey. Neither side wanted a nuclear war.

The missile deal remained secret for years, permitting Kennedy and his supporters to pretend that Khrushchev had blinked.

Exaggeration of the Soviet threat was endemic in American politics in the 1950s. Democratic senators Stuart Symington and John F. Kennedy helped lead public campaigns accusing President Eisenhower of passively tolerating a dangerous Soviet superiority in deploying long-range bombers and missiles. While CIA reconnaissance found that the United States had more of both weapons, Kennedy continued to allege a "missile gap" and accuse Ike of weakness on defense in his presidential campaign against Vice President Richard Nixon in 1960.

After JFK won the election and appointed Robert McNamara as defense secretary, the naïve McNamara discovered that the United States actually had a seventeen-to-one advantage over the Soviets in intercontinental missiles. McNamara decided to set the record straight. He held a background session with reporters—in which they were not permitted to identify him as the source—and told them that there was no gap. *The New York Times* ran the story on its front page.

Kennedy was enraged but could not deny the truth. When he was asked at his next news conference whether there was, in fact, a "missile gap," he replied that the matter was under investigation. A great irony is that Nitze's unwarranted fears of a Soviet nuclear buildup actually came to pass after the Cuban missile crisis. Embarrassed by being forced out of Cuba, the Soviets began a massive program to build up their nuclear forces. By the time Richard Nixon became president in 1969, the Russians had achieved parity with the United States, which Nixon acknowledged in his first press conference.

No discussion of intelligence failures and exaggerated threats would be complete without a look at what happened in the Vietnam War. Simply put, the Vietnam War was brought about by U.S. leaders who exaggerated the influence of communism and underestimated the power of nationalism. In his book *A Look over My Shoulder*, former CIA director Richard Helms wrote that Vietnam was his "nightmare for a good ten years." He recounted, "We tried every operational approach in the book, and committed our most experienced field operatives to the effort to get inside the government in Hanoi. Within the Agency, our failure to penetrate the North Vietnamese government was the single most frustrating aspect of those years. We could not determine what was going on at the highest levels of Ho's government, nor could we learn how policy was made or who was making it."

The Vietnam War ended in 1975, but fear of communism continued to haunt the American government. In 1976, the foreign policy hawks on President Gerald Ford's Presidential Foreign Intelligence Advisory Board pushed the administration to accept a "competitive analysis" of the Soviet threat. The competition—Raymond Garthoff later called it a "bizarre" experiment—would pit a group of CIA analysts known as Team A against a group of outsiders known as Team B. The teams would evaluate the same classified intelligence data and report on their findings. George Herbert Walker Bush, Ford's newly appointed CIA director, agreed. He did so just months after his predecessor, William Colby, had rejected the idea.

But what seemed to be an innocent and well-meaning effort to better understand the Soviet threat was actually a sly political ploy by right-wing ideologues. Since Team B was backed by a virtual directory of politically conservative politicians who staunchly opposed the policy of détente and coexistence with the Soviet Union, Team B would predictably conclude that the CIA had underestimated Soviet military power and misinterpreted Soviet strategic intentions.

Heading Team B was the anti-Soviet hard-liner and Harvard professor Richard Pipes. Backers of the Team B initiative included Dick Cheney, then serving as President Ford's chief of staff; William Casey, who would be Ronald Reagan's CIA director; nuclear bomb physicist Edward Teller; and Norman Podhoretz, the effective founder of the neoconservative movement. Team B advisers included Paul Wolfowitz, who became deputy defense secretary under President George W. Bush and a leading advocate for invading Iraq, and Paul Nitze, who helped to create the Committee on the Present Danger, which advanced the false claim that the U.S. nuclear arsenal was so inadequate that the Soviet Union would be able to eliminate all American weapons in a first strike.

"It would have been impossible for the Soviets to do so, since nuclear submarines and aircraft equipped with weapons would have escaped any land attack, the submarines were invulnerable and their ability to launch a counterattack would have maintained an effective deterrent if the Soviets were foolish enough to consider a first strike," wrote Joseph Cirincione.

Dr. Anne Hessing Cahn of the Arms Control and Disarmament Agency has shown that every specific claim about the Soviet arsenal in the Team B report was wrong: "all of it was fantasy," she said. Columnist Fareed Zakaria has opined that the Team B report was "wildly off the mark." On every substantive point, said Garthoff, Team B stressed and enlarged "the impression of danger and a threat."

But the exaggerated threats continued. In November 1985, Robert Gates, then deputy CIA director, claimed in a speech for a foreign policy group in San Francisco that the Soviets were "laying the foundation that will give them the option of a relatively rapidly deployable nationwide ABM system." Gates said the system, despite its deficiencies, "would give the Soviets a significant unilateral advantage both politically and in time of war."

In fact, documents uncovered by journalist and Soviet expert David Hoffman after the Soviet collapse established that Soviet technology was way behind that of the United States. In his book *The Dead Hand: The Untold Story of the Cold War Arms Race and Its Dangerous Legacy*, Hoffman wrote that Gates in a 1987 memo to President Reagan "failed to grasp the essence of Gorbachev's attempts to reverse the nuclear arms race." Gates insisted that the Soviets were trying to upgrade their nuclear systems when Gorbachev was in fact trying to downgrade. Gates said the Soviets were trying to build a sophisticated system, according to Hoffman, when "the Soviet version [for missile defense] was a shambles and would never be built."

When the CIA issued a major report in 1995 on missile threats to the United States, the document angered the foreign policy hawks who had exaggerated Soviet threats during the Cold War. The CIA's National Intelligence Estimate said that countries trying to build new missile forces—such as Iran and North Korea—would be unable to threaten a strike on the North American continent before 2010. Republicans in Congress responded in 1998 by establishing the Commission to Assess the Ballistic Missile Threat to the United States. Chaired by Donald Rumsfeld, it included many of the same people who had participated in the Team B exercise. The commission said that Iran and North Korea could hit the United States with missiles within five years—by 2003— a prediction that, as we can see, was wrong.

If you want to understand why the CIA has failed so miserably and so often, here is a clue. The vast majority of its $80 billion budget—some $50 billion—goes to spy satellites and high-tech listening devices. The system was basically developed to monitor Soviet nuclear and missile capabilities with spy satellites, which take pictures from high altitude. You can see the value of those pictures by watching again Colin Powell's speech justifying the invasion of Iraq. He showed pictures of buildings and insisted the CIA knew what was in them. In fact, the CIA was just guessing, and guessing wrong.

While the Iraq War offers a dramatic example of the corruption within the CIA, the agency's performance during the forty years of the Cold War is even more troubling. Its repeated overestimation of Soviet military strength—while failing to perceive the inherent economic weakness of the communist system—was used to justify the building and expansion of America's worldwide military empire, with its hundreds of military bases, its vast fleets of ships to dominate oceans, its gigantic nuclear arsenal of land- and sea-based missiles, and hundreds of intercontinental bombers.

I am not arguing that the Soviet Union did not present a threat to the security of the United States. I am arguing that the evidence is substantial that the threat was systematically exaggerated, and that both blood and treasure have been wasted over nearly half a century as a result.

Today the public is being conditioned to believe that we face major national security threats from Iran and from North Korea, when the military capabilities of each are a mere shadow of the threat we faced from the Soviet Union—and that threat was, as we have seen, consistently exaggerated.

The overall record of the CIA is disturbing and difficult to explain. The CIA failed to foresee the collapse of the Soviet Union. It did not perceive that the Soviet Union was in deep trouble until a few months before the Berlin Wall fell in 1989. David Hoffman in his book *The Dead Hand* quotes Secretary of State James Baker as observing, "Our CIA was way, way behind the curve."

The CIA was wrong about the "domino theory," the thinking that if one country falls to communism, other countries in the region will fall to communism, a strategic concept that led to the disaster of Vietnam.

It did not foresee either the construction of the Berlin Wall or, ultimately, the fall of the Berlin Wall—both symbols of Soviet weakness.

It failed to anticipate the 2011 Arab awakening.

The nation has paid an incredible price for these failures in billions of dollars for unnecessary weapons, in thousands of lives lost, in the construction and perpetuation of a national security state that symbolizes who we are as a nation.

Caught in a Culture of Secrecy

Edward Snowden's leaks of classified national security documents in 2013 revealed an underlying problem in America: We are caught in a culture of secrecy that has eaten away at our personal rights. We live amid a vast system of intelligence bureaucracies, and we don't know what they do, how they do it, or what it really costs. When we try to find out, we're told, "Sorry, that's classified."

News stories based on the Snowden files revealed the astonishing scope of surveillance by the National Security Agency. Snowden, who obtained the files while working as an NSA contractor, has been characterized as a hero by some and as a traitor by others. Federal authorities have charged him with espionage. Snowden, who fled to Russia to avoid prosecution, was awarded the Ridenhour Prize in April 2014 for truth-telling that protects the public interest. The prize is named after Ronald Ridenhour, the Vietnam veteran who blew the whistle on the massacre by American soldiers of several hundred civilians, including women and children, in the hamlet of My Lai in March 1968. *The Washington Post* and the *Guardian* were awarded the highest accolade in journalism—the Pulitzer Prize for public service—in 2014 for their coverage of surveillance activities based on the Snowden disclosures.

The United States has seventeen intelligence agencies, including the NSA. Others include the Central Intelligence Agency, the Federal Bureau of Investigation, the National Geospatial-Intelligence Agency, and the Defense Intelligence Agency. Each branch of the military—Army, Navy, Air Force, Marines, and Coast Guard—has its own intelligence agency. The Treasury Department has the Office of Terrorism and Financial Intelligence. The Department of Homeland Security has the Office of Intelligence and Analysis.

Director of National Intelligence James Clapper told Congress in March 2013 that the NSA did not "wittingly" collect information on Americans. After the Snowden leaks revealed that the NSA collected millions of Americans' telephone and e-mail communications as part of its surveillance programs, Clapper apologized to Congress.

Senator Dianne Feinstein, a Democrat from California and chair of the Senate Select Committee on Intelligence, is one of Washington's staunchest defenders of the intelligence agencies. But in March 2014, she delivered a passionate forty-minute speech on the Senate floor excoriating the CIA for interfering with her committee's investigation into what is known as the CIA torture program. She said the agency broke the law by searching computers used by Senate committee staffers researching the CIA's use of waterboarding and other interrogation techniques.

Former CIA director Michael Hayden, who served under President George W. Bush, told Fox News that Feinstein was motivated by a "deep emotional feeling." Senator Mark Udall, a Democrat who serves alongside Feinstein on the Senate Intelligence Committee, called the reference to Feinstein's emotions a "baseless smear" that Hayden wouldn't make against a man.

The committee released a landmark six-thousand-page report in December 2014 on its investigation of the CIA detention and interrogation program, which Senator Feinstein said amounted to torture in some cases.

The report was immediately attacked. In her *Washington Post* commentary responding to critics, published December 17, 2014, Feinstein said, "I understand those involved may want to distance themselves from the terrible acts that were committed, but facts are facts. This study will stand the test of time and hopefully ensure that such mistakes are never made again."

6

THE AMERICAN EMPIRE

Once upon a time you could trace the spread of imperialism by counting up colonies. America's version of the colony is the military base.

—Chalmers Johnson

If the myth of America's role in the world as a champion of peace were true, the story of what has happened since the collapse of the Soviet Union in 1991—nearly twenty-five years ago—would be far different.

With the Cold War over, one might imagine, it would no longer be necessary for America to maintain a worldwide military empire. Logic would dictate that the defense budget could be drastically cut, bases throughout the world closed, aircraft-carrier battle groups in every one of the world's oceans reduced or brought home, and expensive weapons systems cut back or abandoned.

But this has not been the story.

America's global military empire has not been reduced. It has expanded. With the end of the Vietnam War in 1975, some hoped for huge defense cuts that would produce a peace dividend. But the military empire found a new lease on life in the 1980s with President Reagan's military buildup. As the Cold War was ending in the early 1990s, the United States took on a new mission—protection of the Persian Gulf oil fields, companies, and Arab monarchies that supplied the oil essential to the American economy. During that same decade the United States also took on responsibility for responding to humanitarian crises and trying to remake foreign countries such as Bosnia, Kosovo, and Haiti into Western-style democracies.

Having gone that far, the U.S. government took on another massive new mission after the September 11, 2001, attacks: invade, conquer, and rebuild Afghanistan and Iraq, reshaping them as democracies—all with the remarkable tool of its globe-girding Defense Department. And all with tragic results. When the Soviet threat died in 1991, America spent $441 billion on its armed services. Twenty years later, in 2011, it spent $736 billion, diverting needed investments from America's wilting economy and saddling taxpayers with the costs.

The defense budget has continued to consume billions of unnecessary dollars. We continue to build multibillion-dollar sophisticated weapons systems, many of which were designed for the Cold War. Now we have unmanned drones operated by remote control that we can dispatch to kill people that the president and his team decide are our enemies.

Johns Hopkins University's Michael Mandelbaum, one of America's most prominent foreign policy scholars, drove home this idea in his 2010 book, *The Frugal Superpower:* "At the end of 1991 the Soviet Union itself, the great communist multinational empire of Eurasia that the Bolshevik Party had assembled after seizing power in Russia in 1917, collapsed entirely. The threat it had presented disappeared. Yet even in the absence of a major threat—indeed, in no small part *because* of the absence of such a threat—the United States sustained, for the next two decades, a foreign policy with the same extensive geographic reach and the same institutions of foreign policy as it had during World War II and the Cold War. Post–Cold War American foreign policy prominently included, in fact, aspirations for promoting change in other countries that in some ways were even more ambitious than its goals during World War II and the Cold War."

So it is reasonable to ask: Why? What forces are at play? And do Americans understand what has been happening—and why?

The record of the last twenty-plus years strongly suggests that the Cold War produced economic and political forces that today are beyond our control, creating a militaristic culture and institutions, many parts of which have vested interests in war. This American war machine has led our country into military interventions, attacks, and even undeclared wars served up for all manner of flimsy reasons. Many of the attacks were against countries that posed no discernible threat to America's safety.

America's habit of interventions, invasions, and attacks has been steady since the end of World War II. We have lived through an era of almost continuous warfare of one kind or another for more than half a century. U.S. military activism continued when the Soviet Union collapsed in 1991. In that year, President George Herbert Walker Bush went to war against Iraqi leader Saddam Hussein after Saddam invaded Kuwait. The following year, Bush sent U.S. forces into Somalia.

Bush's successor, President Bill Clinton, sent U.S. troops into Haiti. He continued military action against Saddam's Iraq by bombing and firing missiles to enforce a no-fly zone—in effect continuing the war at a low level. In 1999, Clinton ordered heavy air strikes in the former Yugoslavia against Serb forces fighting for control of Kosovo. By 2001, under the second President Bush, we had invaded Afghanistan, and in 2003 we invaded Iraq—on false pretenses, we learned later.

To grasp the scope of American military campaigns around the world, consider our history:

1950 Korean War. United States intervenes against communist forces invading South Korea. The war lasts for three years and results in 33,686 American deaths.

1953 CIA coup deposes democratically elected Iranian prime minister Mohammad Mosaddegh after he nationalized a British oil company. With Mosaddegh gone, CIA installs a puppet, Mohammad Reza Shah Pahlavi.

1954   CIA stages a coup to overthrow Guatemala's elected president, Jacabo Árbenz Guzmán, after his land reform seizes banana farms owned by United Fruit, a U.S. corporation.

1955   Vietnam War begins with U.S. troops and the CIA trying to build a pro-U.S. government against communist North Vietnam. The war lasts nearly twenty years, killing 58,286 U.S. troops and causing an estimated 3.6 million war deaths.

1958   United States sends fourteen thousand troops to Lebanon to back its pro-Western president against leftist opponents.

1961   CIA organizes an invasion of Cuba at the Bay of Pigs by anti-communist exiles but fails to overthrow President Fidel Castro.

1965   United States sends troops to the Dominican Republic to prevent communists from taking power amid civil war.

1965   Lyndon Johnson escalates the U.S. role in the Vietnam War, eventually fielding more than half a million troops.

1969   U.S. Air Force secretly starts intensive bombing of Laos and Cambodia in an effort to destroy North Vietnamese bases there. The carpet bombing of Laos is kept secret.

1970   U.S. troops invade Cambodia to attack North Vietnamese forces that threaten the U.S.-backed South Vietnamese government. This expands the Vietnam War into a neutral country.

1973   CIA backs a military coup to oust Chile's elected president, Salvador Allende, a Marxist, leading to the seventeen-year dictatorship of Augusto Pinochet.

1979   CIA begins supplying arms to Afghanistan's guerrillas—including the Taliban—fighting the Soviet Union's occupation of their country. President Carter sends Brezhnev a message threatening military action if Russia goes any further and warning that "we would not exclude any military weapons that we have."

1981   United States begins sending Special Forces to help lead and train government forces fighting leftist and peasant uprisings in El Salvador.

1982 U.S. Marines sent to Lebanon to support the pro-Western government and facilitate the withdrawal of Palestinian fighters defeated in an Israeli invasion.

1982 United States promises support for contras in Nicaragua. President Reagan signs a secret directive on January 4, 1982, giving the CIA authority to recruit and support the contras with $19 million in military aid.

1983 United States invades Grenada to overthrow a Marxist military junta.

1986 U.S. jets bomb Libya's capital after accusing Libyan leader Mu'ammar al-Gaddhafi of ordering the bombing of a German disco that killed two U.S. soldiers.

1987 United States intervenes on side of Iraq in the Iran-Iraq War. This includes the U.S. Navy's escorting and protecting oil tankers in the Persian Gulf, blocking Iranian attacks in the war with Iraq. In Alan Friedman's book *Spider's Web,* a former White House official explained "that by 1987 our people were actually providing tactical military advice to the Iraqis in the battlefield, and sometimes they would find themselves over the Iranian border, alongside Iraqi troops."

1989 United States troops invade Panama and overthrow its ruler, Manuel Noriega.

1990 United States attacks Iraq to reverse its seizure and occupation of Kuwait. President George H. W. Bush says this attack is necessary to stop Iraqi aggression. Senator Bob Dole declares the attack is about oil.

1991 United States leads air patrols against Iraq to constrain its military, enforcing no-fly zones with periodic bombings and missile attacks. This continues for twelve years.

1992 United States leads a multinational invasion of Somalia to protect international aid groups amid a civil war. The United States withdraws a year later, after a devastating battle in Mogadishu that became the basis for the movie *Black Hawk*

Down, a reference to the helicopters shot down by Somali militia.

1994   United States invades Haiti to oust a military junta and restore an elected president.

1995   United States leads NATO bombing attack on ethnic Serb forces amid civil war in Bosnia.

1999   United States leads NATO in bomb and missile attacks on Serbia and Serb forces in the secessionist province of Kosovo.

2001   United States invades Afghanistan, overthrowing the Taliban government and sponsoring the installation of a pro-Western president, Hamid Karzai.

2003   United States invades Iraq and overthrows President Saddam Hussein, saying it acted because Saddam had built illegal weapons of mass destruction. No such weapons were found.

2004   United States begins years of missile attacks by remotely powered drones against alleged Islamic militant terrorists in Pakistan's tribal zones, Yemen, and other countries.

2011   United States joins a multistate coalition to intervene in the Libyan civil war. The intervention was expected to be brief but lasted eight months and ended with the death of Libyan leader Mu'ammar al-Gaddhafi.

An argument could be made that the Department of Defense should be renamed. Calling it the Department of Offense would better describe its actual function for more than half a century.

While American public opinion has repeatedly turned against military interventions that dragged on too long or killed large numbers of American troops, both Democratic and Republican administrations have won public acquiescence—and even popular support—in launching them, by citing needs to fight communism or terrorism, protect U.S. oil supplies abroad, protect innocent foreign populations, or build democracy.

Here is the great irony. The U.S. Constitution says that Congress shall have the power to declare war, but the last time Congress issued a formal declaration of war was for World War II, more than half a century ago. President George W. Bush did get a congressional resolution supporting his invasion of Iraq in 2003, but no declaration of war.

Since World War II, U.S. presidents have ordered military action on an estimated 125 occasions. This has been possible primarily because of the 1973 War Powers Resolution, which allows the president to deploy limited numbers of troops without prior congressional approval. This arrangement has put much more power into the hands of the president, and Congress likes it this way.

As the conservative lawyer John Yoo explained in a 2013 opinion article, "Congress has no political incentive to mount and see through its own wartime policy. Members of Congress, who are interested in keeping their seats at the next election, do not want to take stands on controversial issues where the future is uncertain. They will avoid like the plague any vote that will anger large segments of the electorate. They prefer that the president take the political risks and be held accountable for failure."

In other words, Congress wants the president to take responsibility for initiating military action. Then members of Congress can vote money for the action and contend that they are just supporting the troops.

The reason inevitably given for the many military actions is "national security." But it was not clear when Ronald Reagan ordered the invasion of Grenada in 1983 why the possibility of a Cuban-built airport in Grenada might represent a military threat to the United States when the United States had lived with a communist state in Cuba for more than twenty years—and Cuba is far closer to the United States than Grenada is.

In 1990, President George H. W. Bush asserted that the United States could not tolerate Iraqi "aggression" in Kuwait even though the United States had supported Iraqi aggression against Iran ten years earlier in the Iran-Iraq War. The U.S.-led coalition drove Iraq out of Kuwait in a quick and decisive victory. But what exactly did Operation Desert Storm, the 1991 Gulf War, under George H. W. Bush, accomplish in the long run? The results are not impressive. Saddam Hussein remained in power. His Republican Guard survived. The emir of oil-rich Kuwait was restored to his position as dictator of a country with a record of opposing pro-democracy activities and limiting the rights of women and foreign workers.

One other result: the U.S. presence in Saudi Arabia during the Gulf War outraged Saudi-born Osama bin Laden, who complained that thousands of "infidel" troops from America were in Saudi Arabia, which contains Islam's two holiest sites, Mecca and Medina. Bin Laden was the mastermind behind the 9/11 terrorist attacks on New York and Washington.

As Barry Lando noted in a 2011 column for the *Huffington Post*, bin Laden and his followers were also "outraged by U.S. support for corrupt, repressive regimes from Saudi Arabia to Egypt to Yemen, as well, of course, for America's backing of Israel." Lando recalled what Osama bin Laden told CNN in March 1997: "The U.S. wants to occupy our countries, steal our resources, impose agents on us to rule us, and then wants us to agree to all this. If we refuse to do so, it says we are terrorists. . . . Wherever we look, we find the U.S. as the leader of terrorism and crime in the world."

While the United States has been quick to send in the troops, there has rarely been a happy ending. Even Robert Gates, a Republican who has held positions both as director of the CIA and as secretary of defense (and who has thus been at the top of the Pentagon machine), acknowledged that the United States has repeatedly launched military actions without knowing what it was getting into. Gates made this observation in a 2011 talk to cadets at West Point. Since the war in Vietnam, he noted, "we have never once gotten it right, from the *Mayaguez* to Grenada, Panama, Somalia, the Balkans, Haiti, Kuwait, Iraq, and more."

So the question is, how do you explain this pattern? In the years since World War II the United States has presumed the right to dictate—with the use of military power if necessary—who should govern other countries. Certainly this was the premise of President George W. Bush in his decision to invade Iraq in 2003. But it has also been the premise of American policy in many other cases where military actions were taken. It was the American premise in Vietnam. It was the American premise when the CIA overthrew the governments of Iran in 1953, of Guatemala in 1954, of the Dominican Republic in 1965, of Chile in 1973, of Panama in 1989.

The list in modern times of American foreign adventures that have gone sour is long. Lyndon Johnson plunged us into Vietnam. We lost the war. Jimmy Carter unleashed the CIA in Soviet-occupied Afghanistan, providing American support to guerrilla fighters, some of whom would later ally themselves with the Taliban. Ronald Reagan sent American "peacekeepers" to Beirut; when a Marine Corps barracks was attacked, Reagan was forced to withdraw. George H. W. Bush invaded Somalia, and the United States unceremoniously withdrew—mission unaccomplished. And of course George W. Bush invaded Iraq, misleading the world with the allegation that Iraq possessed weapons of mass destruction. There were none. How do you explain the forces that have led to this long series of American disasters?

We all know the basic history of what happened to this country after World War II. America inherited a broken world in Europe, the Middle East, and Far East Asia and within a few years perceived itself in a competition with the Soviet Union for control of the world. The competition became known as the Cold War.

Because America was the least damaged by the horrors of the war, we became the leader of the so-called Free World in the confrontation with the Soviets. In assuming that role, we built up a huge nuclear arsenal and a worldwide system of bases. A huge armaments industry evolved to support the military and its hundreds of bases.

It is not clear that many Americans fully understand the dimensions and complexity of what the late Chalmers Johnson, a well-respected scholar at the University of California at San Diego, called "a new form of empire." Johnson—basing his claim on a 2003 Pentagon report—said the U.S. military owned or rented 702 overseas bases in dozens of countries around the world and had military forces in about 130 countries. "Once upon a time," he wrote, "you could trace the spread of imperialism by counting up colonies. America's version of the colony is the military base."

The numbers today are about the same. A Pentagon report for 2010, the latest year for which figures are available, said the U.S. military had

611 military facilities around the world, not counting war zones. When the war-zone bases are added, the total is about 720, with troops in 153 countries.

Experts such as Sherwood Ross, a veteran foreign affairs journalist, have challenged the Pentagon numbers. In a 2012 post on the *Veterans Today* Web site, Ross said the United States had eleven hundred overseas military bases and that the Pentagon, despite the ending of the Afghan War, was continuing to expand its presence around the globe. Many of the new military bases remain secret, he said, because they are in politically sensitive areas.

Critics of the U.S. foreign bases say they have the potential to engender grievances and anger in host countries. David Vine, a professor at American University writing in *Foreign Policy in Focus*, said, "Most dangerously, as we have seen in Saudi Arabia and Yemen, and as we are seeing in Iraq and Afghanistan, foreign bases create breeding grounds for radicalism, anti-Americanism, and attacks on the United States, reducing, rather than improving, our national security."

The neocons agree that the United States has a huge number of bases and troops around the world. And they applaud that. According to a 2003 study by the conservative Heritage Foundation, "No other military in world history has been so widely deployed as that of the United States."

We are certainly far more widely spread than the Roman Empire, the Ottoman Empire, or even the British Empire at it zenith. Locations in which the United States is known to have bases include Germany, Italy, Japan, Portugal, Saudi Arabia, South Korea, Turkey, the United Kingdom, Bahrain, Cuba, Diego Garcia, Greece, Iceland, Spain, Guam, Colombia, Djibouti, the Philippines, Panama, the Azores, Kenya, Egypt, Indonesia, Singapore, Thailand, Malaysia, Australia, New Zealand, Norway, Sweden, Belgium, Antigua, Saint Helena, Ecuador, Pakistan, and the Netherlands Antilles.

The United States has sought to install, buy, enlarge, or rent bases in a number of other countries, including Morocco, Algeria, Mali, Ghana, Brazil, Poland, the Czech Republic, and France. The United States has also sought to establish a military presence in parts of the former Soviet Union—a zone that Russia has always considered vital to its national interests, much as the United States has regarded Central America and the Caribbean. The presence of U.S. bases in formerly Soviet Uzbekistan and Kyrgyzstan has caused consternation in Russia. In fact, we were evicted from a base in Uzbekistan in 2005.

Meantime, the United States has kept most of its existing military facilities, particularly in the Middle East, including its facilities in Bahrain, Kuwait, Oman, Qatar, and the United Arab Emirates.

LOCATIONS WHERE U.S. FORCES ARE STATIONED

As of March 2014, the United States had about two hundred thousand active-duty military personnel serving in about 150 of the world's 196 countries. Locations included:

Japan	50,631
Germany	40,328
Afghanistan	32,800
South Korea	28,500
Kuwait	11,415
Italy	11,080
United Kingdom	9,485
Guam	5,485
Bahrain	3,115
Spain	1,797
Kyrgyzstan	1,649
Turkey	1,518
Belgium	1,203
Guantánamo Bay	801
Other countries	5,300

Source: Defense Manpower Data Center

The Obama administration has never indicated any intent to contract this empire in a significant way. Obama in his presidential election campaigns never suggested any desire to substantially reduce America's vast involvements abroad. Former secretary of state Hillary Rodham Clinton has, in fact, declared, "The United States can, must, and will lead in this new century"—sounding much like many of her Cold War predecessors.

The impact of the 2013 sequestration—a package of laws requiring across-the-board cuts in defense and other programs—is not yet clear. Although former defense secretary Chuck Hagel and others warned that reduced spending will have a draconian impact on national defense, Congress has the power to reverse that impact and even to order increased defense spending.

By the end of 2013, we had about thirty-three thousand troops in Afghanistan, although most had been withdrawn by the end of 2014, as President Obama pledged. As of December 31, 2014, there were 6,839 U.S. troops in Afghanistan, according to Department of Defense statistics. The administration has said it wants to keep some troops in the country as trainers for the Afghan military even though former president Hamid Karzai and other Afghans have voiced concern that the United States may seek a lasting presence in their country that would impinge on Afghan sovereignty.

Retired Army colonel Douglas Macgregor, a decorated combat veteran, argues, "It is a dangerous deluding statement to think that Muslim populations anywhere want U.S. or British conventional forces inside their country. They do not. They want us out."

In his presentation at a 2009 seminar on Pentagon reform, Macgregor said the United States has been on a "trip down this morally self-justifying road that is appealing to many people on the right and on the left for many reasons." He said this notion goes back to the late defense secretary Les Aspin, who said in 1992 that the mission of U.S. armed forces—with the end of the Cold War and the absence of a Soviet threat to America—was to "punish evildoers."

Macgregor said this idea was reinforced by former secretary of state Madeleine Albright, "who described us as the indispensable nation, the nation that presumably has all the answers for everyone else's problems and has this military establishment that can be used anywhere without restraint anywhere it wants—to rectify all the things we don't like in regions, countries, states, and places where there are internal difficulties."

The American role in the world in the past half century has come with a price, and the price is high. The United States now spends as much on defense as the rest of the world.

For a brief period after the collapse of the Soviet Union in 1991, the Pentagon budget began to fall, but that trend did not last long. It began rising in 2000, then skyrocketed after the 9/11 attacks, with the U.S. invasion of Afghanistan followed by the invasion of Iraq. The Pentagon budget has nearly doubled since 2000, which clearly bothered Defense Secretary Robert Gates—a Republican holdover in Obama's administration.

Gates expressed his dismay in a speech in May 2010 at the Eisenhower Library in Abilene, Kansas: "The attacks of 9/11 opened a gusher of defense spending that nearly doubled the base budget over the last decade, not counting supplemental appropriations for Iraq and Afghanistan. Which brings us to the situation we face and the choices we have today—as a defense department and as a country. Given America's difficult economic circumstances and parlous fiscal condition, military spending on things large and small can and should expect closer, harsher scrutiny."

Gates did not seek to analyze the forces at play, although he probably understands them better than almost anyone else in public life as a result of his long government service. Astonishingly, the so-called war against terror has become more expensive than the Cold War. Total spending for national security was about $1 trillion for fiscal 2012, billions more than our country spends on education, science and medical research, and transportation infrastructure.

In 2010 Barney Frank, then a Democratic congressman from Massachusetts, observed that today "we have fewer enemies and we're spending more money." Many scholars have attempted to explain America's policies. One of the most thoughtful is historian Walter Russell Mead. "For the past few centuries a global economic and political system has been slowly taking shape under first British and then American leadership," he wrote. "As a vital element of that system, the leading global power—with help from allies and other parties—maintains the security of world trade over the seas and air while also ensuring that international economic transactions take place in an orderly way. Thanks to the American umbrella Germany, Japan, China, Korea and India do not need to maintain the military strength to project forces in the Middle East to defend their access to energy. Nor must each country's navy protect the supertankers carrying oil and liquefied natural gas. For this system to work, the Americans must prevent any power from dominating the Persian Gulf while retaining the ability to protect safe passage of ships through its waters." Clearly Mead sees that a central element of American policy is to maintain the free flow of oil from the Persian Gulf.

In her book *The Mission,* Dana Priest documents the rise of the U.S. military and "America's growing dependence on our military to manage world affairs." Her introduction is titled "Pax Americana." Priest describes how the military and its top leaders "fill a diplomatic void" that developed in the 1990s due to budget cuts at the State Department, which closed more than thirty embassies and consulates. With fewer foreign diplomats and fewer embassies, the power of the Pentagon's commanders in chief (CinCs) expanded.

To see the American Empire from the point of view of the Pentagon, look at how the generals divide up the world into six regions (see map on page 99), each with a CinC. The regions are known as CinCdoms—a play on *kingdoms.* One of the most active is Centcom, which includes the Middle East, North Africa, and the Central Asian countries of Afghanistan and Iraq. The other five are the European Command (Eucom), the Pacific Command (Pacom), the African Command (Africom), the North American Command (Northcom), and the South American Command (Southcom).

Historian Andrew Bacevich believes what we have witnessed is the evolution of a "new American militarism," the title of his 2005 book. He went further in his 2010 book *Washington Rules: America's Path to Permanent War.* He argued that America's long-standing post–World War II policy of what he called "global interventionism" had "propelled the United States into a condition approximating perpetual war, as the military misadventures of the past decade have demonstrated."

Garry Wills, professor of history emeritus at Northwestern University, has suggested that growing militarism in American foreign policy

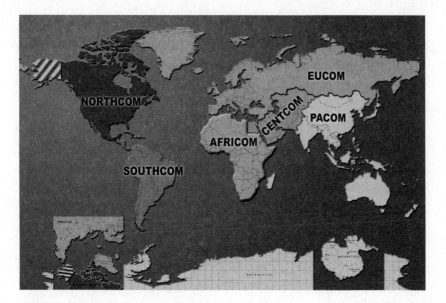

Source: Department of Defense

could be traced to a single underlying factor—the development of the atomic bomb. In his 2010 book, *Bomb Power: The Modern Presidency and the National Security State,* Wills wrote that the bomb has "fostered an anxiety of continuing crisis, so that society was pervasively militarized." In Wills's view, the atomic bomb altered American history "down to its deepest constitutional roots." He continued:

"Since the inception of World War II we have had a continuous state of impending or partial war, with retained constitutional restrictions. World War II faded into the Cold War, and the Cold War into the war on terror, giving us over two-thirds of a century of war in peace, with growing security measures, increased governmental secrecy, broad classification of information, procedural clearances of those citizens able to know what rulers were doing in secret. The requirements became more stringent, not less, after World War II and then again after the Cold War. Normality never returned."

Clearly, the national security state has slipped beyond control—not only of citizens and taxpayers, but also of the government itself. New evidence of this came in a series of shocking stories produced by *The Washington Post* in July 2010. "The government has built a national security and intelligence system so big, so complex and so hard to manage, no one really knows if it's fulfilling its most important purpose: keeping its citizens safe," the *Post* reported. Here is the summary of its findings:

- Some 1,271 government organizations and 1;931 private companies work on programs related to counterterrorism, Homeland Security, and intelligence in about ten thousand locations across the United States.

- An estimated 854,000 people, nearly 1.5 times as many people as live in Washington, D.C., hold a top-secret security clearance.

- In Washington and the surrounding area, thirty-three building complexes for top-secret intelligence work are under construction or have been built since September 2001. Together they occupy the equivalent of almost three Pentagons or twenty-two U.S. Capitols—about 17 million square feet of space.

- Many security and intelligence agencies do the same work, creating redundancy and waste. For example, fifty-one federal organizations and military commands, operating in fifteen U.S. cities, track the flow of money to and from terrorist networks.

- Analysts who make sense of documents and conversations obtained by foreign and domestic spying share their judgment by publishing fifty thousand intelligence reports each year—a volume so large that many are routinely ignored.

The *Post*'s findings, pieced together over two years from unclassified documents, provide a dramatic insight into how the so-called war against terrorism has built a whole new world of vested interests into a national security state. The series—called "Top Secret America"—also revealed the degree to which the national security structure has gotten out of control. What we can see is that America is becoming more militarized than ever before despite the collapse of the Soviet Union and the end of the Cold War.

Many scholars of various ideological persuasions have been predicting an inevitable decline in America's role in the world, an inevitable retraction of the post–World War II American Empire. Yale historian Paul Kennedy in his 1987 book, *The Rise and Fall of the Great Powers,* suggested that great powers in history often devoted so many resources to military adventures that their economies weakened, leading to decline. He wrote, "The United States now runs the risk . . . of what might roughly be called 'imperial overstretch': that is to say, decision-makers in Washington must face the awkward and enduring fact that the sum total of the United States' global interests and obligations is nowadays far larger than the country's power to defend them all simultaneously."

The scholar Michael Mandelbaum has updated that argument, predicting flatly that the United States in years to come will inevitably be forced to reduce its assumed worldwide responsibilities because of domestic demands. "Mounting domestic economic obligations will narrow the scope of American foreign policy in the second decade of the twenty-first century and beyond," he wrote. "Because the United States will have to spend so much more than it has in the past on obligations at home—particularly caring for the ever increasing ranks of its older citizens—it will be able to spend less on foreign policy. Because it will be able to spend less, it will be able to do less."

2013 SPENDING BREAKDOWN
(In Billions of Dollars)

Operation and maintenance	259.7
Military personnel	150.9
Procurement	114.9
Research and development	66.9
Military construction	12.3
Family housing	1.8
Other	1.4
Total	**607.9**

Source: Department of Defense

2010 BUDGET REQUEST FOR BRANCHES OF MILITARY
(In Billions of Dollars)

Army	244.9
Air Force	170.6
Navy	149.9
Defense-wide joint activities	118.7
Defense intelligence	80.1
Marine Corps	4.0

Source: Wikipedia

For every $5 that the United States spent in 2011, about $1 went to defense, about $1 for Medicare and Medicaid, and about $1 for Social Security. David Wessel reported in his 2012 book, *Red Ink*, a detailed breakdown from the White House Office of Management and Budget: 21 percent Medicare and Medicaid, 20.1 percent Social Security, 19.4 percent defense, 15.1 percent benefits other than health, 6.4 percent interest, 18 percent everything else.

As Congress struggles to cut federal spending, the forces for war will continue to exert pressure to maintain a preponderance of American power throughout the world, and rationales will be developed to sustain their arguments. These forces got us where we are and are not likely to retire from the field.

Cato Institute scholar Christopher Preble has studied this problem and has a theory for why Washington can't seem to say no to defense spending. He contrasts the politics of military spending with the politics of regulation. When new government regulations are proposed for any given area, "the people for the regulation push for their position, and the people against the regulation push for theirs," he said. That provides some balance to the debate and the final decision. But with defense spending, the only lobby is the one in favor, the more the better. Anyone who speaks out *against* defense spending risks being called a wimp who is weak on defense. In today's America, that is a politically dangerous label that politicians court at their peril.

The U.S. economic crisis of 2008 and the weak recovery have led to renewed pressure to cut back on defense spending and perhaps even on foreign adventures. But the vested interests for military action and U.S. global domination are too powerful to compel to retreat. The history of our national security state goes back too far.

Dwight Eisenhower was the first—and so far the only—president to fully understand these pressures and to warn publicly against them as strongly as he did, in January 1961. In his 1988 book, *Parting the Waters,* historian Taylor Branch wrote of Eisenhower's concerns about the military-industrial complex a year before he famously warned of them. Eisenhower seemed especially concerned about the Pentagon's lust for more weapons. According to Branch, Eisenhower had "a burning fury against those he considered responsible for creating an atmosphere of feverish demand to spend more money on weapons. The demand had more to do with greed and anxiety than with military judgment, he believed, and was subverting both politics and military professionalism."

Pressures that concerned Eisenhower more than half a century ago exist today and remain poorly understood. The question remains, have forces developed in American society favoring militarization and, ultimately, war grown beyond our control? And what can be done to get America back on track?

AMERICA'S DEFENSE SPENDING AND THE GDP

In recent years, defense spending has consumed less than 4 percent of the nation's GDP (gross domestic product), the measure of the goods and services produced by the nation during one year. This is a critical distinction at the heart of a critical debate over defense spending.

Conservatives typically point to the statistics showing the decline in defense spending as a percentage of GDP as proof that the United States needs to spend more on defense. Liberals and progressives ridicule that interpretation of the data.

As Winslow Wheeler, director of the Straus Military Reform Project, explains in a 2013 blog for *Time* magazine about the decline in defense spending as a percentage of GDP, "These data, while technically accurate, are misused to make a bogus argument. These numbers aren't based on money actually spent, but instead represent the sum of annual Pentagon spending as a slice of the total American economy. Because the American economy has grown faster than defense spending since World War II, the ratio yields numbers that show us dedicating 3.2 percent of the national economic pie to the military in 2014, compared

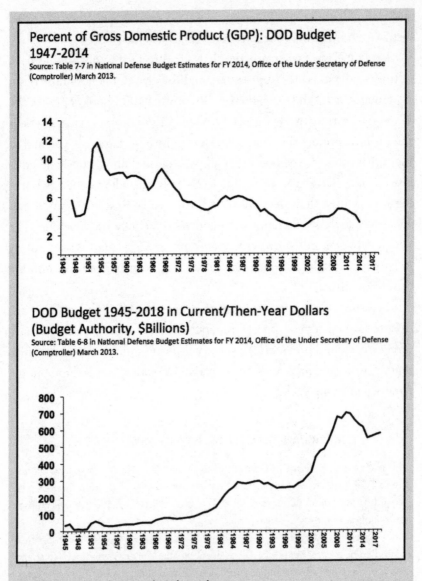

Percent of Gross Domestic Product (GDP): DOD Budget 1947-2014

Source: Table 7-7 in National Defense Budget Estimates for FY 2014, Office of the Under Secretary of Defense (Comptroller) March 2013.

DOD Budget 1945-2018 in Current/Then-Year Dollars (Budget Authority, $Billions)

Source: Table 6-8 in National Defense Budget Estimates for FY 2014, Office of the Under Secretary of Defense (Comptroller) March 2013.

Source: Winslow Wheeler, Center for Defense Information

to a 5.9 percent slice in 1985 during the Reagan-era defense buildup. The key fact is that we are now spending more on our military than during the Reagan Administration."

The 2012 Republican presidential candidate, Mitt Romney, called for committing at least 4 percent of GDP to defense spending. The Center for a New American Security—a progressive Washington think tank—countered with studies showing that Romney's idea would have added as much as $2.3 trillion to the defense budget over ten years from spending levels projected in 2013. An opinion piece about Romney's idea, published August 25, 2012, in *The New York Times*, was headlined, "How Mr. Romney Would Force-Feed the Pentagon."

Except for the Reagan buildup in the 1980s, the spikes in U.S. defense spending as a percentage of GDP have occurred during wartime. The previous page shows two charts that Wheeler developed from Department of Defense statistics. One shows how defense spending has declined as a percent of GDP. The other shows how defense spending has increased.

7

THE VORTEX: THE MIDDLE EAST

You know, some people never get the word. The fight isn't about oil. The fight is about naked aggression that will not stand.

—President George H. W. Bush, 1990

We are in the Mideast for three letters—oil, O-I-L.

—Senator Robert Dole, 1990

I t was President Jimmy Carter, widely described as a political wimp, who laid out the policy that has largely driven America's war machine for more than thirty years. Carter declared on January 23, 1980, that the United States held "vital interests" in the Persian Gulf and would use "any means necessary, including military force," to bar any nation's attempt to dominate that region.

What scholars call the Carter Doctrine has remained a pillar of U.S. policy ever since, enforced by Republican and Democratic presidents alike. True to Carter's promise, the United States has routinely used armed force to defend its "vital interests"—importing, and helping to produce, the petroleum that underpins its economy and standard of living.

In and around the Persian Gulf region, the United States has since 1980 fought three major wars, including the second-longest in U.S. history. It has conducted scores of smaller assaults, interventions, and demonstrations of force. It has built its U.S. Central Command to oversee what in late 2012 were about eighty-five thousand American service members deployed across most of twenty countries in the region, plus the ships and roughly fifteen thousand personnel of the U.S. Navy's Fifth Fleet. The CIA conducted the longest, most expensive covert operation in its history in the Gulf region and used it as the battlefield testing ground for America's newest way of warfare—missile-armed drone aircraft piloted by remote control.

According to U.S. presidents, both Republican and Democratic, our country fights its now-constant Middle East warfare over moral principles. We fight, they say, to promote nonaggression, build democratic nations, ensure self-determination for national groups, protect minorities' rights, or seize hideous weapons of mass destruction. Yet for these noble aims, our country has allied with military dictators and authoritarian monarchs, overthrown a democratically elected government, and armed extremist, antidemocratic guerrilla fighters.

The disconnect between America's declared goals and its actions is resolved only when we understand that our military effort to dominate the region is not primarily about achieving justice or democracy. It's about the oil.

In the region that has brought more war into Americans' lives than any other since Vietnam, oil is one of the two great engines of our policy. And in a nightmare for our efforts to act coherently and sensibly in the region, our oil-driven policy often runs counter to the other engine, which is the U.S. relationship with Israel.

Carter was not the visionary who first saw the need of the Western superpowers for enough control in the Middle East to ensure their access to Persian Gulf oil. That distinction goes to the British navy secretary of 1911, the young Winston Churchill, who foresaw that navies and armies, then fueled by coal, would soon be shifting to petroleum. The race for oil deepened Britain's domination of the Gulf region for three decades, until the United States took the lead in 1945. In that year, President Franklin Roosevelt beat Prime Minister Churchill to a first meeting with Saudi Arabia's founder, King Abdul Aziz Al Saud. Over Arab coffee on a U.S. Navy cruiser in the Suez Canal, FDR and Abdul Aziz opened their countries' oil-for-security partnership, which has remained the centerpiece of American influence in the Gulf region.

The oil-versus-Israel conundrum was present from the start. Sitting knee to knee with Abdul Aziz on the deck of the USS *Quincy*, FDR asked him three times for help in arranging the resettlement of European Jews among the Arabs of Palestine, according to the men's translator, U.S. scholar and diplomat William Eddy. Each time, Abdul Aziz replied that, if the German Nazis had oppressed the Jews, it was they, rather than Palestine's Arabs, who should pay the cost of reparations. Rather than press the issue to the point of disrupting the men's incipient agreement on an alliance, FDR backed down, telling Abdul Aziz that America would never act with hostility toward the Arabs and would not back Jewish immigration to Palestine without Arab agreement. But fifty-seven days later, Roosevelt was dead of a stroke, and that October, President Harry Truman dismissed his predecessor's promise to the Saudi king. He supported the Jewish immigration efforts and, three years later, declared America's recognition and support of the Israeli state just eleven minutes after its formal declaration.

Since then, both oil and Israel have endured as pillars of U.S. policy.

The oil issue appeared seven years before FDR's meeting with Abdul Aziz, when Standard Oil of California struck its first bonanza in the sands of Abdul Aziz's kingdom. During World War II, America's massive war effort would lead it to pump out nearly a third of its own known reserves at the time, an alarming loss. The entire world had seen the lesson that oil meant power, for the United States had defeated Japan in part by cutting off its oil supplies.

So the United States would need foreign supplies of oil, and its imports from the Persian Gulf were on a climb that would peak in 2001. In that year, nearly one-third of U.S. imported oil came from the

Persian Gulf countries. As America's dependence on Gulf oil grew, so did its readiness to fight to keep it.

In 1953, when an elected Iranian prime minister seized British-owned oil facilities in his country, the CIA helped Britain overthrow him and hand absolute power to Iran's military and its shah. But Britain's regional policing power was declining, and by 1969 the United Kingdom was preparing to close its military bases east of the Suez Canal, a step it would formally take in 1971. President Richard Nixon stepped in with an offer to help nations there with defense, by selling them weapons and, in selected cases, offering U.S. forces to assist. The Iranian shah, Mohammad Reza Pahlavi, soon became America's biggest arms customer and military ally in the Gulf region.

A decade later, that fell apart. In February 1979, Iranians overthrew the shah's corrupt, unpopular regime and installed the theocratic Ayatollah Ruholla Khomeini. The Iranian revolution disrupted oil production. Saudi Arabia and some other Gulf countries increased production to offset the Iranian decline, but widespread panic drove up prices worldwide and contributed to a national energy crisis in the United States.

In a TV address in July 1979, President Carter called on Americans to cut "self-indulgence and consumption" by avoiding unnecessary car trips, reducing their thermostats in winter, and using more public transport. But as the United States entered an election year, Republican Ronald Reagan was mounting a political challenge that would decisively defeat Carter by accusing him of failing to build and use American power abroad.

On Christmas Eve 1979, the Soviet Union invaded neighboring Afghanistan, bringing its troops to within striking distance of the straits at the mouth of the Gulf, a strategic choke point for much of the world's oil supply.

Four weeks later, in his State of the Union address in January 1980, President Carter strode into the chamber of the U.S. House of Representatives to tell Congress and the nation that the Soviet invasion of Afghanistan was an unacceptable threat to Persian Gulf oil, and thus to America. This was a matter of economics. "Let our position be absolutely clear," Carter said. "An attempt by any outside force to gain control of the Persian Gulf region will be regarded as an assault on the vital interests of the United States of America and such an assault will be repelled by any means necessary, including military force."

Carter left no doubt about his reasons: "The region, which is now threatened by Soviet troops in Afghanistan, is of great strategic importance. It contains more than two-thirds of the world's exportable oil. The Soviet effort to dominate Afghanistan has brought Soviet military forces to within three hundred miles of the Indian Ocean and close to the Strait of Hormuz, a waterway through which most of the world's oil must flow."

And he went further. He declared that the situation "demands collective efforts to meet this new threat to security in the Persian Gulf and in Southwest Asia. It demands the participation of all those who rely on oil from the Middle East and who are concerned with global peace and stability."

Less than six weeks after his speech, Carter and the military established a new military task force to execute this doctrine, a step toward what in 1983 became the U.S. Central Command. Centcom, as it is known in military jargon, directs U.S. military operations in twenty countries, from Egypt to Kazakhstan, which together contain 60 percent of the world's oil supplies and about 40 percent of the natural gas supplies. Centcom's naval force, the U.S. Fifth Fleet, patrols much of the Indian Ocean, and three of the world's seven major choke points for oil shipping, including the Strait of Hormuz, which still carried 20 percent of the world's oil trade in 2012.

As critical as oil was in 1980, America's addiction to Persian Gulf oil became only more acute in the two decades afterward. Reagan's defeat of Carter in 1980 had schooled American politicians against trying to wean the country from that addiction by urging citizens to voluntarily reduce their consumption.

"The ultimate in U.S. national interests" had become "the removal of any obstacles or encumbrances that might hinder the American people in their pursuit of happiness ever more expansively defined," wrote Andrew Bacevich in his 2005 book, *The New American Milita-rism.* "During the 1980s and 1990s, the U.S. strategic center of gravity shifted, overturning long-established geopolitical priorities that had appeared sacrosanct." American policy that had been fixated on the Cold War, and the danger of a Soviet invasion of Western Europe, now shifted to the worry of what could happen if the United States lost access to Persian Gulf oil. "A set of revised strategic priorities emerged, cen-tered geographically in the energy-rich Persian Gulf but linked inextri-cably to the assumed prerequisites for sustaining American freedom at home," Bacevich wrote. "A succession of administrations, both Repub-lican and Democratic, opted for armed force as the preferred means to satisfy those new priorities."

This fundamental shift in American policy in the post–Cold War world helps explain why defense spending has continued to rise despite the end of the Cold War and why America remains up to its ears in ques-tionable military adventures in the Middle East. None of the presi-dents who have followed Carter have wanted to acknowledge that they have adopted his policy. It is not hard to figure out why. They have not wanted to suggest that the United States would sacrifice the blood of its sons and daughters for oil. But history speaks for itself.

The first president to enforce the Carter Doctrine through a full-blown war was a Republican—George Herbert Walker Bush, who in 1990 sent American forces to throw back Iraqi leader Saddam Hus-sein's invasion of Kuwait. In so doing, did Bush mention Jimmy Carter or any kind of doctrine? He did not. For Bush, Jimmy Carter and his celebrated doctrine never existed. Bush categorically and repeatedly denied that an American interest in oil had anything to do with his decision to go to war to drive Saddam's forces out of Kuwait. The offi-cially stated reason for his decision to go to war was a matter of princi-ple. The United States, he said, simply opposed aggression as a means of settling international disputes.

In announcing his decision on August 8, 1990, within days of the invasion, to send American troops to the area, Bush said, "I took this ac-tion to assist the Saudi Arabian government in the defense of its home-land." When speculation began to appear in the press that American interests in oil might be a factor, Bush denied it. But at least one time, in a speech within the military's bureaucracy, Bush did admit that oil was a motivation. On August 15, 1990, speaking to Defense Department employees at the Pentagon, he repeated the line, standard for him and for other U.S. presidents, that he sought "peace and stability" for the entire world. Then he said, "We are also talking about maintaining access to energy resources that are key—not just to the functioning of this country, but to the entire world. Our jobs, our way of life, our own freedom, and the freedom of friendly countries around the world would all suffer if control of the world's great oil reserves fell into the hands of that one man, Saddam Hussein."

Bush's candor turned out to be a brief, shining moment. Two weeks later, he returned to his standard theme. "Aggression"—not oil— became the official rationale for the war.

In mid-October, when interrupted by war protesters at a GOP fundraising event in Des Moines, Bush declared, "You know, some people never get the word. The fight isn't about oil. The fight is about naked aggression that will not stand." A week later, he repeated this mantra in Vermont.

One skeptic did speak out. In a speech on the floor of the U.S. Senate, Republican senator Bob Dole of Kansas ridiculed the idea that Bush was sending troops to Kuwait because of "aggression" by Iraq, our ally in the earlier Iran-Iraq War. "We are in the Mideast for three letters— oil, O-I-L," Dole declared. "We are there because we do not want Saddam Hussein to get his hand around our throats and jack up the price of oil, which would have a severe impact on the economy."

Bush's self-righteous opposition to Saddam's "aggression" seems at least disingenuous. A few years earlier, the Reagan administration, with Bush as vice president, had sold matériel and provided intelligence help to the same Saddam Hussein after his invasion of Iran.

The U.S. military pushed Iraq's army out of Kuwait in February 1991. With that, America's campaign to dominate the Gulf entered a new phase with a twelve-year-long containment of Saddam's military strength, enforced by economic sanctions and an air war. From 1991 until 2003, the United States and the United Kingdom (with French participation for several years) flew thousands of sorties to prohibit Saddam's government from flying military aircraft over the far north and south of Iraq. These no-fly zones were declared to protect Iraqi minority groups who had faced retribution by Saddam. The groups included Kurds in the north and Shiite Muslims in the south.

The military effect of this operation was to prepare for the U.S. invasion in 2003. With an average of seventy-four hundred personnel and nearly two hundred combat aircraft operating from Saudi and Turkish bases over twelve years, the U.S.-led air forces destroyed Iraqi air-defense missiles and radar systems.

This aerial war of containment, which continued from the Bush administration into that of President Bill Clinton, was part of a pattern that underscored American willingness, under both of its political parties, to use military force to assure military dominance in the Gulf region. Clinton's deployment of forces as president was directed largely toward the Balkans following the breakup of Yugoslavia. Still, Clinton sustained the militarized Middle Eastern policies of his predecessors. Six months after taking office, he ordered twenty-three cruise missiles fired at the headquarters of Iraq's intelligence service as retaliation for what the FBI found was a plot to kill former president George H. W. Bush during a visit to Kuwait. Clinton strengthened the containment of Saddam with repeated cruise missile attacks and bombing raids in response to Iraqi military movements and Iraqi restrictions on UN weapons inspectors. Clinton also ordered waves of cruise missiles fired into Sudan and Afghanistan in retaliation for Al Qaeda's 1998 bombings of two U.S. embassies in East Africa.

In one more critical way, Clinton laid the foundations for the disastrous Iraq invasion that would follow under his successor. In 1998, he signed the Iraq Liberation Act, which made it U.S. policy to seek the overthrow of Saddam's regime. Under the law, the United States would sponsor and finance the creation of the Iraqi National Congress, an anti-Saddam exile group headed by Ahmed Chalabi. Chalabi's group would, in 2002, provide the George W. Bush administration with "intelligence" information, later proved false, which Bush's team used to help launch its nine-year war in Iraq.

Al Qaeda's 9/11 attacks on New York and Washington and the response of George W. Bush's administration brought to full fruition an American policy to seek military dominance in the Middle East. As Andrew Bacevich put it, "Using armed might to secure American preeminence across the region, especially in the oil-rich Persian Gulf, remained the essence of U.S. policy. What had changed was the scope of the military effort that the United States was now willing to undertake in pursuit of those objectives. After September 11, the Bush administration pulled out all the stops in its determination to impose America's will on the Greater Middle East."

It took less than two months and just a small contingent of CIA officers working with anti-Taliban Afghan militias to overthrow Afghanistan's Taliban regime, which had hosted Al Qaeda leader Osama bin Laden, the mastermind of the 9/11 attacks. But Afghanistan was only a sideshow in the younger President Bush's Middle East policy. By March 2002, only twelve weeks after ousting the Taliban, the Bush team was recalling the CIA and military specialists working in Afghanistan to help prepare the main act. By July, the first of them were on the ground in Iraq, to prepare for the overthrow of Saddam.

In his speech to the nation in March 2003, as the United States prepared to invade Iraq, President Bush said, "The people of the United States and our friends and allies will not live at the mercy of an outlaw regime that threatens the peace with weapons of mass murder."

What of the need to sustain U.S. dominance in the Persian Gulf to keep access to oil? Defense Secretary Donald Rumsfeld said it had "nothing to do with oil." But in a 2007 memoir, former Federal Reserve chairman Alan Greenspan wrote that George W. Bush's invasion was driven at least in part by America's lust for Iraq's oil. "I am saddened that it is politically inconvenient to acknowledge what everyone knows: the Iraq war is largely about oil," he wrote.

During a roundtable discussion at Stanford University in October 2007, General John Abizaid, former head of U.S. Central Command and military operations in Iraq in 2007, said the same: "Of course it's about the oil; we can't really deny that."

Chuck Hagel, a former Republican senator, was equally blunt in comments he made in 2007 to a class of law students at Catholic University: "People say we're not fighting for oil. Of course we are. They talk about America's national interests. What the hell do you think they're talking about? We're not there for figs." Despite his remarks, Hagel was confirmed as secretary of defense in 2013.

We know now and have known with certainty since 2004 that there were no weapons of mass destruction in Iraq. Yet American military forces remained there for nine years, until December 2011. Nearly forty-five hundred U.S. military members and tens of thousands of Iraqis died.

Without mentioning oil or the Persian Gulf, President Obama, perhaps unwittingly, paraphrased the Carter Doctrine in addressing troops in Afghanistan in March 2010. "If I thought for a minute that America's vital interests were not at stake here in Afghanistan, I would order all of you home right away." There were those "vital interests" again. But Obama did not tell the troops what he thought those "vital interests" might be.

According to a 2010 study by Princeton University scholar Roger Stern, the United States spent $7.3 trillion from 1976 to 2007 to keep at least one aircraft carrier on station in the Persian Gulf region to make it safe for oil shipments. Stern calculated that cost based on published Defense Department data.

But that is only a portion of the true cost of oil. In 2008, Nobel Prize–winning economist Joseph Stiglitz and Harvard University budget expert Linda Bilmes estimated that the 2003 invasion of Iraq had, until then, cost $3 trillion—adding roughly $5 to the cost of a barrel of oil. Interruption of Iraqi oil production pushed up oil prices, they said. Another price factor was the instability from the war that dampened investment in the Middle East, the largest supplier of oil in the world. Writing two years later, they said that the war's impact actually added at least $10 per barrel—twice their earlier estimate. The true cost, they noted, was incalculable damage to America's economy, the expansion of our federal debt, and damage to America's standing as a global leader.

What do these costs mean at the pump?

Anita Dancs, an associate professor of economics at Western New England College, dug into the numbers and estimated that the U.S.

military cost for securing the free flow of oil was about $166 billion for fiscal year 2010. She said that translated to about fifty-six cents for a gallon of gasoline, a surcharge that we pay through our federal taxes.

That $166 billion, instead of keeping aircraft carriers in the Arabian Sea and defending Gulf emirates, could be reinvested in ways to strengthen our country and economy. Or if we wanted, it could even operate public transportation systems for free in a hundred U.S. cities, Dancs wrote.

One other important fact: the major beneficiaries of the Middle Eastern oil are Japan and Europe. That is becoming more and more true as the U.S. domestic energy supply increases and U.S. dependence on imports decreases.

The question is how long the United States—under pressure to cut government spending—will continue to provide free military force to secure Middle Eastern oil for the rest of the world, making it possible for those countries to put their savings into education, infrastructure, health care, and other domestic priorities.

Energy magnate T. Boone Pickens, for one, thinks that the United States should rethink its strategy in the Middle East. A 2012 *Parade* magazine article quoted him as saying, "It's insane that we have the Fifth Fleet of the U.S. Navy tied up there to protect oil that ends up in China and Europe."

No American administration in the last thirty years—including the Obama administration—has been completely candid about the reasons for America's deep military involvement in the Persian Gulf area. Even after a decade of war in Afghanistan, declarations of its purpose by President Obama and his top military aides remained ambiguous. In his talk to troops in Afghanistan, Obama said the American goal was to prevent a resurgent Taliban from returning to power to again provide a haven for Al Qaeda or other terrorists. That would seem to be a narrow objective. But top officers suggested a broader agenda, stressing the need for political stability in the Persian Gulf area. And that objective changes everything, because the creation of political stability would take years or generations, if it can be achieved at all.

In October 2009, General Stanley McChrystal, the top military commander in Afghanistan, mentioned "stability" as an underlying objective. He didn't mention oil or that Afghanistan is close to the Strait of Hormuz, the busiest passageway for oil tankers in the world—a point that led President Carter to threaten to use nuclear force against the Soviets after they invaded Afghanistan in December 1979.

After delivering a talk in London, McChrystal was asked if he would support a proposal to cut back the American military presence in order to focus on tracking down leaders of Al Qaeda.

"The answer is no," McChrystal said. "A strategy that does not leave Afghanistan in a stable position is probably a shortsighted strategy." He added that Afghanistan was the "key" to stability in South Asia as well as to the security of the United States, Britain, and other Western allies.

General David Petraeus, who was the commanding general in Iraq and later in Afghanistan, is quoted in Bob Woodward's 2010 book, *Obama's Wars,* as saying, "You have to recognize also that I don't think you win this war [in Afghanistan]. I think you keep fighting." At another point, Petraeus said, "You have to stay after it. This is the kind of fight we're in for the rest of our lives and probably our kids' lives."

When he announced his plan to send an additional thirty thousand troops to Afghanistan, President Obama apparently wished to make clear that he did not envision a permanent American involvement. He said he planned to begin withdrawing troops by mid-2011, and that drawdown has been completed. Obama also said he intended to remove all of America's combat forces by 2014. But as of March 2015, there were nearly ten thousand U.S. troops still in Afghanistan. And according to a *New York Times* article published March 19, 2015, the Obama administration is "nearing a decision to keep more troops in Afghanistan" in 2016 than intended because of "roiling violence in the country."

Obama in his speech to American troops on a visit to Afghanistan in March 2010 justified troop increases: "The United States of America does not quit once it starts on something. We keep at it, we persevere, and together with our partners we will prevail."

The president may be excused for a pep talk to American troops, but he should not be excused for misrepresenting fairly recent history that reminds us that there are limits to American power. The historical record is quite clear that the United States ultimately quit in Vietnam, after realizing that it could not win. President Ronald Reagan quit in Lebanon in 1983 after 241 American servicemen were killed in a suicide bomb attack on a Marine Corps barracks.

Ted Koppel, for many years the managing editor of ABC's *Nightline*, pointed out in a 2010 *Washington Post* column that the 9/11 attacks "succeeded far beyond anything Osama bin Laden could possibly have envisioned" by sucking the United States into a vast series of overreactions. Koppel argued that the United States had accomplished its objectives in Afghanistan quickly in its initial 2001 attack by driving the Taliban from power and Al Qaeda into the mountains of Pakistan. But the United States then blundered into Iraq on the false pretenses that Saddam Hussein's regime held chemical or biological weapons and had had some connection with Al Qaeda. Since American troops withdrew from Iraq in 2011, it has come close to being a failed state. Countless bombings have killed thousands of Iraqi civilians. Government corruption is rampant. Koppel's argument is that the George W. Bush administration's military adventures in Afghanistan and Iraq, in ostensible efforts to stabilize the area, have seriously destabilized it.

President George W. Bush declared on more than one occasion that terrorism was the major threat facing the United States, and President Obama appears to have bought into that concept by his aggressive expansion of the war in Afghanistan. But Benjamin Friedman and Christopher Preble of the Cato Institute have pointed out that a war against terrorism cannot justify a huge military. "Most of our military spending goes to conventional forces adept at destroying well-armed enemies," they wrote in 2010. "Terrorists are lightly armed and mostly hidden. The trick is finding them, not killing or capturing them once they are found. Counterinsurgency enthusiasts claim that we can be safe from terrorists only by using ground forces to rebuild the states where they operate. But we have learned the hard way that theory badly overestimates our ability to organize other nations' politics."

They added, "Even if we could master that imperial art, it would not be worth the cost."

No examination of American policy in the Middle East, particularly in Republican administrations, would be complete without noting the close ties of many top officials to the oil industry—and thus to the economic importance of the flow of oil from the Persian Gulf.

President George Herbert Walker Bush made his fortune in Texas with Zapata Petroleum. Kevin Phillips, in his 2004 book about the Bush family, *American Dynasty*, wrote, "Over four generations the vocation of the Bushes has been essentially financial, sometimes with a flow of petroleum or a whiff of natural gas. This background, transcending their Texas experience alone, explained much of their economic worldview: what they perceived to be a good economy, the yardsticks they used to measure it, and what policies they pursued in the White House to promote the necessary outcomes."

Dick Cheney, vice president under George W. Bush, served as chief executive officer of Halliburton, one of the world's largest oil-services companies, after serving as defense secretary for George H. W. Bush. Halliburton was one of the largest private contractors hired by the U.S. military during the U.S. wars in both Iraq and Afghanistan.

George Shultz, who served as secretary of state under Ronald Reagan, was once president of the giant engineering company Bechtel, which, among other things, operates oil refineries.

Before becoming George W. Bush's national security adviser and secretary of state, Condoleezza Rice served on the board of Chevron, one of the world's largest oil companies.

In seeking to understand and explain American policy in the Middle East for the last thirty-plus years, it seems apparent in retrospect that Jimmy Carter was the architect and his successors the implementers. The history of these years demonstrates that administrations of both political parties have believed that the United States has a vested interest in the free flow of oil from the Persian Gulf. In other words, the United States has a vested interest in war in the Middle East.

8

NUCLEAR FOLLY

I see no compelling reason why we should not unilaterally get rid of our nuclear weapons. To maintain them is costly and adds nothing to our security.

—Paul Nitze

No more dramatic example of America's vested interests in war can be found than in the story of the nuclear arms race—a race America has led for more than sixty-five years.

We have created a vast nuclear industry with thousands of employees and spent hundreds of billions of dollars on nuclear weapons and the missiles and bombers to deliver them. But as history has demonstrated over those sixty-five-plus years, these weapons have little value beyond the threat of terror because they can't be used.

Since the United States launched the nuclear age by dropping two bombs on Japan in World War II, we have fought four major wars—in Korea, Vietnam, Iraq, and Afghanistan—in which more than one hundred thousand American soldiers have died. We have launched more than fifty smaller invasions or incursions in which thousands more have died—and our vast nuclear stockpile has stood idle. Because those bombs can't be used.

At the peak of the Cold War, the United States and the Soviet Union wielded about 70,000 nuclear weapons. The total for the United States and Russia as of 2014 was about 16,200. See the chart on page 125 for details.

The principal contribution that America's addiction to nuclear weapons has made to the modern world is to encourage other nations to build nuclear arms as well—thus making the entire civilized world more dangerous.

Proponents of nuclear weapons argue that these weapons have deterred war with the idea of mutually assured destruction (MAD). This principle holds that any state that might start a nuclear war would itself face destruction in a nuclear counterstrike and is thus deterred from beginning such a deadly exchange.

But why 70,000 nuclear weapons? Or 16,200? Isn't it obvious that a few—a dozen perhaps—would perform the same function?

Astonishingly, the consensus among serious students of nuclear arms—Republicans and Democrats, retired generals, NATO commanders, former secretaries of state and of defense, and top nuclear scientists—is that it is time for the world to rid itself of nuclear weapons.

Even Paul Nitze came to this conclusion late in his life. This American cold warrior extraordinaire was the primary author of the infamous 1950 government study NSC-68, which helped to launch the United States on its huge Cold War military buildup to "contain" the Soviet Union. But after the Soviet collapse, he wrote in 1999 in *The New York Times*, "I see no compelling reason why we should not unilaterally get rid of our nuclear weapons. To maintain them is costly and adds nothing to our security."

President Obama agrees and has said so, most notably in a 2009 speech: "So today, I state clearly and with conviction America's commitment to seek the peace and security of a world without nuclear weapons. I'm not naïve. This goal will not be reached quickly—perhaps not in my lifetime. It will take patience and persistence. But now we, too, must ignore the voices that tell us that the world cannot change. We have to insist, 'Yes, we can.'"

In a speech on June 19, 2013, in Berlin, Obama proposed cutting the U.S. nuclear arsenal and called for reducing global nuclear weapons. But no serious possibility exists that this is going to happen anytime soon.

The U.S. Senate in late 2010 approved a nuclear arms treaty with Russia called the New Start, which will cut the number of deployed strategic warheads to 1,550 on each side, a number still large enough for either to virtually destroy modern civilization. But the Obama administration paid a high price to get reluctant Republican support, agreeing to pour billions more dollars into the fool's game of missile defense, a contradiction of the intent of the treaty, and into the modernization of U.S. nuclear weapons production and stockpile stewardship. The treaty lets each side keep thousands of strategic warheads stored in stockpile—just in case. And it does not limit tactical nuclear weapons, of which there are thousands more. The treaty will not have to be fully implemented for seven years.

In his first State of the Union speech in 2010, Obama said that he had "embraced the vision of John F. Kennedy and Ronald Reagan through a strategy that reverses the spread of [nuclear] weapons and seeks a world without them." Obama has made more speeches since then, including the one in Berlin. But a long-sought implementation of the Comprehensive Nuclear Test Ban Treaty is nowhere in sight. The treaty was completed in 1996 and signed by the United States and 183 other nations. While it could conceivably put real brakes on the arms race, the United States has come nowhere near the two-thirds majority needed in the Senate for ratification. Six other countries, including China, must also ratify the accord to bring it into force.

This is the madness of the nuclear arms race and this is the madness of the military-industrial-congressional-think-tank-intelligence complex that dominates American politics. I first became aware of the difficulty of making progress in nuclear arms control from an offhand statement by Secretary of State Henry Kissinger at the close of a summit meeting with the Soviets in Moscow in July 1974.

The summit conference between President Richard Nixon and Soviet leader Leonid Brezhnev had clearly failed to make progress. In the press conference afterward, a disappointed Kissinger said with some emotion, "My impression from what I have observed is that both sides have to convince their military establishments of the benefits of restraint, and that is not a thought that comes naturally to military people on either side." It was an admission that the Pentagon was playing a critical role in arms control policy.

Later, clearly frustrated, Kissinger exclaimed, "One of the questions which we have to ask ourselves as a country is what in the name of God is strategic superiority? What is the significance of it, politically, militarily, operationally, at these levels of numbers? What do you do with it?" He suggested that if the arms race could not be brought under control, the result could eventually be tragic for both sides—a point that remains valid today, more than thirty-five years later.

A curious moment in 1986 showed that leaders on both sides of the Cold War understood and shared the desire to eliminate nuclear arms altogether. In a hastily arranged and poorly prepared meeting in Reykjavík, Iceland, on October 11 and 12, between Soviet leader Mikhail Gorbachev and President Ronald Reagan, the two seriously discussed ridding the world of nuclear weapons. Both leaders stated several times that their most important objective should be total elimination.

Historian Richard Rhodes reports on the meeting in *Arsenals of Folly,* quoting Reagan as stating at the summit's opening session, "I'm proceeding from the assumption that both sides want to rid the world of ballistic missiles and of nuclear weapons in general."

At the same session Gorbachev stated, "Let me precisely, firmly, and clearly declare, we are in favor of finding a solution that would lead eventually to a complete liquidation of nuclear arms."

The two men, along with aides on both sides, discussed detailed timetables seeking to achieve that objective—starting with a 50 percent cut and moving on over some years to total elimination.

Of course it didn't happen at that summit or at any other summit in the years that have followed, and we know why. The reason then and since is Ronald Reagan's fantasy—a fantasy embraced by American administrations to follow—that a perfect system of defense against intercontinental ballistic missiles is possible. And it isn't. I believe it is true that most scientists fully understand that it is not possible. But this knowledge has not restrained American governments of both political parties from continuing to pour billions of dollars into missile defense programs. This fact can only be understood in the context of the economic and political forces that make up the complex that is the subject of this book.

Reagan had announced his proposal to develop a missile shield in March 1983, three years before sitting down with Gorbachev in Iceland. The Reagan proposal, called the Strategic Defense Initiative (SDI), was commonly known as Star Wars. For the Soviets, that proposal overturned the basic principle of deterrence—the notion of mutually assured destruction, of the vulnerability of each side to a counterattack by the other. Reagan declared that his proposal was consistent with the agreement the United States and the Soviets had signed eleven years earlier not to deploy more than token missile defenses. But to the Soviets, Reagan's effort to build a missile shield unbalanced the nuclear calculus and heightened the risk of war.

At Reykjavík, Reagan was determined not to give up on his missile defense fantasy, and that determination killed the dream that both leaders had expressed of eliminating nuclear weapons. Gorbachev proposed that research on missile defense be restricted to the laboratory, a proposal that many American experts—including Secretary of State George Shultz and longtime arms-control specialist Paul Nitze—believed would make it possible to continue the SDI program satisfactorily. But at a crucial moment of decision at the summit, Reagan accepted the advice of his assistant secretary of defense, Richard Perle—a notorious neoconservative hawk and longtime opponent of arms control. Perle had a well-earned reputation as an arch-cold warrior. If ever a situation fit the cliché of a fox in the henhouse, Reagan's reliance on Perle on this occasion certainly was it.

The crucial moment at the summit came on the final day and was recounted by Perle's biographer, Jay Winik, as Perle had described it to him:

"The president first looked at Perle. 'Can we carry out research [on SDI] under the restraints the Soviets are proposing?'"

Perle responded, "'Mr. President, we cannot conduct the research under the terms he's proposing. It will effectively kill SDI.'"

Reagan accepted Perle's judgment over the judgment of his most experienced counselors, Shultz and Nitze. Nitze had said that the Soviet proposal was "the best we have received in twenty-five years." Thus the dream of ridding the world of nuclear arms died for at least a generation on the judgment of an arch-neoconservative most Americans have probably never heard of.

The dream itself, however, has not died. One of the most dramatic cries for sanity in the effort to control nuclear arms came a little more than a decade later from a totally unexpected source—a retired four-star Air Force general, George Lee Butler, who at one time held the trigger to nuclear war in his hand. In 1996, in a speech to the National Press Club, he declared that nuclear weapons should be abolished and that they do not provide security for Americans or anyone else. He said that the theory of nuclear deterrence, the bedrock principle of U.S. national security during the Cold War, was costly, wrongheaded, and dangerous.

HOW MANY NUCLEAR WARHEADS THREATEN THE WORLD?

Knowing how many atomic warheads threaten the world is, at best, guesswork based on careful research. The Ploughshares Fund, a foundation devoted to a world without nuclear weapons, reported in 2014 that the following nine countries have an estimated 17,300 nuclear weapons.

Country	Nuclear Weapons
Russia	8,500
United States	7,700
France	300
China	250
United Kingdom	225
Pakistan	120
India	110
Israel	80
North Korea	10
Total	**17,295**

Few in America were more familiar with the mathematics of a potential nuclear war than Lee Butler. For three years, beginning in 1991, he had been commanding general of the Strategic Air Command, in charge of either launching a nuclear attack or responding to one. He commanded 13,000 personnel controlling an estimated 5,700 deployed strategic nuclear warheads, out of 11,089 then in the U.S. arsenal. He knew every intricate detail of the plans for war—the timing and the targets. For most of a prestigious military career he had accepted the logic of MAD—mutual assured destruction and deterrence, which was and is the basis of American national security policy.

But by 1996, Butler had learned more—perhaps more than he had wanted to know—about the system's essential nature as a formula for mutual annihilation if war should come. "As to those who believe nuclear weapons desirable or inevitable," he told the Press Club, "I would say these devices exact a terrible price even if never used. Accepting nuclear weapons as the ultimate arbiter of conflict condemns the world to live under a dark cloud of perpetual anxiety. Worse, it codifies mankind's most murderous instincts as an acceptable resort when other options for resolving conflict fail." In closing, Butler said, "We can do better than condone a world in which nuclear weapons are accepted as commonplace."

Apparently there was no single moment when Butler concluded that the world would be safer without nuclear weapons. But he told *Washington Post* reporter R. Jeffrey Smith in a 1997 interview that he was dumbstruck in December 1988, on his first visit to the Soviet Union, to find it a poverty-stricken state that looked like a third-world country.

As Butler's plane landed, he noticed pockmarked and uneven runways at the Sheremetyevo Airport. Dozens of the runway lights were broken. On the ride into downtown Moscow, the roads were ill-paved, and government buildings were crumbling and in need of repairs. He told Smith he had expected a country far more modern. Instead, he saw "severe economic deprivation. . . . More than that, it was the sense of defeat in the eyes of the people. . . . It all came crashing home to me that I really had been dealing with a caricature all those years."

In retirement Butler campaigned for ridding the world of nuclear weapons. He told the *Post*, "The simple existence of a nuclear weapon in somebody's arsenal continues to send a message that we can imagine circumstances under which, even in our democratic system with our profound beliefs in the dignity [of] and respect for life and the individual, that somehow we rationalize the employment of that weapon. That's just wrong."

In urging the elimination of nuclear weapons, Butler and Paul Nitze are not alone. More than three hundred current and former heads of state and political and military leaders from around the world have endorsed nuclear zero as a goal. Still, the concept has gained little traction in the mainstream media, and few Americans seem familiar with the proposal—or the idea that it could be taken seriously.

The difficulty of making a nuclear-free world seem credible was demonstrated clearly in January 2007. Four of the most respected figures in American foreign policy publicly made the case for nuclear zero—on the op-ed page of *The Wall Street Journal*, clearly a vehicle to address the corporate world, where weapons are made.

The four: Henry Kissinger, Republican, former secretary of state and the initiator of strategic arms control negotiations with the Soviet Union; Sam Nunn, Democrat, former chairman of the Senate Armed Services Committee; George Shultz, Republican, former secretary of state; and William J. Perry, secretary of defense in the Democratic Clinton administration. The headline: "A World Free of Nuclear Weapons."

The opening paragraphs were a thunderclap:

Nuclear weapons today present tremendous dangers, but also an historic opportunity. U.S. leadership will be required to take the world to the next stage—to a solid consensus for reversing reliance on nuclear weapons globally as a vital contribution to preventing their proliferation into potentially dangerous hands, and ultimately ending them as a threat to the world.

Nuclear weapons were essential to maintaining international security during the Cold War because they were a means of deterrence. The end of the Cold War made the doctrine of mutual Soviet-American deterrence obsolete.

I well remember my astonishment at this article. I looked forward eagerly to what I was certain would happen: other elements of the mainstream media—the television networks, other major newspapers such as *The New York Times,* perhaps *The Washington Post,* the *Los Angeles Times,* even the *Chicago Tribune*—would understand what these veterans of the nuclear arms race had concluded and make their views widely known. This, I was sure, was a true breakthrough.

I was wrong.

If the other major players in the mainstream media even noticed, they were clearly not impressed. Rather than the thunderclap I anticipated, the effect was akin to that of the proverbial tree that fell in the forest with no one around. It seemed virtually unnoticed.

The four foreign policy leaders, however, have not given up. They wrote a follow-up column for *The Wall Street Journal* a year later in which they reported that interest in the issue in the year since their original article had been "extraordinary, with strong positive responses from people all over the world."

But silence continued from significant quarters—the George W. Bush White House and Congress, as well as the mainstream media.

In their follow-up article, the four foreign policy leaders wrote:

The accelerating spread of nuclear weapons, nuclear know-how and nuclear material has brought us to a nuclear tipping point. We face a very real possibility that the deadliest weapons ever invented could fall into dangerous hands.

The steps we are taking now to address these threats are not adequate to the danger. With nuclear weapons more widely available, deterrence is decreasingly effective and increasingly hazardous.

In other words, the problem was getting worse.

The four have lined up public support from a wide range of other former high-level officials, of both political parties, from academics, from scientists, and even from a few retired military figures. Shultz has conducted seminars on the subject at Stanford University, where he has been teaching, and on one occasion the four made a trip to Moscow to make their case to Russian leaders.

An international movement for nuclear disarmament, Global Zero, now counts twenty-two former heads of state and three hundred prominent political, military, diplomatic, and academic leaders as supporters of the campaign. Some of the U.S. public figures—some of whom have since died—on record as supporting nuclear zero are:

- Robert McNamara, former secretary of defense

- Madeleine Albright, former secretary of state

- James Baker, former secretary of state

- Colin Powell, former secretary of state and former chairman of the Joint Chiefs of Staff, and former national security adviser

- Zbigniew Brzezinski, former national security adviser

- Warren Christopher, former secretary of state

- William Cohen, former secretary of defense

- Lawrence Eagleburger, former secretary of state

- Robert McFarlane, former national security adviser

- Andrew J. Goodpaster, former Supreme Allied Commander in Europe

- General John R. Galvin, former Supreme Allied Commander in Europe

- Melvin Laird, former secretary of defense

- Frank Carlucci, former secretary of defense

- General Charles Horner, former commander of the U.S. Space Command

- Alan Cranston, former senator from California

- Paul Nitze, former secretary of the navy, deputy defense secretary, and arms control negotiator

- Admiral Noel Gaylor, former commander in chief of the U.S. Pacific Command

- Admiral Stansfield Turner, former director of the CIA
- Max Kampelman, former arms control negotiator
- Admiral William Crowe, former chairman of the Joint Chiefs of Staff
- Jack Matlock, former ambassador to the Soviet Union

Several other groups have echoed their support of nuclear zero, including one that produced a statement signed by thirty-six American and Soviet generals. General Butler circulated a petition that was signed by eighty people, including physicists, professors, and high-ranking government officials.

President Obama is clearly familiar with the argument for nuclear zero and with steps proposed by leading advocates for how to start getting there. But there is little evidence that he is actually doing anything about it. Without presidential leadership, even with a president who understands the problem, the issue lies dormant.

One question: Where is the mainstream media on this issue? I think the problem is that the mainstream media—I'm talking about *The New York Times*, *The Washington Post*, the *Los Angeles Times*, the major networks, even the major cable networks—have never given credibility to the concept. They have essentially brushed it off as some kind of fantasy. But it is not a fantasy to those former high-ranking officials, to many generals, or to scholars who have studied the problems and the issues.

General Omar Bradley was one of the first to sound the alarm. In 1948, just three years after America dropped nuclear bombs on Hiroshima and Nagasaki, killing about 250,000 people, most of them civilians, Bradley made an Armistice Day speech in which he said:

With the monstrous weapons man already has, humanity is in danger of being trapped in this world by its moral adolescents. Our knowledge of science has clearly outstripped our capacity to control it. We have many men of science, but too few men of God. We have grasped the mystery of the atom and rejected the Sermon on the Mount. Man is stumbling blindly through a spiritual darkness while toying with the precarious secrets of life and death.

The world has achieved brilliance without wisdom, power without conscience. Ours is a world of nuclear giants and ethical infants. We know more about war than we know about peace, more about killing than we know about living. This is our twentieth century's claim to distinction and to progress.

It is time to end the madness and rid the world of nuclear bombs. We can do it. We must do it.

AMERICA'S MOST CONTAMINATED NUCLEAR SITE

In 1943, the U.S. government constructed the 586-acre Hanford Project on the Columbia River in Washington State as part of its secret Manhattan Project to build the first atomic bombs. Hanford produced plutonium for bombs, including the one that destroyed Nagasaki, Japan, in 1945. The plant was decommissioned in the late 1980s.

Today it is America's most contaminated nuclear site, and government agencies are working to contain radioactive waste in aging tanks and groundwater.

Among those who worked at the plant at the height of its operation is the award-winning poet Kathleen Flenniken, who wrote *Plume,* a book of verse about watching friends and neighbors die from mysterious illnesses and about gradually coming to terms with how Atomic City contamination had poisoned the water and sickened residents. In a 2013 interview with National Public Radio, Flenniken said her book is an attempt to make sense of the pride and betrayal she feels about Hanford, her hometown, where workers at the Hanford Nuclear Reservation and their families believed their plutonium production for bombs was helping to protect America at the height of the Cold War. They had no idea that the materials they were handling could kill them.

9

BILLIONS FOR WEAPONS
SEARCHING FOR ENEMIES

Think hard about it. I'm running out of demons. I'm running out of villains. I'm down to [Fidel] Castro and Kim Il Sung.

—General Colin Powell, chairman of the Joint
Chiefs of Staff, 1989–93

Wearing a white suit and a look of determination, First Lady Laura Bush stood in the Newport News shipyard in Virginia and swung a bottle of American sparkling wine toward the steel nose of a new nuclear-powered attack submarine. Splashing wine sparkled in the sun as forty-five hundred people cheered the christening of the USS *Texas* on July 31, 2004. Mrs. Bush said she had simply followed her husband's advice: "He just said, 'Laura, whatever you do, don't miss.'" Everyone laughed.

But there is nothing funny about this giant new submarine with the $3 billion price tag. America was at war, in Afghanistan and in Iraq, against what President George W. Bush said were terrorists of Al Qaeda, the Taliban, and allied groups who posed the central threat to the United States. A logical question: Why a $3 billion submarine if our country's biggest security threat is terrorism? As Representative Barney Frank, a Massachusetts Democrat and chairman of the House Financial Services Committee, put it, "I don't think any terrorist has ever been shot by a nuclear submarine."

The building of the USS *Texas*, the second of at least thirty similar ships, is a symbol of an American national security policy gone terribly wrong. We are building billions of dollars' worth of ships, planes, tanks, and all manner of ultrasophisticated technological military marvels for threats that do not exist. We will not let the absence of a Cold War stop our weapons-building frenzy. Too many jobs and too many careers are on the line.

Critics of U.S. military spending have raised questions about the wisdom of continuing to make and maintain an expensive Cold War arsenal that may be doing more harm than good. As the Institute for Policy Studies, a left-of-center think tank, declared in a 2007 report, the Virginia-class submarine is a "weapon looking for an enemy." President Barack Obama acknowledged this issue in a 2009 speech to Congress. He pledged to "reform our defense budget so that we're not paying for Cold War weapons systems that we don't use."

Defense contractors were quick to respond, hoping to head off more critics. At a March 2009 meeting of subcontractors, John Casey, president of General Dynamics Electric Boat, the prime contractor for the Virginia-class subs, said the industry could not afford to be complacent. "We cannot take for granted that Congress will continue to support the program," he told the meeting. Casey was quoted by MSNBC as saying, "*Cold War* and *Virginia* should never be used in the same sentence. This platform was designed after the Cold War ended, specifically to deal with the threats we face as a nation today."

What else might a man say when contracts worth billions of dollars are at stake?

As of mid-2013, the Virginia-class submarine program was still going forward. The contractors prevailed.

It takes about five years to build each of these submarines. According to an analysis by the nonpartisan Center for Arms Control of the fiscal year 2010 Pentagon spending request, the U.S. Navy listed the cost for one Virginia attack submarine at $3.1 billion. The Navy plans to build thirty of these subs at a total cost of more than $90 billion.

As discussed in chapter 3, the political power to spend billions on unneeded weapons comes in large part from the nationwide spread of contractors' jobs. General Dynamics and its subcontractors have distributed the work on the Virginia-class submarines among tens of thousands—perhaps hundreds of thousands—of workers across the United States, from Northampton, Massachusetts, to Tacoma, Washington. In 2011, *Undersea Warfare,* a magazine published by the U.S. Navy, reported that the Virginia-class submarines "require millions of parts, provided by more than 4,000 suppliers in 47 states and the District of Columbia." In Connecticut alone, home to the shipyard of General Dynamics Electric Boat, that company, plus a nearby Navy submarine base, created 31,500 direct and indirect jobs in 2005, and they add an estimated $3.3 billion to the state's economy every year.

The staggering numbers and costs of America's submarine fleet, and the Navy's plans for it, go far beyond the Virginia-class subs. That fleet in 2010 included "fifty-seven nuclear-powered attack and cruise-missile submarines . . . more than the rest of the world combined," Secretary of Defense Robert Gates said in a speech that May to the Navy League. In mid-2013, the U.S. Navy listed seventy-three submarines in active service, patrolling all of the world's oceans. The Navy has plans for a much larger and more expensive class of submarines called the SSBN-X. These would be twice as big as the USS *Texas* and would cost twice as much. The Navy wants twelve, and the estimated price per ship is between $7 billion and $8 billion.

As heavy a burden as these costs are to America's taxpayers and economy, what is even more important is the unexamined premise on which they are based: America's continued military domination of the planet—a goal on which the American taxpayer has never been asked to cast a vote.

America's dominant military role in the world was assumed, with widespread international support, in the Cold War. But that fundamen-

tal role was never discussed or examined in the 2008 presidential election campaign between Barack Obama and John McCain. Nor did it
surface in the 2012 contest between Obama and his Republican chal-
lenger, Mitt Romney. The dominant role that the United States continues to play has been taken for granted even though the Cold War ended
in 1991. Yet that role is at the heart of such issues as the future of the
Virginia-class submarine and the SSBN-X. Where is the enemy for these
highly sophisticated submarines to confront?

Finding an Enemy

I believe it is fair to suggest that right-wing ideologues with close ties
to military contractors may be relied upon to find an enemy.

At the end of the Cold War, Irving Kristol complained that the end
of the Soviet Union "deprived us of an enemy." He explained, "In politics, being deprived of an enemy is a very serious matter. You tend to
get relaxed and dispirited." Kristol, who died in 2009, was the intellec-
tual godfather of neoconservatism and the founder of the political
magazine *The Weekly Standard*.

In the case of submarines you can already sense a move in the conservative academic community to define a resurgent China as a perfectly suitable rival for control of the waters of the vast Pacific. The
United States has been debating with China the extent of China's right
to limit other countries' uses of the South China Sea. U.S. officials, such
as Hillary Rodham Clinton when she was secretary of state, have referred to a U.S. "national interest" in maintaining free international nav-
igation, including, apparently, military vessels, in swaths of that sea that
China claims as its exclusive economic zone.

Since 2011, when Clinton published an article about America's need
to "pivot" more toward Asia, the Pentagon has indicated that 60 percent
of U.S. ships will be in the Pacific and 40 percent in the Atlantic by 2020,
compared to what has been a 50-50 split. The United States already has
begun expanding a standing deployment of U.S. Marines in northern
Australia, a force that is to reach twenty-five hundred troops in 2016.
China's government and state-run media have criticized the move as a

throwback to the Cold War, reflecting Chinese suspicions of U.S. intentions in the region. It is hard to watch this happening without being reminded that all those Cold War weapons are in need of a new enemy, and that China seems to be the ideal opponent in today's world.

Exactly why do we continue our commitment to Cold War weapons if we are the only remaining superpower and our biggest national security threat is terrorism?

In his May 3, 2010, speech to the Navy League, Secretary of Defense Gates raised questions about America's vast aircraft-carrier fleet and other highly sophisticated ships that no other nation comes close to being able to match. "The U.S. operates eleven large carriers, all nuclear powered," Gates said. "In terms of size and striking power, no other country has even one comparable ship." He asked, "Do we really need eleven carrier strike groups for another thirty years when no other country has more than one?"

Gates laid out other ways in which the U.S. Navy overmatches all other navies: "The U.S. Navy has ten large-deck amphibious ships that can operate as sea bases for helicopters and vertical-takeoff jets. No other navy has more than three, and all of those navies belong to allies or friends. Our Navy can carry twice as many aircraft at sea as the rest of the world combined."

In reference to Navy cruisers and destroyers that use its Aegis radar and missile control system, he said, "Seventy-nine Aegis-equipped combatants carry roughly eight thousand vertical-launch missile cells. In terms of total missile firepower, the United States arguably outmatches the next twenty largest navies. All told the displacement of the U.S. battle fleet—a proxy for overall fleet capabilities—exceeds by one recent estimate at least the next thirteen navies combined, of which eleven are our allies or partners."

Then he raised the question of cost. "At the end of the day we have to ask whether the nation can really afford a Navy that relies on three- to six-billion-dollar destroyers, seven-billion-dollar submarines [the SSBN-X], and eleven-billion-dollar carriers." He said that it was "important to remember that, as much as the U.S. battle fleet has shrunk since the end of the Cold War, the rest of the world's navies have shrunk even more. So in relative terms, the U.S. Navy is as strong as it has ever been." He added, "At 202,000 strong, the U.S. Marine Corps is the largest military force of its kind—exceeding the size of most world armies."

In another speech a few days later at the Eisenhower Library in Abilene, Kansas, Gates asked, "Does the number of warships we have and are building really put America at risk when the U.S. battle fleet is larger than the next thirteen navies combined, eleven of which belong to allies and partners? Is it a dire threat that the United States will have only twenty times more advanced stealth fighters than China?"

Gates deserves a lot of credit for raising these issues. He is the first secretary of defense to try to start a conversation on these kinds of issues. Selecting the Eisenhower Library as the site of his second speech was clearly meant to honor Eisenhower's concerns about a military-industrial complex—concerns he mentioned, approvingly, in his talk.

Congressman Barney Frank took the question far beyond the Navy and its plans. "The major part of our weapons spending and our military commitment overseas has nothing to do with terrorism and little to do with making us safer," he said in a 2010 television interview. In short, the military's lust for Cold War weapons continues to consume vast amounts of American treasure, even though they are of little use against the terrorist threats that have dominated U.S. security concerns since September 11, 2001.

Mission Creep

The economic and political forces that have encouraged the military to hang on to its Cold War mentality have also given birth to the Pentagon's mission creep.

The trend began developing before the 9/11 attacks but has accelerated since then. Simply put, America has allowed—even encouraged—the military to expand its role in the world. The proof of this is the funding of the military, which gets $1 of every $5 that the federal government spends. Since World War II, the United States has maintained air and naval bases in Europe and elsewhere as a part of its national security strategy aimed at promoting American ideals and American interests. We have thousands of soldiers at hundreds of U.S. bases in dozens of countries. We have thousands of nuclear weapons.

With the collapse of the Soviet Union in 1991, General Colin Powell, then chairman of the Joint Chiefs of Staff, summed up, "Think hard about it. I'm running out of demons. I'm running out of villains. I'm down to [Fidel] Castro and Kim Il Sung."

Americans celebrated the prospect of a "peace dividend" that would make it possible for the United States to spend less on defense and more on education, infrastructure, the environment, and other domestic programs. But it never happened.

There is no better example of a weapons system searching for an enemy than the biggest boondoggle of them all: Ronald Reagan's multibillion-dollar pipe dream for a missile defense program, which was dubbed Star Wars by the late Senator Ted Kennedy, a Democrat from Massachusetts.

Reagan announced on March 23, 1983, that the United States planned to develop a program that would make nuclear weapons "impotent and obsolete." The result was the most expensive defense-procurement program in history, with Congress spending $9 billion to $10 billion a year, year after year. What was originally envisioned as a five-year program that would cost $26 billion has failed even as it ballooned in cost. At last count, the United States had pumped more than $200 billion into the program.

In 2008, on the twenty-fifth anniversary of Reagan's announcement of his dream, David Wright and Lisbeth Gronlund published an opinion piece on the Bulletin of Atomic Scientists' Web site that said, "Ronald Reagan's dream of building a viable defense against long-range missiles is still simply that—a dream. And by pursuing this dream, the United States has weakened its own security instead of enhancing it."

They explained: "The Pentagon has yet to demonstrate that the U.S. ground-based missile defense system is capable of defending against a long-range ballistic missile in a real-world situation. The tests have demonstrated that the kill vehicle is able to hone in on and collide with an identifiable target, but only under highly scripted conditions. A February 2008 Government Accountability Office report, 'Assessment of DOD Efforts to Enhance Missile Defense Capabilities and Oversight,' concluded that these tests have been 'developmental in nature, and do not provide sufficient realism' to assess the system's potential effectiveness."

Furthermore, they said, "There's almost no prospect that the United States will develop a defense system that could defend against real-world long-range missiles in the foreseeable future."

Two weeks later, Gronlund took her case to Congress. In testimony on April 16, 2008, before the House Subcommittee on National Security and Foreign Affairs, she made many of the same points that she and Wright had made in their column for the Union of Concerned Scientists, a nonprofit science advocacy group with more than 225,000 members. In her remarks before the subcommittee, Gronlund challenged Reagan's "vision of a shield that would protect us from nuclear missiles just as a roof protects a family from rain." That idea is "very compelling to many people," she said. The question, she said, is whether it is "possible for this system ever to run because if it is not, it is pointless to spend money trying to crawl."

Today there is no credible threat of a nuclear attack by intercontinental missiles against the United States. The Soviet Union, against whom Reagan's program was designed, no longer exists. No other country considered an aggressive antagonist of the United States, such as North Korea or Iran, possesses missiles capable of a serious threat.

As Pentagon bureaucrats and companies, such as Boeing and Raytheon, have developed the rockets and radar systems meant to shield the United States from attacking missiles, they have justified the continued spending of billions of dollars by reporting years of tests that they say show the system can work. But, as others point out, these tests are nothing like the real challenge of hitting missiles that would be launched by surprise, if that threat really existed.

In effect, tests have been rigged. Or as the General Accountability Office explained in an April 2004 report: The ground-based midcourse defense element needed for the system to work "has not been tested under unscripted, operationally realistic conditions." Even under favorable conditions, the Missile Defense Agency has been able to claim success in only half of sixteen intercept tests it had conducted by mid-2013.

The U.S. missile defenses are, in fact, an obstacle to real security, Gronlund said. "Today, the risk of a premeditated Russian or Chinese nuclear attack on the United States is essentially zero. But because Russia continues to maintain a thousand nuclear weapons on high alert (as does the United States), ready to be launched within a matter of minutes, there is still a danger of an accidental or unauthorized attack or of a mistaken launch in response to a false warning."

In his Pulitzer Prize–winning history, *The Making of the Atomic Bomb,* Richard Rhodes points out the folly of trying to build a high-tech shield against nuclear attack from space when a nuclear bomb could be boxed up in a shipping container and detonated as it reaches the entrance to New York harbor. "No such system yet operates to intercept clandestine weapons delivered by aircraft, ships or trucks," Rhodes noted in a 2005 *National Geographic* article. "After sixty years of searching for a fail-safe defense against nuclear attack, none has been found, nor is one likely to be found, against weapons that even in their crudest forms can be made relatively small and portable, and vastly destructive."

The history of this misguided program, initiated by Reagan, is one of the great tragedies of modern diplomacy. By 1972 it had become clear to many in the American scientific community and to both President Richard Nixon and his national security adviser, Henry Kissinger, a longtime student of nuclear weapons, that efforts to build an antimissile system would be counterproductive. That insight led them to initiate the first successful nuclear arms control agreements with the Soviet Union, where Soviet scientists agreed. The result was the Anti-Ballistic Missile (ABM) treaty, signed in the Kremlin in June 1972.

Essentially, they agreed not to spend the money on an antimissile system because it would be virtually impossible to shoot down hundreds of incoming nuclear-laden missiles. The logic was unmistakable. Missiles travel at thousands of miles an hour, meaning that the system would have to be capable of identifying and destroying hundreds of them in less than half an hour—and if even one or two got through, hundreds of thousands of people would be killed.

Reagan's belief that American technology could master such a problem was apparently influenced by nuclear physicist Edward Teller, the father of the hydrogen bomb. He was a far-out conservative, perhaps because of his rich imagination and his background in Hollywood, a world in which fantasy thrives.

The initial concept of Reagan's scheme—not made public at the time—was bizarre. The United States was to launch into orbit 100 to 150 satellites armed with high-powered lasers. If the satellites' sensors detected heat from the launch of a missile, they would have about three minutes to track the rocket, determine that it was a weapon on its way to attack the United States, and destroy it with laser beams. Launching this system would take about five thousand flights of NASA's space shuttles and shuttle-size rockets. The cost would be up to $1 trillion.

It was—and is—a pipe dream. The original program was abandoned after ten years, but the idea was not dead. In its place today, the Missile Defense Agency is working on systems that would use high-speed missiles fired from the ground to intercept incoming warheads. The task often is described as comparable to hitting one flying bullet with another.

As it became apparent that the original concept of laser-firing satellites was beyond achieving, and as the Soviet Union and its threat of nuclear missile attack dissolved, the Pentagon sustained its argument for continuing the Star Wars program by simply identifying a new enemy. Now the potential attacker would be North Korea or Iran.

North Korea has an estimated eight to ten nuclear weapons and Iran has none. The missiles North Korea has developed could at best reach Hawaii and perhaps some parts of Alaska and maybe some parts of the West Coast. They are primitive missiles compared to U.S. and Russian missiles. Iran has no missiles capable of reaching the United States.

Obviously, North Korea, Iran, or any other potential hostile state in the future must be deterred from making a nuclear attack on the United States. But a massively expensive antimissile system is not necessarily the best means of deterrence. Richard Garwin, a member of the

1990s Commission to Assess the Ballistic Missile Threat to the United States, chaired by Donald Rumsfeld, noted in a 2000 essay that it "remains highly debatable as to how secure a missile defense would make the United States." And if some missile defense was required, he said, it should be a much smaller one than the United States was developing.

Even Paul Nitze, the cold warrior who jump-started America's nuclear buildup in the 1950s, declared before his death in 2004 that the best deterrent for North Korea was to monitor its activities and to be prepared to destroy its nuclear capacity with conventional weapons if it showed a readiness and capacity to launch a nuclear attack.

The threat of a nuclear attack against the United States today is far less than it was when President Reagan launched the Star Wars program. At that time the Soviet Union had many thousands of nuclear weapons as well as sophisticated intercontinental ballistic missiles to deliver them. The real risk of a nuclear attack on the United States is not from states wielding intercontinental missiles but from terrorist groups that would deliver a bomb in far simpler ways. In January 2010 the U.S. Army was reported to be training a special squad "to seal off and snatch back" Pakistani nuclear weapons in the event that militants obtained a nuclear device or materials that could make one. U.S. officials refused to comment on their plans. Pakistan's arsenal is believed to number at least 120 nuclear bombs.

Let's assume extremists did obtain a nuclear weapon. How might a terrorist group choose to make its attack? A bomb might be delivered in a shipping container addressed to any metropolitan area in the United States. Or it might be hidden in a steamer trunk. Terrorists could fire a missile from a ship off the U.S. coastline. *Washington Post* columnist David Ignatius has suggested that a missile fired from less than 120 miles offshore would take just eleven minutes to reach its target and could cause thousands, perhaps millions, of casualties if it hit Washington, D.C., or New York City or another major metropolis. He has pointed out that short-range missiles are available on the world's arms bazaars.

Joseph Cirincione, president of the Ploughshares Fund, a global security foundation, has suggested this kind of scenario: "With technical expertise supplied by former Russian or Pakistani nuclear scientists, terrorists would need only twenty-five to fifty kilograms [55 to 110 pounds] of highly enriched uranium to fashion a 'gun assembly' bomb similar to the one dropped on Hiroshima. With half of the uranium packed at one end of a six-foot-long tube and half in a bullet propelled by conventional explosives from the other end, terrorists could create and carry in the trunk of a car a thousand-pound bomb that, if detonated in Times Square, could kill one million New Yorkers."

So we have spent upwards of $200 billion on a missile defense program—$12.3 billion of it in 2011 alone—that is of no value against the real threats in the modern world.

Let's look at this in a slightly different way. Suppose the president of the United States wakes up one morning to learn that a nuclear bomb has been exploded in downtown Manhattan, perhaps on the site of the former World Trade Center. Or maybe in downtown Chicago. Or downtown Washington. He would not know how it got there or who was responsible. At this point the president might wonder what good the U.S. arsenal of some seventy-seven hundred nuclear weapons might be. And he might well wonder about the billions spent on Reagan's antimissile fantasy. It might well occur to him that our vast nuclear arsenal is of no value in today's world.

The American missile defense program is a crowning example of the forces at work in what President Eisenhower called the military-industrial complex, which has grown to include Congress, think-tank hawks, and the intelligence community.

Our Nuclear Triad Makes No Sense

Although former secretary of defense Gates has raised many serious questions about unnecessary weapons, neither he nor any other high-ranking official has publicly raised what may be the most profound question of all. Why, nearly twenty-five years after the collapse of the Soviet Union and the end of the Cold War, does America continue to support a multibillion-dollar strategic doctrine that makes no sense? I refer to the triad, the maintenance of three separate, expensive nuclear-delivery systems designed during the Cold War as deterrents to the Soviet Union.

The three systems—land-based intercontinental ballistic missiles plus submarine-launched missiles and strategic bombers—represent about two thousand strategic nuclear warheads searching for an enemy. But no conceivable enemy is on the horizon. According to a 2015 report by the Congressional Research Service, the cost to maintain and upgrade these nuclear systems is about $30 billion per year over the next thirty years—or about $1 trillion.

The fundamental strategy was built for the prospect of a Cold War nuclear holocaust. If the Soviet Union had threatened the United States with attack by its nuclear arsenal, which reached forty-five thousand warheads in the 1980s, the U.S. triad guaranteed that enough weapons—scattered on land, at sea, and in the air—would survive to launch a devastating counterstrike.

To comprehend the absurdity of maintenance of the triad in today's world requires at least a basic knowledge of what we maintain at huge cost. Here is a summary of America's nuclear strike force, put together by the Congressional Research Service in a March 2015 report for Congress:

- Intercontinental ballistic missiles (ICBMs). The U.S. Air Force has 450 Minuteman III missiles in underground silos at F. E. Warren Air Force Base, Wyoming; Malmstrom Air Force Base, Montana; and Minot Air Force Base, North Dakota.

- Submarine-launched ballistic missiles (SLBMs). The Navy has 533 Trident missiles on fourteen Ohio-class submarines, deployed from Bangor, Washington, and Kings Bay, Georgia.

- Strategic bombers. The Air Force deploys 20 B-2 Spirit bombers at Whiteman Air Force Base, Missouri, and 76 B-52H bombers at Minot Air Force Base, North Dakota, and at Barksdale Air Force Base, Louisiana, that can be equipped for nuclear missions.

The math tells the story. To dismantle the American nuclear deterrent, an enemy would have to destroy more than 540 weapons sites in seven widely separated bases and to have some confidence that it had disabled the submarine fleet.

The obvious question: What nation or what evil terrorist group might conceivably even make a dent in this vast force? The answer is that there is none.

Of the nine nuclear-armed states in 2015, Russia and the United States each had an estimated eighteen hundred weapons deployed and roughly six thousand in reserve or storage, according to a count by the Federation of American Scientists. France, Britain, and China each had a few hundred, with Pakistan, India, and Israel estimated to hold smaller arsenals. North Korea had fewer than ten.

Rather than three systems for destroying any conceivable enemy, one would do. A small portion of the U.S. Ohio-class submarine fleet, with its missiles, would provide an invulnerable nuclear deterrent. The United States would be perfectly safe if it closed down its entire land-based ICBM force as well as its fleets of bombers. Alternatively, Lieutenant General Brent Scowcroft, who served as national security adviser to the elder President Bush, has called for scrapping all the submarines and bombers for a land-based deterrent of about a thousand missile-mounted warheads.

But it is unlikely to happen. Too many jobs would be lost. Too many members of Congress would oppose such a program.

I asked Tom Collina, research director of the Arms Control Association, whether the triad makes any sense since the collapse of the Soviet Union. His answer was simple: "No." I asked whether he was aware of any serious discussion in the Pentagon or in Congress of junking the triad. Not that he was aware of. Politics, he said, would make such a discussion visionary and nonproductive.

A formal Nuclear Posture Review released by the Pentagon on April 6, 2010, stated that the U.S. commitment to the triad would not change.

The Cold War is long since over, but the economic and political forces it created are still with us, and there is no sign on the political horizon that they will go away anytime soon.

Tracking the Cost of Nuclear Weapons

Although the United States does not produce a full accounting of the annual cost of its nuclear weapons, independent experts have sifted through government documents to compile estimates. In a study published by the Carnegie Endowment for International Peace, Steven I. Schwartz and Deepti Choubey reported that the United States spent at least $52.4 billion on nuclear weapons and related programs in 2008. In their report, *Nuclear Security Spending,* Schwartz and Choubey said that the $52.4 billion does not include the nuclear costs for air defense, antisubmarine warfare, classified programs, or most nuclear-weapons-intelligence programs.

U.S. spending on its nuclear weapons programs is hard to track because the money comes from at least seven different agencies, including the Departments of Defense, Energy, Homeland Security, Justice, Labor, State, and Health and Human Services.

The Carnegie report is the latest by Schwartz, who has devoted years of intensive study to this issue. In 1998, he announced at a Brookings Institution briefing that the United States spent nearly $5.5 trillion from 1940 to 1996 on nuclear weapons and related programs. The Brookings study, based on a four-year project, was titled *The Hidden Costs of Our Nuclear Arsenal.*

Schwartz said that building the nuclear explosives themselves was relatively inexpensive. Instead, the majority of the money was spent on the many delivery vehicles for the bombs. These included the strategic bombers and ballistic missiles, artillery shells, depth charges, and nuclear land mines. He said 86 percent of what was spent was for building the launch systems and ensuring not only that they could be fired when ordered but that they would not go off without valid launch orders.

In one example, Schwartz compared the size of the U.S. nuclear stockpile to Hiroshima-equivalent warheads: "In 1960 when the explosive power of the U.S. stockpile peaked, we had the equivalent of nearly 1.4 million Hiroshima-sized bombs. Today, even though the nuclear arsenal is substantially smaller, we still have the equivalent of 120,000 to 130,000 Hiroshima-sized bombs."

Schwartz said the cost of cleaning up from the nuclear weapons program will "come close to or equal the cost of producing the weapons in the first place."

Since 1945, the United States has manufactured and deployed more than seventy thousand nuclear weapons, but the cost of the program has never been fully understood or compiled by the government, Schwartz said. He explained, "In more than half a century Congress has taken action to terminate nuclear weapons programs only a handful of times and has never held a hearing, debate, or vote on the cost, scale, pace, or implications of the overall program."

Schwartz and Choubey's 2009 Carnegie report makes the same point: "Effective oversight of government nuclear security programs is impossible without complete, reliable data on their comprehensive annual and cumulative costs. Such an accounting has never been available to decision makers." To help rectify this problem, the report said that Congress should require the White House to submit an annual unclassified and classified accounting of all nuclear-weapons-related spending for the previous fiscal year, the current fiscal year, and the next fiscal year.

Meantime, the numbers are buried in the bureaucracy.

THE MOST EXPENSIVE WEAPONS IN THE WORLD

To identify the most expensive weapons in the world, Douglas A. McIntyre and Michael B. Sauter of the Web site *24/7WallSt* reviewed figures from the Department of Defense budget and the Government Accountability Office. Their findings were posted January 9, 2012.

1. F-35 Joint Strike Fighter, built by Lockheed Martin and partners. DOD has budgeted for 2,457 of the aircraft. R&D: $58.4 billion. Price per plane: $109.5 million. Total price: $326.5 billion.

2. DDG 51 destroyer, produced by a group of contractors including Bath Iron Works, General Dynamics, and Northrop Grumman. About sixty have been in service since 1991; another fifteen are in the DOD budget. R&D: $1.3 billion. Price per destroyer: $1.3 billion. Total cost: $101.8 billion.

3. Virginia-class nuclear submarine, produced by General Dynamics Electric Boat and Newport News Shipbuilding. Of the thirty in the DOD budget, eight

are in operation. R&D: $7.2 billion. Price per unit: $2.6 billion. Total cost: $83.7 billion. (Note that the Center for Arms Control has estimated the price per unit at about $3 billon and the total program cost at about $90 billion.)

4. F-22 Raptor stealth fighter jet, built by Lockheed Martin/Boeing. DOD has 188 in its budget. R&D: $40.5 billion. Price per unit: $211.6 million. Total cost: $79.2 billion.

5. F/A-18E/F Super Hornet fighter aircraft, built by Boeing. DOD has 556 in its budget. R&D: $7.3 billion. Price per unit: $90.8 million. Total cost: $57.8 billion.

6. V-22 Osprey tilt-rotor transport plane, built by Boeing. DOD has 459 Ospreys in its budget. R&D: $13.6 billion. Price per unit: $95.2 million. Total cost: $57.8 billion.

7. Trident II ballistic missile, built by Lockheed Martin. DOD has 561 Tridents in its budget. R&D: $16.8 billion. Price per unit: $65.7 million. Total cost: $53.2 billion.

8. Joint Mine Resistant Ambush Protected Vehicle, built by different contractors. DOD has 26,552 units in its budget. R&D: $700 million. Price per unit: $1.6 million. Total cost: $41.6 billion.

9. CVN-78–class aircraft carrier, built by Northrop Grumman. The government has ordered three carriers for delivery over the next ten years. R&D: $4.6 billion. Price per unit: $9.78 billion. Total cost: $34 billion.

10. P-8A Poseidon surveillance and antisubmarine plane, built by Boeing. The military has ordered 122 of these planes. R&D: $8.2 billion. Price per plane: $206.5 million. Total cost: $33 billion.

10

SEND IN THE DRONES

Targeted [drone] strikes . . . dramatically reduce the danger to innocent civilians, especially considered against massive ordnance that can cause injury and death far beyond their intended target.

—John Brennan, CIA director

You could see these little figures scurrying, and the explosion going off, and when the smoke cleared, there was just rubble and charred stuff.

—Former CIA officer

Airman First Class Brandon Bryant, twenty-one, stepped into a windowless, air-conditioned metal box at a U.S. Air Force base in Nevada. His head shaved and wearing a khaki flight suit, Bryant settled into a padded chair before glowing video monitors to watch live images from the camera of a Predator drone flying slowly over Afghanistan, on the other side of the world.

It was early 2007, and Bryant was new to his job operating a laser targeting system aboard the Predator. He and the plane's pilot, sitting next to him, saw three Afghan men on the monitors, walking in open terrain not far from where U.S. troops had just come under attack by Afghan insurgents. Bryant and his partner received an order to fire one of the drone's Hellfire missiles at the Afghans.

Six years later, Bryant told National Public Radio what he then saw: Seconds after the Hellfire missile dropped away from the Predator and streaked forward trailing a tongue of flame,

> the guy in the rear . . . runs forward to the two guys in front and then the missile hits. After the smoke clears, there's a crater there. You can see body parts of the people. But the guy who was running from the rear to the front, his left leg had been taken off above the knee, and I watched him bleed out.

> The blood rapidly cooled to become the same color as the ground, because we're watching this in infrared. I eventually watched the guy become the same color as the ground that he died on.

Bryant said afterward that he was not sure whether the men he helped kill were Taliban fighters or simply shepherds carrying rifles or staffs as rural Afghan men routinely do.

Weeks after Bryant's first attack as a Predator crewman, he would follow orders to aim a missile at an Afghan building, only to watch in horror as a small figure walked into the target just before the missile slammed home. Sickened that he might have killed a child, Bryant and his pilot typed a computer message to the officers who had ordered the attack: "Did that look like a child to you?" No, the answer came back, that was a dog.

By the time he left the Air Force in 2011, Bryant and his squadron, which included a small crew of veteran drone operators, had been credited with killing 1,626 "enemies." Bryant said his six years as a "stick monkey" had left him traumatized and physically ill. That is one of many horror stories to emerge from Washington's use of armed drones for killing suspected terrorists around the globe.

Once so secret that the U.S. government would not acknowledge their use, drones have become the focus of serious questions by lawyers, human rights activists, and many others. The drones also have become an essential new element in America's war machine.

Since 2001, America has used drone aircraft to fight terrorists and insurgents in Iraq, Afghanistan, Pakistan, Yemen, Somalia, and Libya. This remote-control warfare can spare government the political costs at home and abroad of putting soldiers on the ground. It is cheaper than troop deployments, which in recent years have cost $1 million annually per soldier.

Officials such as CIA director John Brennan describe the use of drones as a remarkably clean form of war, fought by satellite link from air-conditioned control stations in Nevada or Texas, in which Americans avoid risk to themselves. In a speech at the Woodrow Wilson Center in April 2012, Brennan defended the legality of drones, their ethics, the wisdom of using them, and the standards by which they are approved. "Yes, in full accordance with the law, and in order to prevent terrorist attacks on the United States and to save American lives, the United States government conducts targeted strikes against specific al-Qaida terrorists, sometimes using remotely piloted aircraft, often referred to publicly as drones," Brennan said.

He said targeted strikes "conform to the principles of distinction, the idea that only military objectives may be intentionally targeted, and that civilians are protected from being intentionally targeted." Drones are a "wise choice," according to Brennan, "because they dramatically reduce the danger to U.S. personnel, even eliminating the danger altogether." What's more, he said, drones "dramatically reduce the danger to innocent civilians, especially considered against massive ordnance that can cause injury and death far beyond their intended target."

Despite their value to U.S. military and intelligence forces, the deployment of drones has provoked a controversial new phase in the war against terror. The truth is that combat-by-drone can be as bloody and inhumane as any other form of war, killing innocent civilians as well as enemies and often radicalizing those near the strikes. As targeted enemies are destroyed, new ones emerge.

In particular, the ability of drones to operate in much greater secrecy than conventional military force makes it harder for a democratic society to monitor them. While Brandon Bryant flew drones for the uniformed military in an acknowledged war, the aircraft have become at least as important as America's weapon of choice for covert warfare. The CIA has become a virtual second air force, fighting in Pakistan, Yemen, and Somalia, out of public view.

American wars fought by soldiers on the ground can never be isolated in this way. They can be covered directly by news media. Thousands of American soldiers bring the images of a war home with them. This public witness keeps America's citizenry and policymakers aware of the costs and collateral damage of a war. But secret drone warfare, in its first decade, has reduced American witnesses to a few people such as Brandon Bryant, who absorb those costs as they sit before a video screen. The use of drones has raised agonizing questions for our country about:

- Civilian casualties: In Pakistan, the site of America's biggest clandestine drone war, American officials portray a surgical campaign that killed some two thousand Al Qaeda and allied Islamic militants and fewer than fifty noncombatant civilians in the ten years from 2001 to 2011. Even better, U.S. officials told *The New York Times*, drones in May 2010 to August 2011 had scored a perfect record, killing six hundred militants and not a single civilian. But virtually every other detailed account says otherwise. Evidence from both liberal and conservative U.S. research groups, from two of America's top law schools, from the London-based Bureau of Investigative Journalism, from the New America Foundation, and from Pakistani officials reporting secretly to their own government shows the drone campaign has killed hundreds of civilians and terrorized millions of residents as missiles destroy homes, cars, or gatherings of people without warning.

- The legality and morality of thousands of targeted killings: America's missile strikes are legitimate self-defense following Al Qaeda's 9/11 attacks, according to secret legal opinions that government lawyers submitted to the White House. The Department of Justice memo—finally made public in February 2013—revealed the government's legal case for drone strikes, but the claim of legality is undermined by disturbing tactics. Drones have attacked rescuers and funerals of the casualties from earlier missile hits. Drone strikes have sometimes killed people because surveillance has shown them moving or behaving in patterns like those of alleged militants. In a July 2014 editorial headlined "Reining in the Drones," *The New York Times* declared, "For all the slick technology, there are grave moral and legal questions going unanswered in the government's use of armed drones to kill people considered terrorist threats."

• Accelerated radicalization and destabilization: America's drone campaign began as a handful of strikes, under former president George W. Bush, that targeted a few dozen Al Qaeda leaders. The campaign has broadened under President Obama into hundreds of attacks that have targeted and killed thousands of people in Pakistan and elsewhere. Naturally the desire for revenge from targeted areas has broadened. In Pakistan, the images and numbers of civilian dead, amplified and exaggerated by Pakistan's jingoistic Urdu-language press and by anti-U.S. militant groups, have become a tool for militant protest, recruitment, and radicalization of new members. The same has occurred in Yemen, and as drone attacks highlight the Pakistani and Yemeni governments' failures to protect their countries' sovereignty, they undermine moderate political leaders in lands that the United States wants to tilt toward stable, centrist, civilian rule.

• A more lawless world of covert, robotized warfare: America's often covert warfare by remote control is helping to shape how the world will handle future conflicts. The Government Accountability Office reported in 2012 that seventy-five countries were working to develop drone weapons systems, nearly double the number in 2005. China, India, Israel, Iran, Russia, and Turkey are among countries with armed drones. Meanwhile, the U.S. Defense Department has said it is building new weapons with "a higher degree of autonomy" than today's drones, a step toward a generation of robotic weapons that United Nations and independent human rights advocates say should be banned by international convention.

- The economics of the drone program: The costs are murky because of government secrecy. The CIA drone budget is classified, but *The New York Times* reported in October 2011 that the Pentagon spends nearly $5 billion annually on drone operations. It takes about 150 people to keep a drone flying. That includes those maintaining the drone and its communications links, and those reviewing and analyzing the hours of videos and radio signals needed for a single strike. The Air Force announced in November 2012 that it was buying ten new Reaper drones at a cost of $12.5 million each.

Lawn Mowers in the Sky

Unmanned aerial vehicles date back nearly a hundred years and have been used for military surveillance for decades. They became known as drones because some of them make a constant buzzing sound in flight. Some people say that early models reminded them of lawn mowers in the sky.

Advances in technology helped expand military use of surveillance drones, but not until the turn of the century did new technology make it possible to fire missiles from unmanned drones. The United States did not begin using this new tool of war immediately because of policy principles and legal restrictions. As late as July 2001, two months before the attacks on New York and Washington, the U.S. ambassador to Israel, Martin Indyk, denounced the Israeli government's use of the tactic against violent Palestinian militants: "The United States government is very clearly on record as against targeted assassinations. . . . They are extrajudicial killings, and we do not support that."

The CIA had veered away from such killings following scandals in the 1970s over its plots against five foreign leaders, including a scheme to place an exploding seashell in Cuba at the favorite snorkeling site of President Fidel Castro. President Gerald Ford had signed an executive order in 1976 banning the CIA from political assassinations. As recently as one week before the 9/11 attacks, in a meeting about the use of armed drones, CIA director George Tenet believed that it would be a "terrible mistake for the director of the CIA to fire a weapon like this." This would happen, he said, "over his dead body."

The United States tossed aside those ideas after 9/11. Within days, President George W. Bush gave the CIA permission to assassinate Osama bin Laden and his supporters, effectively lifting the twenty-five-year-old ban on CIA killings. Congress passed the far-reaching Authorization for Use of Military Force—effectively a blank check for armed action.

It was time to send in the drones.

The new rules gave America's war machine the green light to fire drone-borne missiles at suspicious targets in the Middle East and elsewhere. Two different drone programs quickly evolved. One drone program is managed by the U.S. military and is described as an extension of conventional warfare. In June 2011, *The New York Times* reported that the Pentagon had about seven thousand drones, compared with fifty a decade earlier. As of July 2012, the Air Force had more than thirteen hundred drone pilots stationed at thirteen or more bases across the United States, including Hancock Field Air National Guard Base in New York, Creech Air Force Base in Nevada, and Holloman Air Force Base in New Mexico.

The other U.S. drone operation is the covert—and classified—program managed by the CIA, which typically conducts secret drone strikes in Pakistan, Somalia, and Yemen. Just five months after September 11, on February 4, 2002, the CIA conducted its first independent drone killing, separate from the military. The agency's drone operators spotted three men near the eastern Afghan city of Khost. One man was unusually tall, and CIA officers decided they were seeing Osama bin Laden. They were wrong. After the agency fired a missile and killed the men, local residents named them to U.S. and Afghan journalists as villagers who had been out scavenging for battlefield scrap metal, a common occupation among impoverished Afghans.

Despite Brandon Bryant's agonized description of an Air Force drone operation that easily killed innocents in Afghanistan, the vastly more troubling drone wars are the secret CIA attacks. A former CIA officer, quoted in *The New Yorker* magazine in October 2009, described a live drone strike seen on a monitor as both awe-inspiring and horrifying: "You could see these little figures scurrying, and the explosion going off, and when the smoke cleared, there was just rubble and charred stuff."

Since 2004, CIA specialists have flown Predator and Reaper drones over a swath of western Pakistan, circling above craggy mountains and deserts dotted with the villages of ethnic Pashtun tribes. Pakistan does not fully control this border zone with Afghanistan and bars foreigners from entering. Both the Pakistani military and the Taliban threaten journalists there, and neither the U.S. government nor independent monitors are able to directly count the casualties of the drone strikes. The drone strikes in Yemen have taken place in similarly isolated regions with little government control or media access.

These CIA drone wars started small, with occasional attacks to take out top-level commanders of Al Qaeda. The Bush administration conducted 52 reported strikes in Pakistan and Yemen in the fifty-five months before Obama took office. Obama's team escalated these wars to a peak of 132 attacks during 2010, and about 85 each in the next two years—an intensification that multiplied the numbers killed, including innocents.

In Pakistan, the slow-paced strikes of 2002 to 2004 killed "five or six people . . . for each defined high-value target," University of Arizona scholar Leila Hudson and her colleagues estimated in a study of publicly reported casualties. "By 2010, one high-value target was killed per 147 total deaths."

In October 2012, *The Washington Post* reported that the CIA was urging the White House to approve the addition of ten drones to its inventory of thirty to thirty-five—a move that U.S. officials said "would extend the spy service's decade-long transformation into a paramilitary force."

The deep shrouding of the covert battlefields has helped officials such as CIA director Brennan offer a soothing account of wars in which drone controllers wield their hundred-pound Hellfire missiles like a surgeon's scalpel: "A pilot operating this aircraft remotely, with the benefit of technology and with the safety of distance, might actually have a clearer picture of the target and its surroundings, including the presence of innocent civilians. It's this surgical precision, the ability, with laser-like focus, to eliminate the cancerous tumor called an al-Qaida terrorist while limiting damage to the tissue around it, that makes this counterterrorism tool so essential."

As the drone program has become less secret, concern about the ethics, the morality, even the legality, has forced Washington to defend its actions. The drone programs are not exactly transparent, but we do know more about them than we did. Among other things, we have learned that Barack Obama—a Nobel Peace Prize winner, a law professor, and the president of a country based on due process—has a kill list. This became public in May 2012 when *The New York Times* revealed that Obama had the final word in approving targeted killings with American armed drones.

The reaction was immediate. "Too much power for a president," declared a *New York Times* editorial. Michael Brenner, a professor at the University of Pittsburgh and a senior fellow at the Center for International Relations, wrote in a *World Post* blog, "America's moral leadership is gone; we have subverted our own liberties—we have panicked in an unmanly manner."

Although his critics often portray Obama as leftist and even socialist, he has continued and in some cases expanded many of the post-9/11 defense policies that started with President George W. Bush. More drone attacks have occurred under Obama than under Bush. The militant side of Obama began to materialize soon after he was elected to the White House. In his book about national security, *The Way of the Knife,* Mark Mazzetti tells of a scene inside the White House Situation Room early in Obama's first term. General James Cartwright, then the vice chairman of the Joint Chiefs of Staff, asks why the United States is "building a second Air Force" in the form of the CIA's growing armed drone fleet.

Mazzetti quotes Obama as replying, "The CIA gets what it wants."

In April 2012, *The New York Times* described Obama in an opinion-page as "warrior in chief" and called him "one of the most militarily aggressive American leaders in decades." Many others have challenged Obama's use of executive power in waging war against terrorists. *The Washington Post*'s Dana Milbank, in a 2013 column, called Obama's drone warfare program an "extraordinary assertion of the executive's powers. In this new, hidden warfare, unelected officials, without the blessing of a court, or anything else, order killings of suspected terrorists—even American citizens, perhaps on U.S. soil."

The drone program is the newest part of the president's empire, which is largely invisible to the public. Author Garry Wills, in a 2009 article for *The New York Review of Books,* explores this darker side of the presidency and issues a damning indictment of the system. He describes its roots in American military history and warns that the momentum of accumulating powers in the executive is not easily reversed, checked, or even slowed. Here is his interpretation of what the article called the "entangled giant":

"It was not created by the Bush administration. The whole history of America since World War II caused an inertial transfer of power toward the executive branch. The monopoly on use of nuclear weaponry, the cult of the commander in chief, the worldwide network of military bases to maintain nuclear alert and supremacy, the secret intelligence agencies, the entire national security state, the classification and clearance systems, the expansion of state secrets, the withholding of evidence and information, the permanent emergency that has melded World War II with the cold war and the cold war with the 'war on terror'—all these make a vast and intricate structure that may not yield to efforts at dismantling it. Sixty-eight straight years of war emergency powers (1941–2009) have made the abnormal normal, and constitutional diminishment the settled order."

It is easy to see how the secret drone killings initiated by Bush and expanded by Obama fit into the picture that Wills describes. Information about the CIA drone program is closely guarded. But thanks to the work of several nonprofit organizations, some facts have emerged. The British-based Bureau of Investigative Journalism has estimated that CIA drone attacks have killed 2,629 to 3,461 people in Pakistan alone, of whom 475 to 891 were civilians. The New America Foundation estimates from 1,953 to 3,279 killed, of whom 261 to 305 were civilians. In reporting those numbers in February 2013, *Time* magazine was careful to note, "The CIA declined to comment for this story."

The CIA's Secret Drone Operation

One of the best descriptions of how the CIA operates its secret drone program appeared in *The New Yorker* in a 2009 article written by Jane Mayer. As she pointed out, America's military drones operate in recognized war zones, such as Afghanistan. The CIA drone program is aimed at terror suspects not in war zones, in Pakistan and other countries around the world. Intelligence officers as well as private contractors fly the Predator drones for the CIA:

"Within the CIA, control of the unmanned vehicles is split among several teams. One set of pilots and operators works abroad, near hidden airfields in Afghanistan and Pakistan, handling takeoffs and landings. Once the drones are aloft . . . the controls are electronically 'slewed over' to a set of 'reachback operators' in Langley [CIA headquarters outside Washington, D.C.]. Using joysticks that resemble video-game controls, the reachback operators, who don't need conventional flight training, sit next to intelligence officers and watch on large flat screen monitors a live video feed from the drone's camera."

According to Mayer, the operators at Langley can turn the plane, zoom in on the landscape below, and decide whether to lock onto a target. "A stream of additional 'signal' intelligence, sent to Langley by the National Security Agency, provides electronic means of corroborating that a target has been correctly identified." The White House has delegated trigger authority to CIA officials, including the head of the Counter-Terrorist Center. His identity, according to Mayer, "remains veiled from the public because the agency has placed him under cover."

In the bitter controversy that has erupted over drone killings, the U.S. government argues that it is operating within the law and within moral norms to keep Americans safe. Critics don't think so. "These are targeted international killings by the state," says Hina Shamsi, a human rights lawyer at the New York University School of Law.

A 2010 report, "Convenient Killing," explained, "The drone operators themselves are in no danger; they simply shoot at blips on a screen,
then clock off for lunch as someone else takes over the controls." The
report quoted an Israeli military spokesperson as saying, "The drone
computer has no family to be upset if it's killed, so everything's fine."

Time magazine summed up the conflict this way: "The U.S. seems
to be struggling to adapt its 20th century moral code of warfare to the
21st century practice of sending flying robots into other countries to kill
people. It appears that drones are evolving faster than Americans' ability to understand how, legally and ethically, to use them."

The outcry over drone activity reached a fever pitch in early 2013
when President Obama nominated John Brennan to head the CIA, replacing David Petraeus, who resigned after acknowledging an affair
with his biographer, Paula Broadhurst. Brennan was the chief counterterrorism adviser to President Obama and the principal coordinator of
the government kill list.

Just before Brennan's confirmation hearings got under way, *The
New York Times* reported that drone strikes had been launched from a
secret U.S. base in Saudi Arabia. Reporter Scott Shane, who broke the
story, told NPR that the most interesting element "is how we are using
a new military technology in countries where we're not at war to kill
suspected terrorists, how's that going, what are the long-term consequences. Is this the way we'll sort of be dealing with multiple problems
perhaps even beyond terrorism in the future?"

Against this background, Senator Rand Paul, a libertarian and Ken-
tucky Republican, took to the Senate floor on Tuesday, March 5, 2013,
to try to block Brennan's nomination with a thirteen-hour filibuster that
lasted past midnight. What most upset Paul was the drone killing of the
American Anwar al-Awlaki in Yemen, and what Paul saw as the possibility for the American government to use drones to kill Americans in
the United States. "I don't think the president would purposely take innocent people and kill them," Paul said. "I really don't think he would
drop a Hellfire missile on a café or a restaurant like I'm talking about.
But it bothers me that he won't say that he won't . . . to let this nomination go without an answer is a big mistake for us."

Paul also said he thought the Barack Obama of 2007 "would be right down here with me arguing against this drone strike program if he were in the Senate. It amazes me and disappoints me how much he has actually changed from what he once stood for."

The left and the right celebrated Paul's filibuster, but Brennan had enough votes to survive and was confirmed March 6, 2013.

Drama over drones and Brennan's role in the drone program continued to build. On May 22, 2013, Attorney General Eric Holder sent a letter to Congress disclosing that three Americans—in addition to al-Awlaki—had been killed in U.S. drone attacks. This information had previously been classified.

The next day, President Obama made a major televised speech to the nation in which he discussed the "lethal, targeted action" that the United States has taken against Al Qaeda and its associated forces, using drones. "This new technology raises profound questions—about who is targeted and why; about civilian casualties, and the risk of creating new enemies; about the legality of such strikes under U.S. and international law; about accountability and morality."

The president then defended his drone program. "To begin with, our actions are effective," he said, pointing to the removal of dozens of highly skilled Al Qaeda commanders, trainers, bomb makers, and operatives who have been "taken off the battlefield." He argued that America's actions are legal and that care is taken to avoid civilian casualties. In other words, he wants us to trust him and the war machine that he commands.

But can we believe Obama and his administration?

Unintended Consequences

One of the most troubling aspects about the use of armed drones for targeted killings is the law of unintended consequences. Countless civilians in the wrong place at the wrong time have died as a result of the armed drone strikes. Because the government does not disclose the details of its drone activities, the number of people killed by mistake is unknown. But we do know that the family, relatives, and neighbors of the people killed—by mistake or by design—are outraged that America has come into their country with armed drones that are targeting their people for death.

Some scholars say this has helped swell membership in Al Qaeda, even as its top leaders have been eliminated. Gregory Johnson, a Fulbright scholar formerly based in Yemen, now at Princeton University, explained to the *PBS NewsHour,* "Not all of these strikes that the U.S. carries out are successful. So there are some mistaken strikes. There are strikes that kill civilians. There are strikes that kill women and children. And when you kill people in Yemen, these are people who have families. They have clans. And they have tribes. And what we're seeing is that the United States might target a particular individual because they see him as a member of Al Qaeda. But what's happening on the ground is that he's being defended as a tribesman. So you have people flowing into Al Qaeda, not necessarily because they share the same ideology of Al Qaeda, but just so that they can get revenge for their tribesman who has been killed in a drone or an air strike."

The result, Johnson said, is that Al Qaeda on the Arabian Peninsula has grown in less than four years from a group of between two hundred and three hundred people in December 2009 to more than a few thousand fighters in 2013, according to numbers from the U.S. State Department. One of the fighters trained in Yemen was Umar Abdulmutallab, who, at age twenty-three, boarded a Northwest Airlines flight bound for Detroit on Christmas Day 2009 carrying a bomb that had been sewn into his underpants. The bomb did not go off. Abdulmutallab was convicted and is now in jail.

While the drone has become America's weapon of choice against terrorists, questions continue to rage about its advantages and disadvantages. One negative aspect that made headlines in June 2014 was the report in *The Washington Post* that more than four hundred drones have crashed in major accidents around the world since 2001. According to the *Post,* "A $3.8 million Predator carrying a Hellfire missile cratered near Kandahar, Afghanistan, in January 2010 because the pilot did not realize she had been flying the aircraft upside-down. Later that year, another armed Predator crashed nearby after the pilot did not notice he had squeezed the wrong red button on his joystick, putting the plane into a spin."

In another case, an inexperienced military contractor using remote controls to fly an Air Force drone made a series of blunders, ending with the crash of the drone a few minutes after takeoff. The Reaper drone, which was on a classified spy mission, landed at the edge of the Seychelles International Airport, a civilian facility on an island in the Indian Ocean east of Somalia.

That's the bad news. The good news is that the Reaper was not armed with a missile.

Sometimes the drones go *rogue,* the term used when remote control of the drone is lost. In September 2009, the Air Force lost control of an armed drone and had to shoot it down over Afghanistan.

So how much safer are we as a result of our many drone attacks?

As the United States struggles to clarify the scope and limits of its efforts to conduct targeted killings, drones are being used or developed in an estimated seventy-five countries. Will the time come when our enemies will be able to send their armed drones to our cities to target people they oppose? Clear international rules are needed to regulate drone use, just as international rules have been developed for chemical and nuclear weapons. It's not too soon to get started.

For Brandon Bryant, retired from the Air Force and trying to turn his life in a happier direction, the problem with drones is not in their expansion of a government's technical capacities. The problem is the secrecy. "It can't be a small group of people deciding how they're used," he said in a 2013 interview with *GQ* magazine. "There's got to be transparency. People have to know how they're being used so they're used responsibly."

11

THE MEDIA: CHEERLEADERS FOR WAR

I couldn't believe it, the way they blew that story out of proportion. It was something out of Male *magazine, the way they described the "battle." All we needed were naked women running up and down the deck.*

—James Stankevitz, crew member USS *Maddox*, Gulf of Tonkin

Over the past half century, America's mainstream media have repeatedly failed to investigate and report the truth in times of major foreign policy crises. Our big news organizations have without critical thinking accepted official government explanations and passed them along to the public as truths. The media have too often been the mouthpiece for politically motivated government propaganda.

The media's failures have made it possible for America's war machine to grow and prosper without public understanding, in part by helping to create political myths that encourage hawkish public attitudes. Often these myths grow deep into our political culture and continue to be accepted in the public mind long after the truth has been revealed.

When the news media, or individual reporters, publish stories that get too close to the truth and contradict official positions, the government may retaliate. Typically, a reporter who tries to dig beyond the official position will find that his or her sources suddenly dry up. Sometimes the government will go over the reporter's head to editors or corporate officers. President Kennedy was so unhappy with David Halberstam's reporting on Vietnam in the early 1960s that he pressed *The New York Times* to transfer Halberstam. The *Times* refused. In 1971, President Nixon's administration went to court to stop the *Times* and *The Washington Post* from publishing the *Pentagon Papers,* the secret Defense Department history of America's involvement in Vietnam. Nixon lost. On June 30, 1971, the Supreme Court ruled 6–3 in favor of the newspapers, barring the government from using preventive censorship.

Nixon's team also attacked *The Washington Post* and CBS over their coverage of the Watergate scandal, threatening to remove the companies' federal licenses to operate TV stations. Attorney General John Mitchell responded to *Post* reporter Carl Bernstein over a Watergate story by screaming, "Katie Graham . . . is gonna get her tit caught in a big fat wringer if that's published." The *Post* published the story and publisher Graham recounted the threat in her autobiography.

To counter the possibility of negative coverage, the government maintains a huge public relations program—more than $1 billion each year—to spin the news its way. The government is willing to lie to make its points and cover its actions.

In recent years, the Obama administration has increased its targeting of journalists who report government secrets, all in the name of protecting national security. That is almost always the government's argument for trying to control the story.

Following a 2012 Associated Press story about a terrorism plot, Obama's Justice Department secretly seized records of telephone calls by at least one hundred AP reporters in an apparent effort to identify the person who had leaked the information. The department seized e-mail records of a Fox News reporter and named him as a possible "co-conspirator" after he published intelligence information leaked by a government adviser on North Korea. In a third case, the government has been trying to force *New York Times* reporter James Risen to testify about his sources on a failed CIA operation. In January 2015, the

Justice Department withdrew its subpoena to have Risen testify, ending a seven-year legal battle.

Regardless of these pressures, the media have a responsibility to do what they can to ferret out the truth. Unfortunately, the media have failed to do this in some of the most important foreign policy actions of the past half century. One way to understand how the media have failed is to examine several cases in detail. Let's look back at the Cuban missile crisis in 1962, the Gulf of Tonkin incident in Vietnam in 1964, and the Iraq War of 2003 to 2011.

The Cuban Missile Crisis in 1962

When a U.S. spy plane photographed Soviet nuclear missile bases under construction in Cuba on October 14, 1962, the two superpowers plunged into a confrontation that took the world to the edge of nuclear war. A half century later, many Americans still believe the history of the Cuban missile crisis that was crafted by President John F. Kennedy and his aides. Their account is that a courageous young president, wielding military strength, faced down a communist dictator and forced him to withdraw the Cuban missiles, saving the world from nuclear war.

The problem: it's not true.

The truth is that an inexperienced, young president was blindsided by the Soviet military buildup in Cuba, failed to perceive that Soviet leader Nikita Khrushchev believed the United States planned to invade the island, and then nearly stumbled into nuclear war. Kennedy's speeches, and his team's management of American news coverage, delivered the message that the firm use and threat of military force had pushed Khrushchev to retreat. But in fact Kennedy had arranged a secret compromise with Khrushchev, accepting the Soviet leader's demand for the removal of American nuclear-tipped missiles from Turkey. That hidden concession, alongside Kennedy's public agreement not to invade Cuba, had resolved the crisis.

Kennedy insisted on secrecy in the deal because he could not afford politically to appear weak against communism or Cuba—especially since congressional elections were to be held within a few days.

America's mainstream media—television networks, major newspapers, and magazines—accepted Kennedy's politically motivated whitewash and failed to investigate beyond it. In doing so, the media contributed to the building of a political mythology about the crisis that contributed to a militarizing of U.S. foreign policy and helped lead the country into the catastrophic Vietnam War.

On October 16, 1962, Kennedy asked the three major TV networks for airtime to address the nation. His news of the missile crisis transfixed America and its media for days. Yet, as Khrushchev withdrew the missiles, and for weeks afterward, the Kennedy administration provided the public with no details about how the settlement was reached.

In early December 1962, the White House planted its own version in the *Saturday Evening Post*, which at the time was one of the leading general circulation magazines in the country, with a circulation of 6.5 million. Kennedy's team invited two reporters to interview members of the administration to tell the "inside story." The reporters were carefully chosen. One was Charles Bartlett, a Kennedy family friend of long standing—he had introduced Jack to Jackie—who ran the one-man Washington bureau of the *Chattanooga Times*. The other was *Saturday Evening Post* columnist Stewart Alsop, the brother of Joe Alsop, a prominent columnist and Kennedy friend and supporter.

The article they wrote was a sensation. On the magazine's cover was the now-famous quote from Secretary of State Dean Rusk: "We were eyeball to eyeball, and I think the other fellow just blinked." It was perfect shorthand for the myth that the administration wanted to build. The theme of the story was that Khrushchev had backed down under American military pressure. Quoting Kennedy aides it never named, the article portrayed the president as cool and masterful, patiently cornering Khrushchev and winning a major victory.

The article offered anecdotes to burnish Kennedy's image: "Once or twice the president lost his temper on minor matters. But he never lost his nerve," an aide was quoted as saying. The writers added approvingly: "A president's nerve is the essential factor when the two great nuclear powers are eyeball to eyeball."

The story portrayed Adlai Stevenson, the U.S. representative to the

United Nations, as a weakling who "wanted a Munich" because he had suggested trading U.S. missiles in Turkey for Soviet missiles in Cuba. The damning charge against Stevenson was that "he preferred political negotiation to the alternative of military action." The irony is that the Kennedy brothers had resolved the crisis by doing precisely—and secretly—what Stevenson had suggested.

The major U.S. television networks and newspapers never sought to explore or challenge the White House mythology dramatized in the *Saturday Evening Post*. Rather, the news media helped Kennedy's aides portray the crisis as an example of the effective use of military force to confront communist power. When the removal of America's Jupiter missiles from Turkey was announced a few weeks following the crisis, some skeptical legislators asked if there had been a secret deal—but news organizations did not pursue that critical question.

In January 1963, Senator Bourke Hickenlooper, a Republican, asked Secretary of State Rusk to confirm that the removal of the Jupiter missiles "was in no way, shape, or form, directly or indirectly connected" with the missile crisis settlement. Rusk replied, "That is correct, sir." Rusk had, in fact, suggested that Robert Kennedy meet Russian diplomat Anatoly Dobrynin to make the deal.

Secretary of Defense Robert McNamara was asked by Senator John Stennis of Mississippi whether the two missile withdrawals were related: "Absolutely not," McNamara said. "The Soviet government did raise the issue . . . but the president absolutely refused to discuss it."

The news media's failures in covering the crisis were broad. The mainstream news organizations:

- Never mentioned the presence of U.S. missiles in Turkey, Italy, and Great Britain, even though these formed a strategic parallel to the Soviet missiles in Cuba.
- Accepted Kennedy's declaration of Soviet motivation, that the missiles were intrinsically offensive, rather than defensive.
- Accepted administration officials' assertions in background meetings with reporters that the Soviets were threatening American

forces in Berlin, trying to force the United States to abandon the former German capital to the Soviet bloc.

- Overstated the Soviet threat to the United States. *The New York Times* on October 27, 1962, reported on its front page that the Soviet action might have created a "first strike" capability—a superiority in nuclear arms that would let the Soviets destroy the entire American nuclear arsenal before America could respond. This was not remotely possible, as U.S. forces vastly overmatched the Soviet arsenal at the time.

- Never suggested that political considerations might have played a role in the administration's management of the crisis, even though midterm elections were only three weeks away when it began. Political polls during the summer and fall had shown that Kennedy and the Democrats were facing the greatest disapproval among voters on the issue of Cuba.

- Were oblivious to the fact that the United States had for years been attempting to sabotage the communist government of Cuban leader Fidel Castro, including plotting to assassinate Castro.

William LeoGrande, a political scientist at Washington's American University, studied the media's performance in years that followed and wrote, "The press approached the missile crisis with the same Cold War worldview as the policymakers in the Kennedy administration, framing events and issues in exactly the terms in which the administration portrayed them. The press almost never questioned the basic assumptions and arguments advanced publicly and privately by administration spokesmen. . . . The press exhibited no independent judgment and did not treat seriously the views of anyone who dissented from the administration position."

After Kennedy's assassination on November 22, 1963, close Kennedy associates did their best to amplify the myth. Among those who helped was Ted Sorensen, JFK's speechwriter and confidant. Another was historian Arthur Schlesinger, Jr., whom Kennedy had recruited for the White House staff. In his book *A Thousand Days,* published in 1965,

Schlesinger waxed eloquent in describing Kennedy's management of the crisis: "To the whole world it displayed the ripening of an American leadership unsurpassed in the responsible management of power." What's more, "it was this combination of toughness and restraint, of will, nerve and wisdom, so brilliantly controlled, so matchlessly calibrated, that dazzled the world."

Robert Kennedy, the president's brother, decided to spill the beans about the secret deal several years after the crisis, in a book he wrote entitled *Thirteen Days,* published in 1969. The Kennedy family recruited Ted Sorensen to edit the book after Robert Kennedy was assassinated in 1968. Sorensen discovered what Robert Kennedy had written about his meeting with Dobrynin, in which the missile-exchange deal was made. True to his commitment to keep the secret, Sorensen edited that scene out. Sorensen didn't publicly admit to making that deletion until 1989, and he only did so under direct prodding from Dobrynin at a conference in Moscow in the waning years of the Cold War.

Meantime, Schlesinger discovered the secret deal in Robert Kennedy's memoirs, which the Kennedy family had asked Schlesinger to edit after Robert Kennedy was killed. The astonished Schlesinger reported his finding in the preface to the memoir, *Robert Kennedy and His Times,* published in 1978—sixteen years after the crisis.

Some files on the Cuban missile crisis and Robert Kennedy's "back-channel effort . . . to avoid nuclear war" were declassified in October 2012 on the fiftieth anniversary of the crisis. But we still don't know the full story. In summary, we didn't learn about the secret deal until 1978. We didn't learn the details of the 1962 deal until after the Soviet Union collapsed in 1991 and historians found the exact text of Dobrynin's cable in Soviet records. Details of the American version of the deal are still missing.

In reporting the Cuban missile crisis, news organizations accepted President Kennedy's claim that the Soviet Union had taken an offensive act in Cuba without provocation. In fact, Soviet leader Khrushchev had felt provoked by at least two major U.S. policies:

- American construction of a vastly superior nuclear missile force, with some missiles deployed just outside Soviet borders.

- American attacks on Cuba, a Soviet ally. Not only had the United States attempted an invasion, with émigré proxies at the Bay of Pigs in 1961, but Kennedy had then promptly directed the CIA to organize a bigger program of attacks in 1962.

Khrushchev was deeply concerned about American nuclear superiority, which was very real. He was worried about American missile bases in Great Britain and Italy and especially about a U.S. base in Turkey, planned in the Eisenhower administration but established in the Kennedy administration. All had missiles capable of reaching Moscow. Khrushchev had no similar capability to counter U.S. power and decided on a bold move to correct the imbalance. In 1965 a government-supported study by the RAND Corporation concluded, "The introduction of strategic missiles into Cuba was motivated chiefly by the Soviet leader's desire to overcome . . . the existing large margin of United States strategic superiority."

Roger Hilsman, the brisk, energetic head of State Department intelligence during the missile crisis, has since written that the Soviet decision seems to have been a "solution to a whole set of problems—the overall U.S. strategic advantage and the 'missile-gap-in-reverse,' the exigencies of the Sino-Soviet dispute, and the impossible demands on their limited resources."

But that's not what President Kennedy told the nation in a televised address after the Soviet missiles in Cuba were discovered. Kennedy's exact words about the Soviet motivation were "the purpose of these bases can be none other than to provide a nuclear strike capability against the Western Hemisphere." It was yet another case of Americans exaggerating the threat from the Soviet Union, and one that went unchallenged by the U.S. news media.

Kennedy also falsely said that the United States had done nothing to provoke the Soviet action. In fact, there had been considerable provocation. Immediately after the Bay of Pigs fiasco, the United States developed a new secret plan aimed at the overthrow of the Castro regime by whatever means might ultimately be necessary. JFK selected his brother Robert to oversee the plan, to be run by the CIA and known as Operation Mongoose. A directive for the project said, "The U.S. will make use of indigenous resources, internal and external, but recognizes that final success will require decisive U.S. military intervention."

Revealed to the American public in Senate hearings in 1975, Operation Mongoose—the largest operation within the CIA—had a budget of $100 million and more than four hundred U.S. employees and two thousand Cuban recruits. Its operatives had made systematic attempts to sabotage the Castro regime, including efforts to assassinate Castro.

In his 1962 televised address, Kennedy overstated the threat of Soviet missiles. With midterm elections only a few weeks away, the Soviet missiles did represent a political threat for Kennedy, but they did not increase the Soviet military threat. At one of the early meetings of the special committee—known as EXCOM (Executive Committee of the National Security Council)—that Kennedy assembled to give him advice on how to handle the crisis, Defense Secretary McNamara was asked whether he believed the Soviet missiles changed the strategic balance. McNamara replied, "As I suggested, I don't believe it's primarily a military problem. It's primarily a, a domestic, political problem." That was also Roger Hilsman's opinion: "The United States might not be in mortal danger . . . but the administration certainly was."

McNamara was right about the military irrelevance of the missiles' placement in Cuba. The number of nuclear-armed missiles wielded by the two sides in 1962 is now known. The Soviet Union possessed 250 nuclear warheads and 24 to 44 ICBMs capable of delivering them. The United States, with about 3,000 warheads and nearly 300 missile launchers, was far superior.

McNamara was also right about Kennedy's political difficulty should he appear weak on Cuba. Two years earlier, Kennedy had narrowly won the presidency in part by sharply attacking his Republican rival, Vice President Richard Nixon, as weak in opposing communism. Kennedy accused Nixon and President Dwight Eisenhower of creating "communism's first Caribbean base" by failing to prevent Castro's revolution in Cuba.

Only eighteen months before the missiles appeared, Kennedy had had a humiliating failure when Castro's forces crushed the U.S.-backed invasion attempt at the Bay of Pigs. Now, just days before the midterm congressional elections, opinion polls showed that American voters were doubting Kennedy's resolve on Cuba. In a 1987 interview, McNamara explained, "You have to remember that, right from the beginning, it was President Kennedy who said that it was *politically* unacceptable for us to leave those missile sites alone. He couldn't say *militarily*, he said *politically*."

Five days after Kennedy revealed the Cuban missiles and announced his naval quarantine of the island, his political predicament shaped the conversation that his brother Robert had with Soviet ambassador Dobrynin at a secret Saturday-night meeting at Robert Kennedy's Justice Department office. Robert Kennedy offered the Soviet diplomat a simple deal: you take your missiles out of Cuba; we will take our Jupiter missiles out of Turkey. But Kennedy laid down an inviolable condition: the exchange had to be kept secret. If it was made public, Kennedy said, the deal was off. Then Kennedy went further. He said his brother, the president, was under tremendous pressure from the Pentagon to attack Cuba. He said the United States would have to invade Cuba by the following Monday morning if the Soviets did not accept the proposal. To avoid war, Washington needed a swift response from Khrushchev and wanted to hear back the following day.

Dobrynin immediately cabled Robert Kennedy's message to Moscow, where it arrived on Sunday morning. Within hours, Khrushchev met with his advisers and issued a statement on Moscow radio that the Soviets would take their missiles out of Cuba. In the United States the public was led to believe that the Soviets had backed down.

Obviously, the news media faces difficult problems in trying to tell the truth when top government officials flat-out lie, as they did in the Cuban missile crisis. But as William LeoGrande has pointed out, the press exercised no independent judgment on the crisis, did not raise obvious questions, and for the most part simply bought the administration's politically motivated line.

The triumph of the Kennedy mythology about the crisis warped the powerful lessons of the missile crisis. Many scholars and the U.S. public came away from the confrontation believing that military force was the way to deal with the threat of communism. The reality was that negotiation and compromise had saved the world from nuclear war.

Among those kept in the dark about the secret deal was Vice President Lyndon Johnson, who became president a year later, after Kennedy's assassination. And Johnson, in the years that followed, would try to deal with the communist threat in Vietnam with military force.

Gulf of Tonkin, August 1964

In August 1964, the U.S. government announced that North Vietnamese torpedo boats had attacked an American Navy destroyer conducting routine patrols in international waters in the Gulf of Tonkin. President Johnson ordered the ship, named the USS *Maddox*, and a companion ship to return to the scene of the attack to show the North Vietnamese that the United States could not be intimidated.

Two nights later, during rough weather, the ships reported sonar and radar contacts suggesting a second attack. Hours afterward, even as the *Maddox* radioed follow-up reports casting doubt on the overnight account of attacks, President Johnson went on national television and announced that he had ordered retaliatory bombing raids against North Vietnam.

Within seventy-two hours, Johnson would win from Congress a resolution letting him expand America's war in Vietnam. After the Gulf of Tonkin incident America would begin overt conventional warfare in Vietnam, a war that would drag on for eleven more years, killing fifty-eight thousand American military and millions of Vietnamese. The war would topple Johnson from office, deepen the Cold War, and become America's greatest foreign policy catastrophe of the twentieth century.

Unfortunately, it was all based on a mistake. The August 4 attack that triggered Johnson's response never happened.

Caught in thunderstorms on a moonless night, the *Maddox*'s officers and crew mistook the images on their sonar and radar for attack boats. Years later, the historian of the National Security Agency would report that the NSA deliberately distorted intelligence reports about the August 4 incident to cover intelligence mistakes. Even the defense secretary at the middle of those August events, Robert McNamara, would eventually concede that the attack never occurred.

Let's set the scene: Lyndon Johnson had succeeded to the presidency just eight months earlier, following President Kennedy's assassination. He was seeking a full term in the White House, with election day just three months away in his race against a conservative Republican, Senator Barry Goldwater. Throughout the campaign, Goldwater had been accusing Johnson of being soft in Vietnam. Goldwater was advocating use of nuclear weapons and defoliating the jungles. Johnson wanted to run as a peace candidate but he was fearful of appearing weak, which was unacceptable in American politics then as now.

Johnson had already escalated the U.S. role in Vietnam, sending about sixteen thousand military advisers to help the fractious, military-run government of South Vietnam try to build a competent army to fight off communist guerrillas backed by North Vietnam's communist government. The CIA had told Johnson in May that this escalation would lead North Vietnam to put a hold on its own covert war against South Vietnam and seek an international conference to halt the covert U.S. campaign. The CIA was wrong.

One part of Johnson's secret war was called Operation 34-A, a program of attacks, assassinations, and propaganda directed at North Vietnam. Op 34-A included CIA-directed commando and shelling raids on the North Vietnamese coast, using boats bought and maintained by the U.S. Navy to carry South Vietnamese units under U.S. command. The United States conducted such attacks on two North Vietnamese coastal islands around midnight on July 31, 1964. On Sunday, August 2, Radio Hanoi reported these raids and complained that the United States was behind them.

In a separate but complementary intelligence program, the U.S. Navy was sending destroyers with electronic listening equipment into the Gulf of Tonkin to monitor North Vietnamese military and government message traffic, notably when it spiked following the U.S.-run raids. Captain John Herrick, the senior officer aboard the *Maddox*, received orders in July to conduct such a patrol. His orders said that "activity in 34-A Operations has increased."

Some hours after the 34-A attacks on the North Vietnamese islands, the *Maddox* entered the Gulf of Tonkin and immediately began picking up North Vietnamese naval communications. The intercepts suggested that the North Vietnamese were trying to determine whether the *Maddox*'s appearance off the coast was connected to the island raids.

Shortly after 3:00 P.M. on August 2, three North Vietnamese PT boats approached the *Maddox*, apparently mistaking it for a South Vietnamese escort vessel. Fearing an attack, the *Maddox* fired first. The patrol boats fired machine guns and torpedoes, which missed the *Maddox*. Captain Herrick called the nearby aircraft carrier USS *Ticonderoga* for air support. Three airplanes appeared and fired on the North Vietnamese boats, which retreated. Two of them appeared to be damaged. The *Maddox* left the area, awaiting instructions.

In tracking the Johnson administration's handling of what happened, it is important to note the twelve-hour difference in time between the Gulf of Tonkin and Washington, D.C. For example, 7:00 P.M. August 2 in the gulf would be twelve hours earlier in Washington, or 7:00 A.M. that same day of August 2. So it was Sunday morning, August 2, when Washington got word of the attack. President Johnson was briefed while dressing for church. At 10:15 A.M. the Pentagon issued a public announcement of the Tonkin incident.

After the attack, Captain Herrick reported that his ship was vulnerable and recommended canceling the mission. But on Monday, August 3, President Johnson instead ordered a second destroyer, the *C. Turner Joy*, to accompany the *Maddox* in returning to the Gulf of Tonkin to show America's resolve.

At the State Department, Secretary Dean Rusk told the Bureau of East Asian and Pacific Affairs to "pull together" material for a draft of a congressional resolution giving the president broad powers to handle any contingency that might arise in Southeast Asia.

On August 3, the United States directed new raids under Operation 34-A on North Vietnam. Hours later, the *Maddox* and the *C. Turner Joy* steamed north into the Gulf of Tonkin. On the morning of August

4, the *Maddox*'s sonar equipment went out. Other electronic equipment also failed. Repairmen did what they could to get everything working again, but with limited success. With darkness came rough seas, rain-squalls, and high swells. Herrick remembers it as "numerous thunderstorms, no moon, completely dark, ink dark."

Suddenly, with the use of their communications systems, the *Maddox* intercepted what seemed to be North Vietnamese attack orders. Herrick notified the Pentagon, which received the message at 9:20 A.M., Tuesday, August 4. Half an hour later Herrick cabled that an attack was under way.

Crew members began to see images on radar and other equipment suggesting that North Vietnamese PT boats were nearby and about to attack. The *C. Turner Joy* also saw blotches on its radar screen and began firing, hoping to hit something. As the ships twisted and maneuvered, Herrick asked the *Ticonderoga* for air cover. Eight planes arrived and dropped flares, searching for targets.

The leader of the air flight was James Stockdale, who wrote about his experience years later: "Our destroyers were just shooting at phantom targets—there were no PT boats there. . . . There was nothing there but black water and American fire power." Stockdale, a highly decorated officer, said he was ordered to keep quiet about the details of what he saw that night.

Around midnight, the *Maddox* crew saw the biggest target of the night on radar and prepared to fire their biggest artillery. The man in charge of the firing key for the five-inch-gun mounts was about to push the trigger when he realized that the image on the radar might be the *C. Turner Joy*. The triggerman said he wasn't going to fire until he knew where the *C. Turner Joy* was. The ship was asked to turn on its lights so the *Maddox* could see it. Sure enough, the *Maddox* had been preparing to fire on its partner. "If I had fired, it would have blown it clear out of the water," the gun director later reported.

Just after midnight, the *Maddox* and the *C. Turner Joy* left the North Vietnamese coast, heading south at full speed out of the Gulf of Tonkin. By now it was noontime in Washington, and the reports of a second attack had sent the administration into high gear. McNamara,

Rusk, and the Joint Chiefs of Staff began a series of meetings in an atmosphere of crisis. At noon President Johnson convened the National Security Council and held a lunch with McNamara, Rusk, CIA director John McCone, and McGeorge Bundy. Johnson ordered the drafting of a target list for retaliatory raids.

Meantime, on the other side of the world, Herrick began to have doubts that there had been an attack. He sent a second message to Admiral Ulysses Grant Sharp, Jr., commander of all naval forces in the Pacific, which said, "Review of action makes many reported contacts and torpedoes fired appear doubtful. Freak weather effects of overeager sonar men may have accounted for many reports. No actual visual sightings by *Maddox*. Suggest complete evaluation before any further action."

Secretary McNamara went to lunch concerned about exactly what had happened. He told friends after returning from lunch, "I wish to hell we had more information about what's going on out there. . . . Is the Navy's pony express out of order?"

In his 1995 memoir, *In Retrospect,* published thirty-one years later, McNamara reports that he was still not certain—as late at 4:08 P.M.— that an attack had taken place. He says he phoned Admiral Sharp on a secure line and asked him for the latest information on the action:

"The latest dope we have, sir," replied Sharp, "indicates a little doubt on just exactly what went on." Sharp added, "It may be just as well to wait an hour or so, if we have to, to be certain."

But the Pentagon's plans for a strong military response were by then well under way. At 4:49 P.M. Washington time—about seven hours after the first message of the attack had flashed into the Pentagon—the formal execution order for the reprisals was transmitted to Honolulu, according to the *Pentagon Papers,* which were written under McNamara's direction.

At 6:00 P.M. Washington time, the Pentagon issued a statement: "A second deliberate attack was made during darkness by an undetermined number of North Vietnamese torpedo boats on the USS *Maddox* and the *C. Turner Joy*" while the two were on "routine patrol" in the Gulf of Tonkin, sixty-five miles from land. "The attackers were driven off with no U.S. casualties, no hits and no damage to either destroyer. It is believed that two PT boats were sunk and two others were damaged."

At 11:36 P.M., Tuesday, August 4, America's networks interrupted their programs to let Johnson report a naval battle that had in fact not occurred. Johnson told the nation that U.S. retaliatory strikes were under way.

In covering the Gulf of Tonkin incident, U.S. news organizations added fictional drama to the government's story with accounts like this one in *Time* magazine: "The night glowed eerily with the nightmarish glare of air-dropped flares and boats' search lights. For 3½ hours the small boats attacked in pass after pass. Ten enemy torpedoes sizzled through the water. Each time, the skippers, tracking the fish by radar, maneuvered to evade them. Gunfire and gun smells and shouts stung the air. Two of the enemy boats went down. Then at 1:30 A.M., the remaining PTs ended the fight, roared off through the black night to the north."

Reading an account of the incident in *Time* magazine, *Maddox* crew member James Stankevitz was astonished. "I couldn't believe it, the way they blew that story out of proportion. It was something out of *Male* magazine, the way they described the 'battle.' All we needed were naked women running up and down the deck. We were disgusted, because it just wasn't true. It didn't happen that way, all that . . . drama and excitement."

U.S. News and World Report and *Life* magazine added fanciful details—that the attacking gunboats had hit the *C. Turner Joy* with gunfire and had brazenly used searchlights to find their target.

The Pentagon issued a press release declaring that there had been an "unprovoked attack" on the *Maddox*. President Johnson told an audience at Syracuse University that the "attacks were unprovoked." *The New York Times* carried three stories on its front page on August 5, 1964, about the "attack." One article declared that North Vietnamese PT boats made a "deliberate attack" on two U.S. destroyers patrolling international waters in the Gulf of Tonkin. Another story described "renewed attacks against American destroyers in the Gulf." The third story quoted Defense Secretary McNamara saying that North Vietnamese PT boats "attacked two United States destroyers in international waters."

The *Washington Post* headline on August 5, 1964, declared, "American Planes Hit North Vietnam After 2nd Attack on Our Destroyers: Move Taken to Halt New Aggression."

Neither the *Post* nor other major U.S. newspapers explored the story beyond the government's version in a way that would take Americans significantly closer to the truth.

Yet a great deal of information that contradicted the official account was, in fact, available, according to political scientist and media analyst Daniel Hallin in his 1989 book, *The "Uncensored War": The Media and Vietnam*. Hallin pointed out that the news media failed to address the question of whether the United States had provoked the August 2 attack—even though earlier reports had said that the United States was supporting covert South Vietnamese attacks against North Vietnam. He said the U.S. media paid little or no attention to North Vietnam's denial of any battle on August 4.

The weakness of efforts by U.S. news organizations to dig beyond the false U.S. government story about the Gulf of Tonkin incident is underscored by the actions of news media in other parts of the world. Hallin cites an August 8 analysis by the French daily *Le Monde* that noted holes in the official U.S. story about the August 4 events and suggested that no attack had occurred.

The U.S. press coverage was constrained by an underlying belief in American moral superiority that led news organizations to present a "classic John Wayne image for American behavior; the quiet man who is not easily provoked, but whose wrath is devastating when he is pushed too far," according to historian Edwin Moïse in his 1996 book, *Tonkin Gulf and the Escalation of the Vietnam War.*

Both McNamara and Rusk lied in testimony to Congress when asked about the South Vietnamese raids. McNamara told the Senate Foreign Relations Committee in August 1964, "The *Maddox* was operating in international waters, was carrying out a routine patrol of the type we carry out all over the world at all times. It was not informed of, was not aware, had no evidence of, and, so far as I know today, has no knowledge of, any possible South Vietnamese actions in connection with the two islands."

This was a lie. A Senate investigation years later produced copies of cables providing proof that the *Maddox* was a spy ship and that the ship's captain was aware of the secret U.S. operations supporting the South Vietnamese. Rusk also told Congress flatly there was no connection.

In the summer of 1967, cracks began to appear in the official government version of the Gulf of Tonkin incident. This is an example of what can happen when the press does its job. A new investigative unit of the Associated Press got the names of some *Maddox* and *C. Turner Joy* crew members and interviewed them. The AP's resulting story pointed out the grave doubts about sonar reports of torpedoes and other events on the critical stormy night of August 4.

Unfortunately—and this is an example of media failure—none of the nation's big, influential newspapers published the AP story. *The New York Times* ignored it and so did *The Washington Post*.

But the story did appear in the *Arkansas Gazette,* the Little Rock newspaper whose faithful readers included Senator J. William Fulbright, an Arkansas Democrat. He eventually called the hearings that helped open the door to the truth about the Gulf of Tonkin incident and reveal that it never occurred.

Twenty years after the war's end, McNamara went to Hanoi and met with North Vietnamese leaders. By this time, 1995, he had written his book, *In Retrospect,* in which he said the first attack had occurred, and the second attack "appears probable but not certain." After the meeting McNamara finally came clean after talking with General Nguyen Giap. "I am absolutely positive the second attack never took place," McNamara said. He promised to correct the second edition of his book.

United States Invades Iraq in March 2003

One of the most recent, most obvious, and most tragic failures of the media was in its coverage of the government's invasion of Iraq in March 2003. Here is Bill Moyers's damning 2007 characterization of media performance:

> Four years ago this spring the Bush administration took leave of
> reality and plunged our country into a war so poorly planned it

soon turned into a disaster. The story of how high officials misled the country has been told, but they couldn't have done it on their own. They needed a compliant press to pass on their propaganda as news and cheer them on. Since then thousands of people have died, and many are dying to this day. Yet the story of how the media bought what the White House was selling has not been told in depth on television. As the war rages into its fifth year, we look back at those months leading up to the invasion, when our press largely surrendered its independence and skepticism to join with our government in marching to war.

The most distinguished pro-war journalists were at *The New York Times* and *The Washington Post*—traditionally the cream of the nation's newspapers, the leading opinion makers, and supposedly the best-informed reporters and editors in the country. But they failed to do their job in the run-up to the Iraq War.

In May 2004, a year after the invasion, *The New York Times* published an article in which executive editor Bill Keller said there had been at least six faulty stories about the threat posed by Iraq. Judith Miller wrote or cowrote four of the six articles suggesting that Iraq had weapons of mass destruction. Her source, we now know, was Ahmed Chalabi, an Iraqi exile who had been funded by the U.S. government but was subsequently discredited for delivering fabricated intelligence information to U.S. officials. As Judith Miller became a kind of press secretary for Chalabi, the *Times* added to the credibility of her stories by displaying them prominently. Meanwhile, between March 2002 and the invasion a year later, *New York Times* columnist Bill Safire wrote "twenty-seven opinion pieces fanning the flames of war," according to political commentator Bill Moyers.

In February 2003, Secretary of State Colin Powell went before the United Nations to make the case for invading Iraq on the grounds that its leader, Saddam Hussein, had illegally built or sought biological, chemical, and nuclear weapons that he might use on his neighbors and even on the United States. After the war, when no WMD were found, Powell ruefully agreed with critics that his argument had been based heavily on false evidence.

But most of the American press had fallen for it hook, line, and sinker.

The New York Times published three glowing articles about Powell's speech on its front page. Reporter Steven Weisman said Powell's presentation took "the form of a nearly encyclopedic catalog that reached further than many had expected." *Times* reporter Patrick Tyler wrote that an "intelligence breakthrough" had made it possible for Powell "to set forth the first evidence of what he said was a well developed cell of al-Qaeda operating out of Baghdad." The speech, Tyler wrote, was "a more detailed and well-documented bill of particulars than many had expected." Reporter Michael Gordon wrote that Powell's speech was "vigorously argued and revealed an administration determined to use all means to make its case."

The Washington Post headline summed up the Powell story this way: "Data on Efforts to Hide Arms Called 'Strong Suit' of Speech." On its editorial page, the *Post* declared, "Irrefutable," and said, "It is hard to imagine how anyone could doubt that Iraq possesses weapons of mass destruction." The *Post* opinion page had four pieces, all full of praise, including Jim Hoagland's column, "An Old Trooper's Smoking Gun," and Mary McGrory's "I'm Persuaded."

Some doubts were expressed in the *Post*. But these stores were routinely played down and placed deep inside the paper rather than on the front page. Walter Pincus, the *Post*'s veteran investigative reporter, began a detailed probe of Powell's charges and concluded, "You could see that it was all inferential. If you analyzed all the intercepted conversations he discussed, you could see that they really didn't prove anything."

But Pincus had to fight to get a piece raising these questions into the paper. At first the editors were simply not interested, he said, but Bob Woodward, who was researching a book on the subject, intervened. In one Pincus story that ran on page A17, the lead was "Despite the Bush administration's claims about Iraq's weapons of mass destruction, U.S. intelligence agencies have been unable to give Congress or the

Pentagon specific information about the amounts of banned weapons or where they are hidden."

Pincus later said that it was no accident that these stories were buried. Here's how he described the problem for *The New York Review of Books*: "The front pages of *The New York Times*, *The Washington Post*, and the *Los Angeles Times* are very important in shaping what other people think. . . . They're like writing a memo to the White House." But the editors of *The Washington Post*, Pincus said, "went through a whole phase in which they didn't put things on the front page that would make a difference." Neither did *The New York Times* or most other major newspapers.

Meantime, two reporters at the Washington bureau of Knight Ridder, a national newspaper chain where I worked for more than twenty years, which is now owned by McClatchy, began digging into the Bush administration's allegations that Iraq had stockpiled weapons of mass destruction. Jonathan Landay and Warren Strobel found that a significant number of officials within the administration had serious doubts about the claims. With the backing of bureau editor John Walcott, Landay and Strobel wrote stories about those doubts, some of which were published.

But the stories they wrote had little impact on Washington policymakers. The Knight Ridder chain had no newspapers in Washington or in New York, the country's other center of influence. And as Strobel explained, "There was a lot of skepticism among our editors because what we were writing was so at odds with what most of the rest of the Washington press corps was reporting, and some of our papers, frankly, just didn't run the stories. They had access to *The New York Times* and *The Washington Post* wire and they chose those stories instead."

But Landay and Strobel—who had forty years' experience between them covering foreign affairs and national security—kept digging. In their reporting, they were hearing two different stories. They said the official government story was that Iraq and its WMD were a threat. But, Strobel said, "That was so different from what we were hearing from people on the inside." When Vice President Cheney declared in August 2002 that "we now know that Saddam has resumed his efforts to acquire nuclear weapons," Landay's sources said that little evidence supported that claim. He wrote a story about his findings, but it got no attention in Washington or New York.

Instead, *The New York Times* published a story by Michael R. Gordon and Judith Miller on its front page, quoting anonymous administration sources saying that Saddam had launched a hunt for materials to make an atomic bomb. The headline was "Hussein Intensifies Quest for A-Bomb Parts." The day it appeared, September 8, 2002, Cheney went on NBC's *Meet the Press* and pointed out the story, saying it was now public knowledge that Saddam was trying to enrich uranium for a bomb. In other words, the government leaked the story to *The New York Times* and then used what the paper printed to support its position. How bizarre, but how perfectly in keeping with how the government seeks to control a story.

Knight Ridder editors and reporters, meantime, kept trying to inject some reality into the days leading up to the war. After interviewing more than a dozen military-intelligence and diplomatic officials about the case for war, Landay and Strobel reported, "These officials charge that administration hawks have exaggerated evidence of the threat that Iraqi leader Saddam Hussein poses—including distorting his links to the al-Qaida terrorist network—have overstated the amount of international support for attacking Iraq and have downplayed the potential repercussions of a new war in the Middle East. They charge that the administration squelches dissenting views and that intelligence analysts are under intense pressure to produce reports supporting the White House's argument that Saddam poses such an immediate threat to the United States that pre-emptive military action is necessary."

But reports like that were drowned out as the media drumbeat for war continued.

The United States invaded Iraq on March 20, 2003. What was to be a quick war with local people welcoming American soldiers turned into a disaster. By the time the United States left Iraq in December 2011, 4,486 U.S. soldiers had been killed. More than one hundred thousand people are estimated to have died during the war, including about sixty-six thousand civilians.

And the cost to the U.S. economy? The Bush administration's top budget official said eleven weeks before the invasion that the war would cost up to $60 billion. U.S. budget figures put the government's direct budget appropriations for the Iraq War at $567 billion by 2008. But America's overall cost from the wars in Iraq and Afghanistan is likely to reach $4 trillion to $6 trillion, according to Harvard University scholar Linda Bilmes. Those estimates include the expense of future care for combat veterans and interest paid on funds borrowed to finance the wars.

A *Washington Post* analysis published in September 2010 concluded that the cost of the wars "added substantially to the federal debt" and compounded the 2008 financial crisis.

12
THE RECKONING

Every gun that is made, every warship launched, every rocket fired, signifies, in the final sense, a theft from those who hunger and are not fed, those who are cold and are not clothed.

—President Dwight D. Eisenhower

Many early Americans opposed having a standing army. They argued that it was a threat to their newly won liberty and a form of tyranny. Patriot leader and lawyer Josiah Quincy, of Boston, summed up the prevailing attitude in 1774 when he wrote, "What a deformed monster is a standing army in a free nation." Founding father Samuel Adams, a member of the Continental Congress and a cousin of President John Adams, declared in a 1776 letter, "A standing Army, however necessary it may be at some times, is always dangerous to the Liberties of the People."

James Madison, our fourth president, was just as adamant in his 1787 speech to the Constitutional Convention: "A standing military force, with an overgrown Executive, will not long be safe companions to liberty. The means of defense against foreign danger have been always the instruments of tyranny at home. Among the Romans it was a standing maxim to excite a war, whenever a revolt was apprehended. Throughout all Europe, the armies kept up under the pretext of defending, have enslaved the people."

For 170 years, America acted on the reservations of its founders, repeatedly demobilizing its wartime forces after each succeeding conflict. After World War II ended in 1945, the U.S. Army's swift reduction from 8 million men and women in uniform to 1.5 million led General George C. Marshall to observe, "It was no demobilization, it was a rout."

But just a few years later, the United States saw itself in an unprecedented light—as a global superpower defending the "Free World" from a broad onslaught by the communist bloc. The Cold War and fears of communism overthrew America's traditional aversion to a large standing army during peacetime. The military had peaked at 3.6 million in 1952 during the Korean War, but instead of demobilizing when the war ended in 1953, the military kept a force of more than 2.5 million.

As of 2013, the United States sponsored a military of 1.4 million that controls the world's oceans and skies and that has the global reach to drop forces into any other country at any time. To maintain its position as the reigning superpower and to support its war machine, the United States spends about as much on defense as the rest of the world combined. In fact, the United States now spends more on its armed forces than during the Cold War. The most expensive Cold War year was 1985, during the Reagan military buildup, when the Pentagon budget was $552 billion. That compares to $604.2 billion for 2013. Those dollar figures are adjusted for inflation.

But the time for a reckoning has come.

The United States is now struggling to move forward from the 2008 economic crisis and to address the huge deficits that stem in part from the Bush wars in Iraq and Afghanistan. This has triggered what promises to be a showdown in Congress between those who want to protect entitlement programs such as Social Security and Medicare and those who would cut entitlements and other federal spending in order to continue massive military commitments.

The New York Times summed up the dilemma this way in a November 2013 editorial: "With the Iraq war over and troops coming home from Afghanistan, the military budget must be reduced. The question is whether we can be smart about it."

The editorial quoted the then defense secretary Chuck Hagel as saying that future investment in defense should focus on special operations forces, unmanned surveillance aircraft, and cyber weaponry to protect against adversaries. Hagel and many others now believe it is unnecessary, even foolish, for the United States to maintain a Cold War land army that cannot be effective against the terrorists who are supposed to be our biggest enemy. Instead, the bloated military needs to trim down its traditional army and bulk up smaller Special Forces, which are more nimble and can move quickly and less expensively. But the hawks are resisting changes in the military and its defense budget.

In a proposal released in February 2014, Hagel revealed plans to shrink the U.S. Army to its smallest force since before the World War II buildup and eliminate an entire class of Air Force attack jets. Officials said it was the first Pentagon budget to aggressively push the military off the war footing adopted after the terror attacks of 2001. Explained a senior Pentagon official, "You have to always keep your institutions prepared, but you can't carry a large land-war defense department when there is no large land war."

Some members of Congress immediately declared their opposition to the plan. "It's dead on arrival," said Senator Lindsey Graham, a Republican from South Carolina. Defense contractors whose programs face cuts are fighting Hagel's proposal, along with military and veterans groups worried about losing benefits.

As *Time* magazine reported in a November 4, 2013, article by Mark Thompson, "A force built to fight the Cold War is now battling changes to its size, shape and mission." Among the points that Thompson made:

- In an era of unconventional threats, the Army continues to train against an enemy that looks a lot like the former Soviet army.

- U.S. weapons are getting bigger and heavier, not smaller and lighter. The thirty-five-ton Bradley Fighting Vehicle was built to take on the Soviets. Its replacement could be 50 percent heavier.

- The force is increasingly top-heavy. The United States had two thousand generals and admirals in World War II commanding 12 million troops (one commander for every six thousand commanded). Today nine hundred officers are in charge of 1.4 million (one for every fifteen hundred).

- In budget terms, the military looks increasingly like an employee-benefit program. Pay and fringe benefits have increased 52 percent since September 11, 2001, more than twice what the private sector has seen in that period. The military's health-care bill has jumped from $19 billion to $50 billion in ten years.

Given the obvious need for trims, will the congressional hawks agree to reductions in their beloved defense budget—and the jobs that come with military spending?

The answer: Only if they get enough heat from their home districts. Only if voters begin to elect leaders who are willing and able to make tough decisions about defense. And right now the hawks are in control.

The leading congressional hawks include House Armed Services Committee chair Mac Thornberry of Texas, Senate Armed Services Committee chair John McCain of Arizona, and Senator Lindsey Graham of South Carolina. The three Republicans pushed for billions more in defense spending after complaining that Obama's fiscal 2016 request for defense spending was inadequate.

Thornberry, a fifth-generation Texan, was appointed chair of the House Armed Services Committee in 2015, replacing another hawk, Howard P. (Buck) McKeon, who served as chair from January 2011 until his retirement in January 2015. McKeon represented a sprawling congressional district dotted with Air Force, Marine Corps, and Navy facilities, and his top nine contributions in 2012 came from the defense industry according to the nonpartisan Center for Responsive Politics. In 2013, *Politico*'s Austin Wright and Byron Tau reported that Buck McKeon's family was also involved in the "defense lobbying game." The congressman's brother, Joe McKeon, and nephews Steve and Daniel McKeon served as principals in the California-based company Golden Oak Consulting, the news organization said.

McKeon, a Republican, seemed to believe it was his job to protect the Pentagon from budget cuts. He made that clear during an October 13, 2011, hearing by his House Armed Services Committee on the future of national defense and the military: "There are some in government who want to use the military to pay for the rest, to protect the sacred cow that is entitlement spending. Not only should that be a nonstarter from a national security and economic perspective, but it should also be a nonstarter from a moral perspective." He said cuts should be made not to "the protector of our prosperity" (the military) but to the "driver of the debt" (Medicare and other entitlement programs).

McKeon's remarks were promptly challenged by peace protesters in the gallery shouting, "The driver of our debt is our military-industrial machine!" Capitol Hill police arrested several of them, including Leah Bolger, vice president of Veterans for Peace. As she was carried away, she gave one final cry of outrage: "The war machine is killing this country!"

Those who oppose the budget-breaking defense allocations favored by McKeon, Thornberry, and their allies are not just peace protesters, pacifists, and political liberals. They include fiscally and politically conservative analysts at the libertarian Cato Institute as well as defense specialists at the Henry L. Stimson Center, a nonpartisan think tank named for one of the twentieth century's most influential Republican foreign policy leaders.

The Stimson Center issued reports in 2012 and 2013 on a range of reforms and budget cuts to move toward a more flexible and financially sustainable U.S. military. By reducing top-heavy bureaucracies within the Pentagon, and by trimming military forces and weapons that were built against threats of the Cold War, the Stimson Center estimates, the United States could save about $50 billion per year in military spending. These budget cuts are proposed by a group of seventeen security and political specialists that includes six retired generals and admirals, including a former vice chairman of the Joint Chiefs of Staff.

Specific actions they recommend include changes in retirement and health benefits that could save $22.4 billion, changes in force structure such as a reduction in active-duty forces and nuclear forces that could save $21.4 billion, a slowing in purchases of F-35 jets and ballistic missile submarines, and the freezing of other programs such as the U.S.-based missile defenses that could save $5.7 billion.

Another smart idea under discussion would be to require Washington to tell the public how the next foreign intervention would be financed *before* sending in the troops. This would help alert the public to the cost of military actions and hopefully help avoid the kind of quagmires we experienced in both Iraq and Afghanistan.

Senator Al Franken of Minnesota introduced the Pay for War Resolution in Congress in 2011, proposing that America and its lawmakers decide how to pay for war before launching one. The financial cost of war should be clear, not hidden, Franken said. "Iraq and Afghanistan have cost us well over a trillion dollars," Franken said in his floor speech. "And it's been financed through debt, through borrowing from other countries, and emergency supplemental spending bills. What's more, the Iraq War was accompanied by a massive tax cut. That failed fiscal experiment created the impression that going to war requires no financial sacrifice. We know that's just not true. The question is, who will bear that financial sacrifice—the generation that has decided to go to war, or its children and grandchildren?" The proposal "reestablishes the connection between the citizenry of the United States and the costs of going to war."

Franken found just two cosponsors for the bill, which immediately stalled in the Senate Budget Committee, where no vote was taken on it.

Others continue to endorse the idea of a war tax. R. Russell Rumbaugh, an Army veteran and a senior associate at the Stimson Center, said in a February 2013 column in *The New York Times* that the need for a war tax is urgent, given the possibility of American involvement in the many trouble spots around the world, including civil wars in Syria and Mali. Rumbaugh wrote, "By tying military action to additional revenue, the president would actually have a freer hand in deciding when to use force. Every argument the Obama administration makes for military action would explicitly include a call for increased taxes, forcing the question of whether the stakes in the military situation are worth the cost. If the American people agree they are worth it, the president will get both

350,000
DIRECT WAR DEATHS

AFGHANISTAN,
IRAQ, and PAKISTAN
2001 - APRIL 2014*

Civilians: 220,000

Opposition Forces: 88,024

Humanitarian Workers: 438
Journalists: 344
US Military: 6,802
US Contractors: 6,787
Allied Military and Police: 30,499
Other Allied Troops: 1,432

*Does not include indirect deaths,
which may total many hundreds of thousands more

Source: costsofwar.org

This report, the work of a nonpartisan, nonprofit initiative, was released in 2011 and is regularly up-dated at costsofwar.org.

the political support and financing he needs. . . . If military action is worth our troops' blood, it should be worth our treasure, too—not just in the abstract, but in the form of a specific ante by every American."

In its Costs of War Project report, a Brown University team developed a series of ideas aimed at avoiding future war mistakes. To begin, the report says, the public needs to understand the damages in blood and treasure from the Iraq and Afghanistan Wars by a public accounting of all the deaths and injuries in the war zones, including troops, contractors, and civilians. The Brown team has estimated that 350,000 direct war deaths occurred between 2001 and April 2014, with the wars costing about $4 trillion.

Here is a summary of some of the Brown University team's recommendations for greater transparency in future government decisions to go to war:

- Refrain from funding war through special or emergency appropriations.

- Include future obligations to veterans when estimating the cost of war.

- Include the estimated costs of paying interest on war borrowing and the estimated difference in cost between borrowing for war versus raising taxes or selling war bonds.

- Estimate the costs of war that are passed on to state and local governments and to private individuals.

- Estimate the macroeconomic effects of war spending on the U.S. economy.

- Insist that the Pentagon meet accounting standards that every other department of government meets.

- Fully describe and audit the use of private contractors.

- Make public the National Intelligence Program budget that is directly related to war, such as the CIA drone intelligence and strike program.

Changing the warlike mentality in Washington and other parts of the nation won't be easy. The pressure from Americans who want the United States to operate as world policeman and to impose American values around the world will continue. The challenge is to educate people on the ways in which our militarism has made us less safe, not more safe. Another part of the solution is to make sure the public understands the economic cost of war.

The numbers tell the story.

In World War II, the government financed the war by selling war bonds and "taxing the hell out of everybody," according to defense-spending expert Gordon Adams. Congress raised taxes to pay for the Korean War in the early 1950s. In 1969, at the height of the Vietnam War, Congress imposed a tax surcharge, adding between 5 and 10 percent to most corporate and personal income tax bills. That helped pay for the Vietnam War, which cost $686 billion for the years 1965 to 1975, according to the Congressional Research Service.

But in 2001 and the decade that followed, no additional taxes were imposed for the Iraq War or the Afghanistan War. Washington leaders apparently feared that imposing a war tax would trigger public opposition to military action. Neither the president nor Congress wanted to risk that. Instead of raising taxes to cover the $859 billion cost of two wars from September 2001 to June 2008, Congress reduced taxes.

During the Vietnam War, Johnson wanted war costs included in the basic defense budget. He thought that strategy would somehow conceal the cost of the war, although he privately lamented, "That bitch of a war is killing the woman I love"—his antipoverty programs aimed at building what he called the Great Society.

President George W. Bush wanted war costs handled separately from the defense budget. His administration arranged for the war costs for Iraq and Afghanistan to be channeled through supplemental budgets outside the traditional Pentagon budget. With this approach the Bush White House suggested that the war costs were not really adding to national defense costs. Explains budget expert Adams, "Historically, the government has built the war budget back into the base defense budget. Bush chose not to do that. It was a wonderful game, treating it [war costs] as not part of the budget. There was this huge optical illusion. You say the defense budget has not gone up that much and [you say] pay no attention to the war budget. It will go away." Adams said the Pentagon loved the Bush approach "because for ten years they could park anything they wanted into the war budget."

But the cost for the two Bush wars was real. It did not disappear. Instead, it became part of the federal deficit and helped trigger the 2008 meltdown of the U.S. economy. Harvard University professor Linda J. Bilmes says the Iraq and Afghanistan Wars together are the most expensive in U.S. history. Their total cost could be as much as $6 trillion, she said in a 2013 study, *The Financial Legacy of Iraq and Afghanistan*. That estimated price tag includes long-term medical care and disability compensation for service members and their families. It also includes the likely costs of replenishing military stocks and paying general social and economic costs from the wars.

Bilmes said:

The largest portion of that bill is yet to be paid. Since 2001, the United States has expanded the quality, quantity, availability, and eligibility of benefits for military personnel and veterans. This has led to unprecedented growth in the Department of Veterans

Affairs and the Department of Defense budget. These benefits will increase further over the next forty years.

Additional funds are committed to replacing large quantities of basic equipment used in the wars and to support ongoing diplomatic presence and military assistance in the Iraq and Afghanistan region. The large sums borrowed to finance operations in Iraq and Afghanistan will also impose substantial long-term debt-servicing costs. As a consequence of these wartime spending choices, the United States will face constraints in funding investments in personnel and diplomacy, research and development, and new military initiatives.

Bilmes said the legacy of Iraq and Afghanistan is debt—"promises and commitments that extend far into the future."

In April 1953, President Eisenhower delivered the first of two major speeches during his presidency that addressed the dangers of military spending. Speaking several weeks after the death of Soviet dictator Joseph Stalin, Ike offered what has become known as his "Chance of Peace" speech, telling American newspaper editors that an arms race with the Soviets would impose domestic burdens on both countries:

Every gun that is made, every warship launched, every rocket fired, signifies, in the final sense, a theft from those who hunger and are not fed, those who are cold and are not clothed. This world in arms is not spending money alone. It is spending the sweat of its laborers, the genius of its scientists, the hopes of its children.

The cost of one modern heavy bomber is this: a modern brick school in more than thirty cities. It is two electric power plants, each serving a town of sixty thousand population. It is two fine, fully equipped hospitals. It is some fifty miles of concrete pavement. We pay for a single fighter with a half million bushels of wheat. We pay for a single destroyer with new homes that could have housed more than eight thousand people.

Ike's warning about the cost of military spending fell on deaf ears.

The Cold War, which developed in 1947 with the end of World War II, had expanded. The nation was shivering from a Red Scare fueled in part by Senator Joseph McCarthy, a Republican from Wisconsin, who claimed in the early 1950s that communists and Soviet spies were inside the federal government. Unable to prove his claims, he was censured by the U.S. Senate.

Meantime, a hot war was under way in Korea. The United States had sent 1.3 million troops to help the Republic of South Korea after it was invaded by communist-supported North Korea in 1950. The United States reported 33,686 combat deaths in the conflict, which ended with an armistice in July 1953.

In a break with its history, the U.S. government did not demobilize the army after the Korean War, as it had done after earlier wars. Instead, the nation would support a standing army and a hefty postwar defense budget as fears of communism roiled the Free World.

In January 1961, at the end of his eight years in office, Eisenhower tried again to warn of an unprecedented danger in American life: a standing military force and new political and financial constituencies that would seek to maintain and enlarge it. In what became known as the bookend to his 1953 speech, Ike spoke directly to the nation on live television, urging citizens to "guard against the acquisition of unwarranted influence, whether sought or unsought, by the military-industrial complex." In some drafts of the speech, Eisenhower was more pointed in his description of the complex, characterizing it as "the conjunction of a large and permanent military establishment and a large and permanent arms industry."

Susan Eisenhower has said her grandfather's farewell speech was not an afterthought. In a 2011 opinion piece in *The Washington Post* marking the fiftieth anniversary of Ike's speech, she wrote, "As early as 1959, he began working with his brother Milton and his speechwriters in a decidedly unsolemn time, offering sober warnings for a nation giddy with newfound prosperity, infatuated with youth and glamour, and aiming increasingly for the easy life."

But again, his words went unheeded. Most immediate news coverage of the speech focused on his remarks about the economy, while his warnings were interpreted as the musings of the "old soldier" and buried deep inside newspapers.

For me, the Eisenhower speech had a deeper and more personal meaning. As a veteran of World War II combat in France and Germany, I had witnessed the brutality of war. I had learned to scramble for safety when I heard the scream of incoming artillery that could spray shrapnel into a man's head, killing him instantly or leaving him forever maimed. I had seen the widespread destruction that comes with war and saps the spirit of the survivors.

The movies and the propaganda would have you believe that war is glorious. It is not that. It is hell on earth.

As a private in the U.S. Army, I served under General Eisenhower, the supreme commander of the Allied forces in Europe in World War II. I never saw him or any other major military leader during the war. But as a Washington-based correspondent starting in 1960, I was able to interview top officials in the Pentagon and other branches of government. I covered national security debates in Congress and in the White House and reported on decisions to send U.S. troops to fight in trouble spots around the world. I reported from more than thirty countries, including Vietnam and the Middle East.

I have done my best over the past five decades to focus on the expansion of the military-industrial complex and what has become an American war machine. I have sought to portray its threat to democracy and how it has made us less safe, not more safe. I have never believed that this complex was some kind of conspiracy. No, it isn't that. Instead, I think it is the result of a kind of groupthink. Psychologists say that groups affected by groupthink tend to believe in the rightness of their cause and ignore alternatives. Members of the group are under pressure not to express arguments against any of the group's values.

The Cold War ended in 1991 with the collapse of the Soviet Union, but the forces that make up the complex remained powerful. They gained new clout with the attacks of September 11, 2001, and the decision by President George W. Bush to declare war on terrorism and invade Afghanistan and Iraq. Congress gave the military a blank check in the name of national security.

The money funded a new war on terrorism and provided America's war machine with a new mission. U.S. combat troops have been withdrawn from Iraq and only a few thousand remain in Afghanistan, but there is scant evidence that the United States is ready to relinquish its role as global cop or its willingness to use military force around the world. In essence, the constituencies for war and interventions that have dominated U.S. policymaking since the start of the Cold War are alive and flourishing.

Historian and retired Army colonel Andrew Bacevich wrote in his 2010 book, *Washington Rules,* that the United States, in exercising global leadership, maintains military capabilities "staggeringly in excess of those required for self-defense." He noted that Americans prior to World War II viewed military power and institutions with skepticism, if not outright hostility. "In the wake of World War II," Bacevich said, "an affinity for military might emerged as central to the American identity."

Army general Martin Dempsey put it this way at Buck McKeon's 2011 congressional hearings on the future of the U.S. military: "I didn't become the chairman of the Joint Chiefs to oversee the decline of the armed forces of the United States, and an end state that would have this nation and its military not be a global power. That is not who we are as a nation."

General Peter Pace of the Marine Corps, in prepared remarks for the committee, said it was wrong to look at defense "from a dollar-and-cents perspective." He said it would be better to consider risks and threats from Iran, North Korea, and China.

Talk like that has helped fuel America's war machine for decades. This kind of Cold War mind-set hurts the nation, spoils our reputation at home and abroad, and diverts tax money that could otherwise be spent on education, health care, and the environment.

The best way to rein in the excesses of the complex—and make us safer—is for well-informed voters to elect the kind of enlightened leaders we need to bring about change. Eisenhower's advice, delivered in 1961, still rings true today: "Only an alert and knowledgeable citizenry can compel the proper meshing of the huge industrial and military machinery of defense with our peaceful methods and goals, so that security and liberty may prosper together."

COSTS OF WAR

How much have the wars in Afghanistan, Iraq, and Pakistan cost in human and economic terms? A nonpartisan, nonprofit team of thirty scholars—economists, anthropologists, political scientists, legal experts, and physicians—analyzed this question for Costs of War, a project at Brown University's Watson Institute for International Studies.

The group found that, from 2001 until April 2014, these wars killed 350,000 people, not counting those who have died indirectly from destruction, illness, and privations.

The wars have cost the United States more than $4 trillion. How much is that? Enough for the United States to have financed a four-year, private-university bachelor's degree—tuition, room, and board—for each of the 30 million college-age Americans counted in the 2010 census.

The Costs of War team's research papers, including graphics and videos, are posted and summarized on the Web site costsofwar.org. Among the findings:

- The wars directly killed more than 350,000 people, including soldiers, militants, police, military contractors, journalists, humanitarian workers, and civilians. More than half of these dead, roughly 220,000, were civilians.

- Beyond these 350,000, many more were killed indirectly, through disease, hunger, impoverishment, and homelessness—all spread by the destruction of homes, roads, power grids, water supplies, sewerage systems, and other infrastructure. These indirect deaths go uncounted and are difficult to even estimate.

- The number of war refugees and displaced persons is estimated at 6.7 million—nearly equivalent to displacing the population of the city of New York.

- Vastly greater than the number of those killed was the number of people injured or sickened in ways that permanently mark their lives. While 6,802 U.S. soldiers died in the wars, the Veterans Administration had approved more than 750,000 disability claims by mid-2012. New disabilities, notably including traumatic brain injuries, spinal-cord damage, amputations, and post-traumatic stress disorder, continue to be registered.

- These human and economic costs of the wars will continue for decades, and some will not peak until midcentury.

- Many of the wars' costs are invisible to Americans because they are buried in a variety of budgets. While most people think the Pentagon war appropriations are equivalent to the wars' budgetary costs, the true numbers are twice that, and the full economic costs are much larger yet.

- The U.S. federal price tag for these wars is estimated at $4 trillion, a figure that includes some future costs, but not the cost of future interest to be paid on the U.S. government's borrowing to finance the wars. Harvard professor and budget expert Linda J. Bilmes has estimated that the total costs could be as much as $6 trillion when future costs of long-term care and disability compensation for service members and veterans are counted.

In conclusion, the Brown University report said, "All of the costs of these wars have been consistently minimized, misunderstood, or hidden from public view." More transparency is needed because "the U.S. government's arguments about national security are a poor excuse for leaving everyone but the people of the warzone itself ignorant of what the use of force accomplishes."

EPILOGUE
by Molly Sinclair McCartney

Naturally, the common people don't want war; neither in Russia nor in England nor in America, nor for that matter in Germany. That is understood. But . . . the people can always be brought to the bidding of the leaders. That is easy. All you have to do is tell them they are being attacked and denounce the pacifists for lack of patriotism and exposing the country to danger. It works the same way in any country.

—Nazi leader Hermann Göring

On the morning of Wednesday, February 5, 2003, Jim and I sat down in our Florida condo, overlooking Tampa Bay, to watch Secretary of State Colin Powell's televised speech to the United Nations Security Council. We knew from advance news coverage that Powell was going to argue the Bush administration's case to invade Iraq. We wanted to see whether Powell had the evidence to prove that Saddam Hussein had weapons of mass destruction and should be removed by force. We listened carefully and watched as Powell presented audiotapes and satellite images to back up his claims.

In the end, Jim was not convinced. As a Washington-based national security reporter for more than three decades, he had learned to distinguish fact from fiction. In Jim's view, Powell had delivered a handful of smoke.

A few days later we hosted a dinner party for eight friends. After the meal, we gathered in a circle to talk. Jim's question for the evening: Should we invade? Each person responded, and to our surprise they said they believed Powell. They accepted his assertions that Saddam possessed WMD and might use them against the United States. They favored invasion.

Jim spoke last: "You are all wrong. They have no proof. They have pictures of buildings, but they don't know what is in those buildings. They are making a terrible mistake. They don't know what they are getting into, and people are going to die because of it."

This was vintage Jim—always willing to challenge the official government line and able to defend his position.

But Jim didn't stop with our friends. He made his doubts about the U.S. invasion the centerpiece of his speeches, his columns, and his classes. Because he could speak with authority and passion, people listened. Then someone in the audience would urge him to write a book explaining why America was so willing to go to war. Others wanted to know what could be done to change the system.

In response, Jim began work on this book, which he titled "America's War Machine," as a way to reveal the truth about the policies and the forces that drive American militarism. He believed that one of the ways to loosen the grip of the machine is for people to understand how it works and why it is dangerous. He had drafted much of the manuscript for this book when illness overtook him. He died May 6, 2011. At a memorial service for him, a friend from our local library—who had heard Jim speak—urged me to finish his book and propose some solutions.

The issues are so complex and the system is so rigged that I felt like throwing up my hands in dismay at such a daunting suggestion. That is probably how many people feel about this issue. But Jim never gave up, and I wasn't willing to give up, either. I applied to the Woodrow Wilson International Center for Scholars, based in Washington, D.C., near the White House, for a fellowship to research and complete Jim's book.

Michael Van Dusen, who headed the center at that time, offered me an appointment and provided me with an office there in 2012. I went to work interviewing experts on national security and defense. I reviewed the literature and writings on this subject. I read again the speeches that Jim made and the columns he wrote. I completed the book as close as possible to what I believe he intended. In closing, I am listing twelve recommendations for change that I think he would have wanted, starting with the need to promote peace rather than militarism and endless war.

1. Curb America's militarism and the worship of war that makes us less safe.

During the International Military Tribunal war-crimes trial at Nuremberg in 1946, American psychologist G. M. Gilbert interviewed Nazi leader Hermann Göring in his jail cell about war. Here is their exchange, based on Gilbert's book *Nuremberg Diary:*

> GÖRING: Naturally, the common people don't want war; neither in Russia nor in England nor in America, nor for that matter in Germany. That is understood. But, after all, it is the leaders of the country who determine the policy and it is always a simple matter to drag the people along, whether it is a democracy or a fascist dictatorship or a Parliament or a Communist dictatorship.

> GILBERT: There is one difference. In a democracy, the people have some say in the matter through their elected representatives, and in the United States only Congress can declare wars.

> GÖRING: Oh, that is all well and good, but, voice or no voice, the people can always be brought to the bidding of the leaders. That is easy. All you have to do is tell them they are being attacked and denounce the pacifists for lack of patriotism and exposing the country to danger. It works the same way in any country.

Despicable as Göring was, he spoke an uncomfortable truth.
We need to curb America's militarism and worship of war. A network

of think tanks and public policy groups that have worked closely with the military, defense contractors, and government agencies have in recent years shaped our public view of ourselves as a nation. This foreign policy complex has sought to promote American exceptionalism—the idea that the United States is different from other nations and has a national mission to serve as global police and to establish freedom and democracy in other nations, particularly undeveloped nations. This was one of the ideas—but not the only one—behind the Bush invasion of Iraq.

This complex of forces has developed along with a change in the balance of power within our government. Congress has ceded its war-making authority to the president. Fearful of the money behind the forces that shape national-security and defense policies, our elected representatives see tampering with the military budget as a political third rail. Too many of our leaders wave the flag and scorn anyone who doesn't fall in line.

In Iraq, this militarism gave the militant terrorists of Al Qaeda and their allied groups a propaganda victory and a recruiting tool. They wanted American tanks rolling through the streets of a major Muslim country, and they got it with our invasion of Iraq. They wanted examples of American torture of Muslims and we gave them Abu Ghraib. They wanted evidence of Muslim civilians dying from American drone attacks and we have delivered.

Our system is warped. We need a national awakening. We need to avoid the mistake of thinking that inside every foreigner is an American and that it is our responsibility to liberate that person.

After the Cold War ended in 1991, American political leaders from both parties called for reduced defense spending that could provide a peace dividend. But these voices were essentially silenced after the attacks on September 11, 2001, when it became unpatriotic and practically treasonous to oppose the gross expansion of defense and security spending.

Christopher Preble at the libertarian Cato Institute has said there is no effective counterweight to challenge defense spending. Congress hears only the proponents. We need more opponents—more voices to challenge the forces that prevail and that lead to congressional support of excessive military spending.

Some individuals and groups do question the current system. Winslow Wheeler, the director of the Straus Military Reform Project at the nonpartisan Project on Government Oversight (POGO), is an expert budget analyst who tracks military issues and writes about them with clarity. POGO has recently called for greater transparency in government information about its drone strikes and continues its traditional work exposing excessive military spending, such as the military's purchase in the 1980s of $7,600 coffeemakers.

In Florida, three Sarasota veterans questioned the government's plan to invade Iraq in 2003 and the idea that the Iraqis would greet American troops as liberators. Because their local veterans groups were promoting the invasion, rather than opposing it, the three men found other like-minded veterans and formed Florida Concerned Veterans, which is still active on these issues.

These projects and people provide a good beginning, but we need to grow a bigger movement if we are going to curb American militarism and the worship of war.

2. Recognize the cost of war and be prepared to pay for it.

The economic cost for the Iraq and Afghanistan Wars could amount to as much as $6 trillion when the future costs of long-term care for veterans and service members are included, according to Linda Bilmes, a leading national expert on financial and budgeting issues.

The human costs are incalculable.

Because of improvements in battlefield medicine and practices, the rate at which wounded soldiers die has reached a wartime low. Nearly fifty-five hundred American troops were wounded in action in Afghanistan in 2010. Fewer than 7.9 percent of them died, compared to 11 percent the previous year and 14.3 percent in 2008, according to a *New York Times* report.

According to a 2006 article in the *Christian Science Monitor,* studies by University of Pennsylvania demographers have found that the fatality rate among servicemen and servicewomen in Iraq and Afghanistan is much lower than in the Vietnam War and "the ratio of combat-zone deaths to those wounded . . . dropped from 24 percent in Vietnam to 13 percent in Iraq and Afghanistan" as of 2006.

In other words, wounded soldiers are much more likely to live than to die in today's wars. It's wonderful that their lives can be saved. But it means that more returning soldiers and veterans need help now and into the future as they grapple with extensive physical and psychological injuries.

Tragically, the Department of Veterans Affairs hasn't been doing its job. The head of the agency, Eric Shinseki, resigned in May 2014 amid a firestorm of reports that a number of veterans had died waiting for care at VA hospitals. CNN reported that the delays at a Phoenix VA facility may have played a role in the deaths of forty veterans.

This is a disgrace. We are responsible for providing the best care possible for the people we put in harm's way. This is the human cost of war. It is also a fundamental element in the economic cost of war that we should consider before we deploy our troops.

We should never go to war again on a credit card, as we did with Iraq and Afghanistan.

3. Consider reinstatement of the draft or some form of national service.

Strong arguments exist on both sides of this issue, but Israel has had a successful conscription program that requires both men and women to serve their country for two to three years.

America's military brass have traditionally favored volunteers over draftees, but General Stanley McChrystal, who led U.S. forces in Afghanistan and the Joint Special Operations Command, supports reinstatement of a wartime draft. "I think we ought to have a draft," he told the Aspen Ideas Festival in 2012. "I think if a nation goes to war, it shouldn't be solely represented by a professional force, because it gets to be unrepresentative of the population."

Thomas E. Ricks, a fellow at the Center for a New American

Security, has written that a revived and more equitable draft for men and women in the United States is the "best way to reconnect the people with the armed services." He argues that the draft did not keep President Lyndon Johnson from getting into a ground war in Vietnam, but it did encourage people to pay attention to the war and decide whether they should support it. "The drawbacks of the all-volunteer force are not military, but political and ethical," Ricks has written. "One percent of the nation has carried out almost all the burden of the wars in Iraq and Afghanistan, while the rest of us essentially went shopping. When the wars turned sour, we could turn our backs."

Ricks wrote that a retired general told him that the United States would probably not have invaded Iraq if there had been a draft.

A revived draft for conscripts coming out of high school should include options. Ricks has suggested three levels of service: Some could choose the military with low pay but excellent postservice benefits, including free college tuition. They would not be deployed but could perform tasks currently outsourced to private contractors at great cost to the Pentagon, such as paperwork, painting, and other lower-skills jobs. After eighteen months, they could opt to move into the professional force.

Those who don't want to serve in the military could perform civilian national service for two years and receive some benefits, including college tuition aid.

Those who object to the draft could opt out but would forfeit all government benefits—no Medicare, no subsidized college loans, and no mortgage guarantees. "Those who want minimal government can have it," Ricks wrote.

Andrew Bacevich, the political scientist and retired Army colonel who became an outspoken critic of American militarism and the Bush invasion of Iraq, argues that the draft has merits because it might correct the inequities inherent in our existing military system. But he doesn't think a revived draft is likely to happen. As he explains in his 2008 book, *The Limits of Power,* "Relying on a small number of volunteers to bear the burden of waging an open-ended global war might make Americans uneasy, but uneasiness will not suffice to produce change. Indeed the privatization of war—evident in the prominence achieved by armies-for-rent such as the notorious Blackwater—suggests a tacit willingness to transform military service from a civic function into an economic enterprise, with money rather than patriotism the motive. Americans may not like mercenaries, but many of them harbor an even greater dislike for the prospect of sending their loved ones to fight in some godforsaken country on the other side of the world."

Unlikely though a return to the draft might be, it still bears consideration. It would provide a democratic solution to what we have now. It would close the distance between the average citizen and the Washington war-making deciders. It would give people a stake in what we do with our military might.

4. End the secrecy of drone warfare.

Since the 2001 attacks, the United States has operated two drone programs to target and kill terrorists and extremists around the world. One is operated by the U.S. military as an extension of conventional warfare and is therefore subject to conventional military rules. But the other drone operation is the covert program operated by the CIA.

As drone operations have become less secret, the debate over their ethics, morality, and legality has raged. It's clear we need to end drone secrecy. As Rachel Maddow argues in her 2012 book, Drift, "Let's do away with the secret military. If we are going to use drones to vaporize people in Pakistan and Yemen and Somalia, the Air Force should operate those drones, and pull the trigger. And we should know about it. If the CIA is doing military missions, the agency needs to be as accountable as the military is, and the same goes for the policymakers giving them their orders. The chain of command should never be obscured by state secrets."

A July 2014 report by a bipartisan panel of military and intelligence veterans went further, declaring that the Pentagon should run drones alone, without sharing that authority with the CIA. The report, released by the nonpartisan Stimson Center, said, "The United States should not conduct a long-term killing program based on secret rationales."

5. Abolish nuclear weapons.

Nuclear weapons are supposed to keep us safe. But America's top nuclear experts—and many from other countries—now agree that we need to get rid of all nuclear weapons to be safe. Although estimates vary, the Ploughshares Fund, a foundation committed to a world without nuclear weapons, reported in 2014 that nine countries had about 17,300 nuclear weapons. The United States and Russia have a combined total of 16,200.

In 2007, *The Wall Street Journal* published an article written by four foreign policy experts. They said that the thousands of nuclear weapons that protected America during the Cold War were obsolete and of no value. They endorsed the goal of a world free of nuclear weapons and warned, "Unless urgent new actions are taken, the United States soon will be compelled to enter a new nuclear era that will be more precarious . . . [and] even more costly than [the] Cold War."

The four authors of the article included two Republicans and two Democrats—each with an impressive résumé and each an acknowledged expert in nuclear arms. They were George P. Shultz, a former secretary of state; William J. Perry, a former secretary of defense; Henry Kissinger, a former everything; and Sam Nunn, a former chairman of the Senate Armed Services Committee.

Many other elite members of the foreign policy establishment have joined the group of four in calling for an end to all nuclear weapons. The list includes many former top-level generals and admirals who for many years were in charge of pushing the buttons that would have launched nuclear-armed missiles.

We can't use our nuclear bombs. We need to rid the world of them before there is an accident—and before they fall into the hands of the terrorists. Let's do it now. Let's do it while there is time to save ourselves and the world.

6. Reform intelligence operations.

From its beginning in 1947, the Central Intelligence Agency has been going rogue. The disclosures of what these spies were doing—political assassinations, botched operations such as the failed Bay of Pigs invasion, and dirty tricks—led to the 1975 Senate hearings and new rules aimed at eliminating the worst of the excesses. Following the 2001 attacks, President George W. Bush—backed by Vice President Dick Cheney—unshackled the spies and provided them with executive orders and legal opinions to justify torture and other actions.

Cheney explained why in a television interview on *Meet the Press* five days after the 9/11 attacks: "We've got to spend time in the shadows in the intelligence world. A lot of what needs to be done here will have to be done quietly, without any discussion, using sources and methods that are available to our intelligence agencies, if we're going to be successful." The Cheney-Bush move to the dark side led to secret prisons outside the United States where terrorists could be interrogated—using waterboarding and other methods—without worry about legal limits.

President Obama has outlawed or mitigated many of the dark programs initiated under Cheney-Bush, but not all of them. We need less secrecy and more honesty about the operations of our intelligence agencies—all seventeen of them. This includes the National Security Agency, which collected millions of Americans' phone calls and e-mails as part of a massive government surveillance program. Director of National Intelligence James Clapper lied to Congress about the scope of the surveillance, then apologized after the publication of news stories based on the leaks by NSA contractor Edward Snowden. The national debate continues over the balance between national security and individual privacy, but clearly we need more transparency in this critical area.

7. Stop starving the State Department.

Too often, Congress has starved the State Department while giving the Pentagon more money than it needs or even wants. This pattern got much worse after the 2001 attacks.

In her 2004 book, *The Mission,* Dana Priest describes the new military in which teenage soldiers with guns are expected to act as peacemaker, diplomat, and nation builder—in addition to waging war. The reason for the transformation, Priest said, is "the military simply filled a vacuum left by an indecisive White House, an atrophied State Department and a distracted Congress."

We need to fund the State Department adequately to do its job, and this includes enough money for security so that we don't risk another Benghazi, the 2012 attack by extremists on the U.S. consulate there, which resulted in the death of Ambassador Chris Stevens and three other Americans.

8. Reduce dependence on oil and other fossil fuels.

Despite what Washington says, oil is the primary reason for our involvement in the Middle East and has been since the 1940s. We have lost thousands of lives and spent trillions of dollars to protect Middle Eastern oil. We are as addicted to oil as drug users are addicted to heroin, cocaine, and other drugs.

Developing clean and renewable energy would help reduce our dependency. Because of the finite supplies of oil and gas and other forms of fossil fuels, we are someday going to have to move to renewable sources of energy. The sooner we switch, the better for the environment, the economy, and the soldiers we send off to protect our supply of energy and to help us maintain our addiction.

A good start would be a new push for energy efficiency and some kind of carbon tax. A gasoline tax at the pump would encourage efficiency while providing needed funds to rebuild roads and bridges.

9. Wider and deeper media coverage of national security and defense.

The awarding of the 2014 Pulitzer Prizes—the highest awards in journalism—to *The Washington Post* and *The Guardian* for their disclosure of widespread U.S. government surveillance programs was an important step toward better media coverage of national security and defense.

The stories published by the *Post* and *The Guardian* were based on documents leaked by government contractor Edward Snowden. Denounced by some as a traitor and hailed by others as a hero, Snowden fled to Russia after turning over thousands of documents to Barton Gellman of the *Post* and Glenn Greenwald of *The Guardian*. The reporters developed their stories after considerable research, including interviews with government officials, to confirm accuracy and scope.

The articles sparked a national debate over government spying and demonstrated the power of the press to focus public attention on a critical issue. The Pulitzer judges said that the *Post* won for its "revelation of widespread secret surveillance by the National Security Agency, marked by authoritative and insightful reports that helped the public understand how the disclosures fit into the larger framework of national security."

In their selections, the Pulitzer judges endorsed the concept of reporting in this sensitive area. That recognition is sure to encourage other media to pay more attention to national security and foreign policy issues.

The second move in this direction is the University of Maryland's decision in 2014 to name *Washington Post* investigative reporter Dana Priest to the new James L. Knight Chair in Public Affairs Journalism. Her focus will be on national security. Priest has written several books and won two Pulitzers for her reporting. She brings unquestioned mastery of national security issues to her new job at the University of Maryland, which is seeking to become a premier training ground for students and professional journalists focused on global intelligence matters.

Some government secrecy is essential, even in a democracy, but we need to restore balance. An energetic press can help.

10. Audit the Pentagon.

Former senator Tom Coburn, a Republican from Oklahoma, noted that the Department of Defense was the only federal agency that had never fully complied with financial management laws. Coburn said a Pentagon audit would result in about $25 billion in projected savings each year for the next ten years. The Pentagon has been on the Government Accountability Office's high-risk list for waste, fraud, abuse, and mismanagement every year since 1995. "Auditing the Pentagon is critically important not just because it is the law, but also because our ignorance of how we spend defense dollars undermines our national security," Coburn said.

An effective audit—under the direction of an independent agency such as the Government Accountability Office—could help weed out waste and reduce corruption.

11. Close the revolving door between military and industry.

We need some effective way to address the "rent-a-general" problem, whereby generals and other high-ranking officers retire and promptly go to work for defense contractors. The contractors hire the generals to gain access to contract decision makers. The generals get to collect big paychecks from the contractors in addition to their government retirement benefits.

Why not require military officers to wait two or three years after retirement before accepting new jobs in the defense industry? Any military officer who wants to go to work immediately for a defense contractor would forfeit retirement and other benefits.

12. Rethink what we do in Muslim countries.

We know that the terrorist leader Osama bin Laden was enraged by the presence of American soldiers in Saudi Arabia in 1991 and that he swore revenge. As retired Army colonel Douglas Macgregor, a decorated combat veteran, has said: "It is a dangerous deluding statement to think that Muslim populations anywhere want U.S. or British conventional forces inside their country. They do not. They want us out."

Let's stop kicking the hornet's nest and rethink what we do in the Muslim world.

All the suggestions described above are possible if we can summon the public and political will to support them and make them happen. We know from past experience that we can make progress when we come together.

CLOSING NOTE

by James McCartney

When people would ask me if change is possible, I would always say yes, and I would explain why I think so, despite the troubles we face in this new century.

Yes, the Middle East is in turmoil. Yes, we still live with the threat of terrorism. Yes, the world is full of suicide bombings, genocide, and all the other terrible ways that men have found to kill each other. But when I look back over my eighty-five years, as of this writing, I can point to many reasons why I have hope.

One is the unimagined rebuilding and rebirth of Europe. When I landed in France in October 1944, as an Army private with the One Hundredth Infantry Division in the third wave of the Allied invasion of southern France, I had not a shadow of a doubt in my mind that we were going to win. The Russians had turned the tide of the war at Stalingrad. Paris had been liberated. Allied armies were pressing relentlessly toward the German borders. But we had not the vaguest notion of what the end of the war would bring. In my memory, the France of 1944 was a wasteland of defeated and hungry people, barren farmlands, and dismally sad villages and cities.

When I finally entered Germany with the Forty-Fifth Infantry

Division in the spring of 1945, it was even worse. I remember the bombed-out centers of Nuremberg and Munich, acres and acres with nothing but piles of bricks and stone, the twisted frames of shattered buildings, the smell of death so strong that it seemed difficult to breathe. After the war, I was based for several months in Le Havre, on the English Channel. It was leveled. What had been downtown looked exactly like the photographs of Hiroshima.

Paris had been spared, but its spirit seemed dead. My most vivid memory is of crowds of prostitutes, screaming for business, at every entrance of the American Red Cross building on the boulevard des Capucines.

This was the image of Europe in my mind for more than twenty years after the war. In 1969, I returned for the first time as a journalist, accompanying the recently elected president, Richard Nixon, on a diplomatic trip.

I can still recall my astonishment at the new Europe, for the miracle was well under way. Paris was alive. Cities that I had seen flattened had been rebuilt with gleaming towers, charming restaurants, and prosperous people.

What seemed to me a personal miracle occurred in Bonn, Germany. I was lunching with a press attaché of the German chancellor in the Bonn Press Club. We had a friendly toast, clinking wineglasses. As I glanced across the table, it occurred to me that he was about my age. I asked that inevitable question: Where were you during the war?

Comparing notes, we found that in the winter of 1944–45—a quarter of a century earlier—we were both soldiers, on opposite sides of the line, probably no more than a mile or so apart, in Alsace-Lorraine, in the Vosges Mountains. We had been trying to kill one another. Now we were breaking bread and sipping wine together.

Since then I have witnessed other miracles.

In November 1977, just before Thanksgiving, Egyptian president Anwar Sadat flew to Jerusalem on a historic mission for peace. He was greeted with warm ceremony and profound hope before beginning the first top-level discussion between an Arab and an Israeli in the history of the Jewish state. This stunning effort came after a series of four wars between Israel and nearby Arab states, including the 1973 Yom Kippur War, in which Sadat had been a principal player.

I was there when Sadat's gold-striped Boeing 707 touched down at Ben Gurion Airport. I heard Israel's twenty-one-gun salute for an Egyptian leader and marveled at the colorful and moving military ceremony of welcome. Waiting to greet Sadat was Israeli prime minister Menachem Begin.

"Wonderful to have you," Begin said as he walked with Sadat down the El Al Airline ramp.

Of course, there are no steps forward without some steps back. Sadat's overture to Israel outraged the Arab League, which denounced Egypt a few months later, in September 1978. A group of Egyptian army officers assassinated Sadat on October 6, 1981. Yet the Egyptian peace with Israel has continued for the most part for more than three decades.

Another miracle I have witnessed is the fall of the Berlin Wall on November 9, 1989.

It was stunning. And it was broadcast live on television so that viewers such as me were able to see the demonstrators climb on the wall and break through to the forbidden other side. In the twenty-eight years between the building of the wall in 1961 and its fall, about two hundred people were killed trying to cross into free West Berlin from communist East Berlin. Then suddenly I turn on my TV and see East Berliners climbing to the top of the Berlin Wall. Some were said to be dancing. Guards were on duty but not shooting anybody.

Then, after a brief period of mostly domestic calm in the 1990s, came the terrorist attacks of September 11, 2001, setting into motion a huge American military buildup, an expansion of laws curbing civil rights, and a massive expansion of Homeland Security measures.

America's war machine—the complex of forces that drive our foreign policy and defense spending—reacted immediately.

This book is based on the speeches I have made and the articles I have written over many years, but in particular the years since 2003. From my perspective, the Bush invasion of Iraq was the latest in a series of mistakes and misjudgments by the war machine forces, and I believe their actions and policies have made us less safe, not more safe.

Now we are paying the price for what we have done—and we will continue to pay that price as the self-appointed policeman of the world, intervening in other countries around the world. In addition to the thousands of war dead at home and abroad, we have the injured who have come back from combat badly damaged in body, soul, and spirit. Families around the world have been torn apart. The deficits from our war spending have damaged our economy.

And for what? Our combat troops left Iraq in 2011, but that country remains in chaos with ethnic bombings that have killed hundreds, probably thousands, of people and destroyed homes and businesses. Our troops were supposed to depart Afghanistan at the end of 2014 after thirteen years. But we don't know what will happen after that. We do know, however, that in Afghanistan tribal traditions and political corruption prevail, and that the Taliban and other extremists groups are waiting for their chance to seize power.

In pursuit of the terrorists that are considered our number one security threat, the United States has developed an aggressive drone program that makes it possible for unmanned aircraft to kill people on the other side of the world. Although the targets are identified in advance as enemies who pose a threat to the United States, the attacks sometimes kill others either by mistake or because they are too close to the target.

These programs operated by the U.S. military and by the CIA have outraged people throughout the Middle East.

Even against this background, I continue to have hope for the future, hope that there will be more miracles in the days and years ahead.

I believe the people in this nation are good people who want to do the right thing. Ultimately that could produce leaders who want to pull the nation back from the militarism of recent years and who have the courage to reform our spending so that our tax dollars are channeled from the military to infrastructure, education, and health care. But it won't be easy and it won't happen quickly. The forces driving America's war machine will cling to their power and their perks as long as they can.

ACKNOWLEDGMENTS

This book began with Jim McCartney's speeches about America's love affair with war and the listeners who urged him to write about the dangers of our national-security and defense policies. He had a manuscript well under way when he died in May 2011. Friends at his memorial service urged me to complete the book, which he had titled "America's War Machine." Among those who encouraged me to go forward was Judy McClarren, a member of the lecture committee at the Anna Maria Island Library, where Jim gave his last lecture.

With the help of many others I have been able to finish Jim's book and update the material to reflect recent events. I especially want to thank Michael Van Dusen, who showed his confidence in the book by arranging a research fellowship for me at the Woodrow Wilson International Center for Scholars, where he served as vice president for many years. Janet Spikes, the center's librarian, helped me with print and computer research. I am grateful to my former *Washington Post* colleague Caryle Murphy for her encouragement. Helping me navigate the issues of defense spending and national security was the knowledgeable Mark Thompson, who once worked with Jim and who has devoted his professional life to understanding and writing about the military.

James Rupert, a former *Washington Post* editor, provided valuable editing, fact-checking, and context that strengthened the book. Martin Schram, one of Jim's colleagues, led me to the perceptive agent Ronald Goldfarb, who believed in the book and placed it with veteran editor Thomas Dunne at St. Martin's Press.

A special thanks to Jim's children, Bob McCartney and Sharon Allexsaht. Bob, another *Washington Post* colleague, combed through his father's manuscript and recommended the reporting needed to finish the book. Bob and Sharon read and approved the finished product. My daughter Kathleen Garrett Muckleroy and her husband, Dean Muckleroy, boosted my spirits.

I want to emphasize that I have had the benefit of the work of many national security experts. My home library is full of their books and articles, which have provided a strong base for understanding the issues.

Many people took the time to give thoughtful responses to my many questions. Winslow Wheeler, the indefatigable director of the Straus Military Reform Project of the Project on Government Oversight, provided important background in interviews and a stream of e-mails. Retired army colonel Lawrence (Larry) B. Wilkerson, former chief of staff to Secretary of State Colin Powell, met with me in coffee shops around Washington to share his essential insight.

Renaissance man Gordon Adams, who divides his time between policy work on national security issues, teaching, and professional acting in Shakespeare productions, offered facts, figures, and considerable wisdom. Adams is a professor of international affairs at American University, the author of several books, and a former White House official for national security. He loves acting when he has downtime because it gives him an opportunity "to exercise my right brain."

Arms control expert Jack Mendelsohn, who was a source for many of Jim McCartney's stories, reviewed the material on nuclear folly. Bill Hartung and Christopher Preble answered questions and provided important background information.

Doug Balz and Jane Scholz, friends since our days together at the *Miami Herald,* sent many e-mails recommending ideas and sources for material to bolster the book. Help also came from Bob Boyd, Jim's bureau chief at Knight Ridder, who looked at the early manuscript and told me that it had substance and was worth finishing. Bill Vance, one of Jim's colleagues in the Washington bureau, cheered me onward. Clark Hoyt, who worked with Jim, came through with an important suggestion as I wrestled to finish the manuscript.

Margaret Dunkle staged an early book party and invited her neighbors to hear me talk about the book and answer questions. Frank Greve and Jane Chalmers offered encouragement and warm hospitality that included gourmet meals. Anne Ridder, who knew Jim from his teaching days at Georgetown University, was a constant source of support.

Janet Duke opened her comfortable guest room for me during my time in Washington and treated me to elegant dinner parties with informed friends and sparkling debate. My other hostess was Trish Clark, who turned over her Georgetown house to me while I was at the Wilson Center.

Many thanks to others, including Barbara Matusow, Miriam Goulding, Nancy Schlossberg, Wally and SonYong Turner, Jan Schneider, Nancy Feehan, David and Kim Hackett, Tom Coler, Susan Burns, Glenda Bridges, Susan Hahn, Sue Johnson, Dick Ryan, and Craig Settlage.

In closing I also want to thank Ken Freed, a buddy from my Nieman year at Harvard University, for a final read of the manuscript, and to the brilliant Bill Kovach for coming up with a key quote.

I have sought to base the material in the book on facts and to provide readers with a guidebook to defense issues. Any mistakes are mine.

With the help of all these friends and colleagues, I have worked to honor the manuscript that Jim left and that I hope will shine a light on America's war machine and the need to rethink our national-security and defense policies as we move forward in a new century.

NOTES

Opening Note

ix "We must guard against": President Dwight D. Eisenhower, Farewell Address, January 17, 1961, Eisenhower Presidential Library, http://www .eisenhower.archives.gov/research/online_documents/farewell_address /1961_01_17_Press_Release.pdf. Press release containing text of speech, which was printed in many major newspapers the day after delivery.

x "old soldier": Peter Lisagor, "Ike Ready to Give Up Reins: Packs Mementoes, Leaves Warning," *Chicago Daily News*, January 18, 1961.

x part of Ike's speech that made the front page: James McCartney, "Economic Outlook Bright, Ike Insists," *Chicago Daily News*, January 18, 1961.

x "a pickup in business shortly": *Wall Street Journal*, "What's News— Business and Finance," January 19, 1961.

x "Eisenhower Predicts Early Economic Upturn": Lee M. Cohn, "Eisenhower Predicts Early Economic Upturn," *Evening Star*, January 18, 1961.

x "President Warns Red Struggle Will Go On": Walter Trohan, "President Warns Red Struggle Will Go On," *Chicago Tribune*, January 18, 1961.

x "In a farewell address to the Nation": Edward T. Folliard, "Ike Warns Red Peril Will Linger, *Washington Post*, January 18, 1961.

x "Ike Warns of Danger in Massive Defenses": Robert Hartmann, "Ike

Warns of Danger in Massive Defenses," *Los Angeles Times,* January 18, 1961.

x "Eisenhower's Farewell Sees Threat to Liberties": Felix Belair, Jr., "Eisenhower's Farewell Sees Threat to Liberties," *New York Times,* January 18, 1961.

Prologue

1 "Judge the mind of a man": Pierre-Marc-Gaston de Lévis (French politician), *Maximes et réflexions sur différents sujets de morale et de politique* (Paris: Chez Ant. Aug. Renouard, 1812). This quotation is often misattributed to Voltaire.

3 "We must not fail . . . structure of our society": President Eisenhower, Farewell Address, January 17, 1961, Eisenhower Presidential Library, http://www.eisenhower.archives.gov/research/online_documents/fare well_address/1961_01_17_Press_Release.pdf.

4 defense spending: United States, Department of Defense, Office of the Under Secretary of Defense (Comptroller), *National Defense Budget Estimates for FY 2014,* May 2013, http://comptroller.defense.gov/Portals /45/Documents/defbudget/fy2014/FY14_Green_Book.pdf. Defense spending figures in this book are from the Green Book 2014 base budgets for the Department of Defense, adjusted for inflation. DOD base budgets, sometimes referred to as Pentagon budgets, represent only about half of all federal defense spending because the DOD base budgets do not include spending for nuclear, veterans affairs, Homeland Security, or other defense-related activities. Numbers assembled from Green Book FY 2014 by Todd Harrison, Center for Strategic and Budgetary Assessments.

4 "During the 1980s": "Weapons the Pentagon Doesn't Want," Center for Defense Information, December 27, 1992, http://libertyparkusafd.org /lp/Hale/Special%20Reports%5CMilitary%20Industrial%20Intelligence %20Complex%5CWeapons%20The%20Pentagon%20Doesn't%20Want %20--%20Video%20Transcript.htm.

4 killed more than 350,000 people: Costs of War Project report, first released in 2011, by a nonpartisan, nonprofit team based at Brown University's Watson Institute for International Studies. The Web site is updated on a regular basis, and as of July 28, 2015, the team reported that the "recorded dead—including armed forces on all sides, contractors, journalists, humanitarian workers, and civilians—shows that 370,000 people have died due to direct war violence" resulting from the U.S. invasions of Iraq and Afghanistan, http://watson.brown.edu/costsofwar/files/cow

/imce/Costs%20of%20War%20Executive%20Summary.pdf. Summary
at http://watson.brown.edu/costsofwar/.

4 budget for the new Department of Homeland Security: United States, Department of Homeland Security, *Budget-in-Brief: Fiscal Year 2013,* p. 6,
http://www.dhs.gov/xlibrary/assets/mgmt/dhs-budget-in-brief-fy2013.pdf.

4 240,000 employees: www.dhs.gov/about-dhs.

4 United States spends as much on its military as next nine countries combined: International Institute for Strategic Studies, *The Military Balance 2012*; and Winslow Wheeler, "The Military Imbalance: How the
U.S. Outspends the World," *Breaking Defense,* March 16, 2012, http://
breakingdefense.com/2012/03/the-military-imbalance-how-the-u-s
-outspends-the-world/ (summarizes the IISS report and includes the IISS
graphic showing the defense budgets for the top ten countries).

5 United States now spends nearly $1 trillion annually on defense: Win-
slow Wheeler, Straus Military Reform Project, Project on Government
Oversight, 2014. Wheeler's table showing breakdown of $1 trillion has
been posted on various Web sites, including Tipping Point North South,
http://tippingpointnorthsouth.org/2014/03/17/usas-2015-budget-for
-defence-is-1-trillion-not-496-billion/.

5 price could reach $4 trillion: Ernesto London, "Study: Iraq, Afghan War
Costs to Top $4 Trillion," *Washington Post,* March 28, 2013. The story is
based on a study by Harvard public-policy professor Linda J. Bilmes,
The Financial Legacy of Iraq and Afghanistan, March 2013, https://
research.hks.harvard.edu/publications/workingpapers/citation.aspx
?PubId=8956.

5 $75,000 for every American household: Peter Foster, "Cost to US of Iraq
and Afghan Wars Could Hit $6 Trillion," *Telegraph,* March 29, 2013,
reporting that a study by Harvard University professor Linda J. Bilmes
found that cost could be "$75,000 for every household in America."

5 estimated 260 organizations: Dana Priest and William M. Arkin, "A Hidden World, Growing Beyond Control," *Washington Post,* July 19, 2010,
http://projects.washingtonpost.com/top-secret-america/articles/a-hidden
-world-growing-beyond-control/2.

6 no-fly zone over Libya opposed by Defense Secretary Robert Gates: David
E. Sanger and Thom Shanker, "Gates Warns of Risk of a No-Flight Zone,"
New York Times, March 2, 2011.

7 thirty thousand troops to Afghanistan: President Barack Obama, address to the nation on the way forward in Afghanistan and Pakistan, U.S.
Military Academy at West Point, New York, December 1, 2009, White

House, Office of the Press Secretary, https://www.whitehouse.gov/the
-press-office/remarks-president-address-nation-way-forward-afghani
stan-and-pakistan.

7 "to rebuild our strength . . . among national programs": Ibid.

8 "permanent war footing": President Obama, State of the Union address,
January 28, 2014, White House, Office of the Press Secretary, https://
www.whitehouse.gov/the-press-office/2014/01/28/president-barack
-obamas-state-union-address.

1. Military Might and Money: The Pentagon Rules

9 "U.S. foreign policy is still too dominated": Admiral Mike Mullen, then
chairman of the Joint Chiefs of Staff, speech at Kansas State University,
March 3, 2010. This remark was not in Mullen's prepared text but can be
heard in the video of his speech at http://ome.ksu.edu/lectures/landon/bio
/mullen10.html. John J. Knuzel wrote about Mullen's remark in his article
"Mullen Urges More 'Soft' Power in Afghanistan," American Forces Press
Services, and his story was included in the Department of Defense News,
http://www.defense.gov/news/newsarticle.aspx?id=58170.

10 "Today as never before": Bacevich, *New American Militarism*, introduction, 1.

10 outspends the rest of the world: International Institute for Strategic Studies, *The Military Balance 2012*; and Winslow Wheeler, "The Military Imbalance: How the U.S. Outspends the World," *Breaking Defense*, March
16, 2012, http://breakingdefense.com/2012/03/the-military-imbalance
-how-the-u-s-outspends-the-world/ (summarizes the IISS report and
includes the IISS graphic showing the defense budgets for the top ten
countries).

12 seventy-five hundred military musicians: Eliot Cohen, quoted in "U.S.
Short of Diplomats for Iraq, Afghanistan Reconstruction," Asia One
News, April 29, 2008, http://news.asiaone.com/News/AsiaOne+News
/World/Story/A1Story20080429-62385.html. Eliot Cohen, counselor to
then Secretary of State Condoleezza Rice, is quoted as saying the State
Department employs fifty-five hundred diplomats compared to seventy-
five hundred military band musicians. The article said Cohen told reporters at a briefing on April 28, 2008, that "the generals are shocked"
when he tells them the State Department has only fifty-five hundred
diplomats.

12 "What is clear to me": Defense Secretary Robert Gates, Landon Lecture,

Kansas State University, November 26, 2007, http://www.k-state.edu/media/newsreleases/landonlect/gatestext1107.html.

12 State Department was too short on money: Nicholas Kristof, "Make Diplomacy, Not War," *New York Times,* August 9, 2008.

12 diplomacy and negotiations . . . killed or arrested: RAND National Defense Research Institute, *How Terrorist Groups End: Lessons for Countering al Qa'ida,* July 29, 2008.

14 "the driving force in American foreign policy": Mann, *Rise of the Vulcans,* 365.

14 "You are going to be the owner": Woodward, *Plan of Attack,* 150.

14 sent a team to Saudi Arabia: Woodward, *Commanders,* 254 and 262.

14 Cheney had two objectives: Woodward, *Commanders,* 262–64.

15 "satellite photographs of Iraqi tanks": Ibid., 267–68.

15 "SCUD launchers": Ibid., 268.

15 "no evidence of a massive Iraqi presence": MacArthur, *Second Front,* 173. He quotes a front-page story that appeared January 6, 1991, in the *St. Petersburg Times* by Washington bureau reporter Jean Heller.

15 "cautiousness overcame curiosity . . . nothing was reported": MacArthur, *Second Front,* 173.

15 Pete Williams: Ibid, 175.

16 armed forces shrank: Max Boot, "Overspending the Peace Dividend," *Los Angeles Times,* January 8, 2012.

16 defense budget declined: United States, Department of Defense, Office of the Under Secretary of Defense (Comptroller), *National Defense Budget Estimates for FY 2014,* May 2013, http://comptroller.defense.gov/Portals/45/Documents/defbudget/fy2014/FY14_Green_Book.pdf.

16 defense budget nearly doubled: Ibid.

16 State Department budget stood: Office of Management and Budget, http://www.whitehouse.gov/omb/factsheet_department_state.

16 comparison of ten countries: International Institute for Strategic Studies, *The Military Balance 2012*; and Winslow Wheeler, "The Military Imbalance: How the U.S. Outspends the World."

16 more than the combined: Wessel, *Red Ink,* 21.

16 $1 of every $5: Ibid.

17 "gusher": Gates, speech in Abilene, Kansas, May 8, 2010, http://www.defense.gov/speeches/speech.aspx?speechid=1467: "The attacks of September eleventh, 2001, opened a gusher of defense spending that nearly doubled the base budget over the last decade."

17 "we were ill-prepared": Max Boot, opinion article, "Impact of Defense Cuts Should Warn of Risks," *Washington Post,* July 30, 2010.

18 twenty-one thousand troops: James Kitfield, "Afghanistan Is Obama's War Now," *National Journal,* October 17, 2009.

18 called a *Washington Post* columnist: Woodward, *Obama's Wars,* 158. Excerpts were published in the *Post* on September 27, 2010. One excerpt said, "In September 2009, Petraeus called a *Washington Post* columnist to say that the war would be unsuccessful if the president held back on troops." Woodward did not identify the columnist who got the phone call.

18 "that the war would be unsuccessful": Ibid, 159.

18 Mullen . . . said much the same thing: Mullen, testimony before Senate Armed Services Committee, September 15, 2009, reported by Thom Shanker, "Military Chief Suggests Need to Enlarge U.S. Afghan Force," *New York Times,* September 15, 2009.

18 sixty-six-page assessment: Bob Woodward, "McChrystal: More Forces or 'Mission Failure,'" *Washington Post,* September 21, 2009.

18 "would likely result in failure": Ibid.

19 shot down an alternative approach: John F. Burns, "McChrystal Rejects Scaling Down Afghan Military Aims," *New York Times,* October 1, 2009. Burns reported that General McChrystal used a speech in London to reject an option supported by Vice President Joe Biden.

19 "The short answer": Ibid.

19 contradictory decision: President Obama, address to the nation on the way forward in Afghanistan and Pakistan, U.S. Military Academy at West Point, New York, December 1, 2009, White House, Office of the Press Secretary, https://www.whitehouse.gov/the-press-office/remarks-president -address-nation-way-forward-afghanistan-and-pakistan.

19 "Obama asked . . . agreed as well": Alter, *Promise,* 390. This Obama conversation with his team also published in *Newsweek* in an article written by Jonathan Alter, "Jonathan Alter: Obama, Year One, The Promise," *Newsweek,* October 14, 2009.

20 "I need you to tell me": Woodward, *Obama's Wars,* 326.

20 "terms sheet . . . almost everything": Ibid., 327.

20 *Rolling Stone* magazine: Michael Hastings, "The Runaway General," *Rolling Stone,* June 22, 2010. The article captured McChrystal openly mocking the White House and led to the general's downfall.

20 little choice but to fire him: Obama fired McChrystal June 23, 2010, saying in a White House Rose Garden statement that the general's conduct "undermines the civilian control of the military that is at the core of our

democratic system," https://www.whitehouse.gov/the-press-office/statement
-president-rose-garden.

20 $4.7 billion . . . foreign audiences: Associated Press, "Pentagon Spending
Billions on PR to Sway World Opinion," Fox News, February 5, 2009,
http://www.foxnews.com/politics/2009/02/05/pentagon-spending
-billions-pr-sway-world-opinion/.

21 "This year . . . State Department": Ibid.

21 thirty-eight hundred: "Assistant Secretary of Defense for Public Affairs,"
Wikipedia, http://en.wikipedia.org/wiki/Assistant_Secretary_of_Defense
_for_Public_Affairs.

21 ten, down from twenty-three: Jodi Enda, "Abandoned Agencies," *American Journalism Review*, June/July 2010.

21 "analysts" for U.S. television: David Barstow, "Message Machine: Behind
TV Analysts, Pentagon's Hidden Hand," *New York Times*, April 20, 2008;
and "One Man's Military-Industrial-Media Complex," *New York Times*,
November 29, 2008. Barstow won a Pulitzer Prize for his work.

22 "tenacious reporting": "Investigative Reporting," *The Pulitzer Prizes*, http://
www.pulitzer.org/bycat/Investigative-Reporting.

22 "Is there any limit": Charles Kaiser, "Kaiser on NBC News and the
Military-Industrial Complex," *Columbia Journalism Review*, December
1, 2008, http://www.cjr.org/full_court_press/above_the_fold_complex
_analysi.php. His comment was a way of expressing his dissatisfaction with
the seeming nonreaction by NBC News to *The New York Times* stories on
the military "analysts" such as NBC's General Barry McCaffrey.

22 "That is one of several questions . . . as long as possible": Ibid.

2. Industry at the Wheel

26 "Until the latest of our world conflicts": Eisenhower, Farewell Address,
January 17, 1961, Eisenhower Presidential Library, http://www.eisenhower
.archives.gov/research/online_documents/farewell_address/1961_01_17
_Press_Release.pdf.

27 "Pressure's on for Profits": James McCartney, "Pressure's on for Profits,"
Chicago Daily News, November 14, 1961.

27 "We staged huge selling campaigns": Ibid.

28 Gregory "Speedy" Martin: Bryan Bender, "From the Pentagon to the
Private Sector," *Boston Globe*, December 26, 2010.

28 "such apparent conflicts": Ibid.

28 "For most, moving into what": Ibid.

29 "The easy movement": Senator William Proxmire, quoted in article by

Robert E. Phelps, "Ex-Military Gain in Industry," *New York Times,* March 23, 1969. Senator John McCain repeated the Proxmire quote in a statement on the Senate floor, December 15, 2011, http://www.mccain .senate.gov/public/index.cfm/floor-statements?ID=42987243-f045-7da7 -6952-e32c98949a64.

29 2,072 retired . . . procurement system: Ibid.

29 *USA Today* published the first: Tom Vanden Brook, Ken Dilanian, and Ray Locker, "Military's 'Senior Mentors' Cashing In," *USA Today,* November 18, 2009.

29 Pentagon ordered a review: Tom Vanden Brook and Ken Dilanian, "Gates Orders 'Mentors' Review," *USA Today,* December 17, 2009.

29 Gates tightened the rules: Tom Vanden Brook and Ken Dilanian, "Gates Sets Limits for Military 'Mentors,'" *USA Today,* April 2, 2010.

29 2011 letter . . . "serious inquiry": Tom Vanden Brook and Ray Locker, "McCain Blasts Air Force on Role of Senior Mentor," *USA Today,* December 2, 2011.

30 Panetta eventually responded to McCain: Tom Vanden Brook, "Retired General Had No Conflict of Interest, Panetta Says," *USA Today,* February 20, 2012.

30 Boeing won the $51 billion contract: Tom Vanden Brook and Ray Locker, "McCain Blasts Air Force on Role of Senior Mentor," *USA Today,* December 2, 2011.

30 more contractors in Iraq than troops: Molly Dunigan, "A Lesson from Iraq War: How to Outsource War to Private Contractors," *Christian Science Monitor,* March 19, 2013.

30 108,000 contract workers in Afghanistan: David Francis, "Pentagon Has No Idea What 108,000 Contractors Are Doing," *Fiscal Times,* June 3, 2013. Article based on Congressional Research Service report.

30 privatization unprecedented in modern warfare: Molly Dunigan, "A Lesson from Iraq War."

30 As of June 2012: David Isenberg, "Joe Biden's Uncounted Angels," *Huffington Post,* September 11, 2012, http://www.huffingtonpost.com/david -isenberg/joe-bidens-uncounted-angels_b_1867971.html.

30 Blackwater employees engaged in firefight: David Johnston and John M. Broder, "F.B.I. Says Guards Killed 14 Iraqis Without Cause," *New York Times,* datelined November 13, 2007, and published November 13, 2007.

30 "It was a horror movie": Jennifer Daskal, "Blackwater in Baghdad," *Salon,* December 14, 2007, http://www.salon.com/2007/12/14/blackwater_6/.

31 "elite services provider": Academi, http://academi.com.

31 "keeping soldiers around the world . . . bathe in contaminated water":
Griff Witte, "Army to End Expansive, Exclusive Halliburton Deal," *Washington Post,* July 12, 2006.

32 lush facilities to entertain Pentagon brass: James McCartney, "11 Firms
'Primed' Pentagon," *Akron Beacon Journal,* October 22, 1975. Also, James
McCartney, "Contract Abusers List Grows," *Philadelphia Inquirer,* October 22, 1975.

32 "potential loopholes": Associated Press, "Pentagon Closing Loopholes,"
Independent Record, November 25, 1975.

32 Asked about: *Time,* "Adjusting the Bottom Line," February 18, 1985.

32 reports of $660 ashtrays: Eric Wuestewald, "The Long, Expensive
History of Defense Rip-Offs, *Mother Jones,* December 18, 2013, http://
www.motherjones.com/politics/2013/12/defense-military-waste-cost
-timeline.

32 "our attack on waste and fraud": President Ronald Reagan, radio address
to the nation on Armed Forces Day and defense spending," May 18,
1985, American Presidency Project, http://www.presidency.ucsb.edu/ws
/?pid=38654.

32 Boeing charged the Army $1,678: Eric Wuestewald, "The Long, Expensive History of Defense Rip-Offs."

32 $69 billion: Walter Pincus, "Sen. Tom Coburn Cuts the Fat at Pentagon in
his 'Department of Everything' Report," *Washington Post,* November
19, 2012. The article focuses on Senator Coburn's study, "Department of
Everything," which proposed cuts of $69 billion over ten years.

32 "Using defense dollars": Ibid.

33 Fat Leonard: Christopher Drew and Danielle Ivory, "Navy Was Warned
of Contractor at Center of Bribery Inquiry," *New York Times,* November
20, 2013. Also, Mark Thompson, "Navy Sinks in Hookers and Bribes
Scandal," *Time,* December 16, 2013.

33 $2,700 per capita: Mark Thompson, "Not NATO News," *Time,* June 10,
2011.

33 "to skimp on theirs": Ibid.

33 "both directly, making things": Jennifer Rizzo, "Defense Cuts: The Jobs
Numbers Game," CNN, September 22, 2011, http://security.blogs.cnn
.com/2011/09/22/defense-cuts-the-jobs-numbers-game/.

34 average annual salary: *Time,* "$80,175," March 9, 2012.

34 market research report has estimated: Mark Kleszczewski, "Barracuda
for K-12," *BPT Online,* June 18, 2014, http://bossierpress.com/new-oppor
tunities-in-cybersecurity/.

34 "The issue du jour is cyber warfare . . . reality": Senator Tom Carper, opening statement, U.S. Senate Subcommittee on Federal Financial Management, Government Information, Federal Services, and International Security of the Committee on Homeland Security and Governmental Affairs, October 29, 2009, http://www.gpo.gov/fdsys/pkg/CHRG -111shrg53852/html/CHRG-111shrg53852.htm.

34 Clapper, who told Congress . . . not collecting data: Bill Chappell, "Clapper Apologizes for Answer on NSA's Data Collection," NPR, July 2, 2013, http://www.npr.org/sections/thetwo-way/2013/07/02/198118060/clapper -apologizes-for-answer-on-nsas-data-collection; and Steve Contorno, "James Clapper's Testimony One Year Later," *Tampa Bay Times* Politi fact.com, March 11, 2014, http://www.politifact.com/truth-o-meter/article /2014/mar/11/james-clappers-testimony-one-year-later/.

34 Clapper later apologized: Bill Chappell, "Clapper Apologizes for Answer on NSA's Data Collection," NPR, July 2, 2013.

35 480 private companies: "Top Secret America," *Frontline,* PBS, September 6, 2011, http://www.pbs.org/wgbh/pages/frontline/iraq-war-on-terror /topsecretamerica/transcript-6/.

35 "Contractors have become essential": Tim Shorrock, "Meet the Contractors," *Salon,* June 10, 2013.

35 "our $25 billion tug of war": James McCartney, "Our $25 Billion Tug of War," *Chicago Daily News,* November 13, 1961.

35 $536.8 billion: Paul Toscano and Jill Weinberger, "The Ten Biggest U.S. Government Contractors," CNBC, June 13, 2012, http://www.cnbc.com /2011/04/08/The-10-Biggest-U.S.-Government-Contractors.html.

35 "The ongoing war on terror . . . international bodies": Polaris Institute corporate profile of Lockheed Martin, November 2005, https:// d3n8a8pro7vhmx.cloudfront.net/polarisinstitute/pages/29/attachments /original/1410802113/Lockheed_Martin.pdf?1410802113.

36 ten biggest defense contractors . . . technology services, and intelligence analysis: Paul Toscano and Jill Weinberger, "The Ten Biggest U.S. Government Contractors," CNBC, June 13, 2012.

37 SAIC faced a scandal . . . $2.75 million: *Washington Post,* April 21, 2012.

37 L-3 Communications . . . Department of Veterans Affairs: Paul Toscano and Jill Weinberger, "The Ten Biggest U.S. Government Contractors," CNBC, June 13, 2012.

38 defense contractors have learned: Brandon Michael Carius, "Procuring Influence: An Analysis of the Political Dynamics of District Revenue

from Defense Contracting" (master's thesis, Georgetown University, May 25, 2009).

38 Arms merchants: Zach Toombs and R. Jeffrey Smith, Center for Public Integrity, "Why Is the U.S. Selling Billions in Weapons to Autocrats?," *Foreign Policy,* June 21, 2012.

3. Congress and the White House: A Vital Part of the Problem

40 "the 'military-industrial-congressional' complex": Senator John McCain, Senate floor statement on the "military-industrial-congressional" complex, December 15, 2011, http://www.mccain.senate.gov/public/index.cfm/floor -statements?ID=42987243-f045-7da7-6952-e32c98949a64.

40 Cheney wanted Congress to fund: Leslie Wayne, "The Plane That Won't Die," *New York Times,* May 24, 2006. The Wayne story links to a 1990 article with more detail by Michael R. Gordon, "Cheney Proposes Sharp Reductions in New Warplanes," *New York Times,* April 27, 1990.

41 Gates . . . told Congress: Defense Secretary Gates, congressional testimony, April 6, 2009, Department of Defense press operations, http:// www.defense.gov/speeches/speech.aspx?speechid=1341.

41 C-17 program supports 650 suppliers: Boeing news release, "Boeing to Complete Production of C-17 Globemaster III in 2015," September 18, 2013, http://boeing.mediaroom.com/2013-09-18-Boeing-to-Complete -Production-of-C-17-Globemaster-III-in-2015; and David Kesmodel and Nathan Hodge, "Boeing Looks Afar for New C-17 Jet Sales," *Wall Street Journal,* March 29, 2012.

41 "It's a Bird, It's a Plane": Ben Elgin and Keith Epstein, "It's a Bird, It's a Plane, It's Pork!," *Bloomberg Business,* October 29, 2009, http://www .bloomberg.com/bw/magazine/content/09_45/b4154046738593.htm.

41 "I am convinced . . . policy and politics": James McCartney, "How Lawmakers Vie for Defense Plums," *Chicago Daily News,* November 15, 1961.

42 "we could save a billion dollars . . . Political constraints": James McCartney, "In the Pentagon, Packard Spoke the Unspeakable," *Chicago Tribune,* December 15, 1971. This article quotes David Packard's remarks at his outgoing press conference as the outgoing number two man at the Pentagon.

42 "Dave Packard": Defense Secretary Melvin Laird, quoted in James McCartney's "In the Pentagon, Packard Spoke the Unspeakable."

42 "no one ever comes up to him": Archival notes of Eisenhower meeting, March 1956, as described in Secretary Gates's speech at the Eisenhower

Presidential Library, Abilene, Kansas, Saturday, May 8, 2010," http://www.defense.gov/speeches/speech.aspx?speechid=1467.

42 Barbara Boxer urged funding of the C-17: Senator Boxer's press release, August 18, 2006, https://www.boxer.senate.gov/press/release/boxer-state ment-on-boeings-decision-to-begin-shut-down-of-c-17-production-line/.

43 Boeing employs five thousand in Boxer's state: Michael Hiltzik, "Billions Are Spent to Defend 5,000 Jobs at Boeing C-17 Plant," *Los Angeles Times*, October 8, 2009.

43 "We need these planes": Ben Elgin and Keith Epstein, "It's a Bird, It's a Plane, It's Pork!"

43 "continuing attention": President John F. Kennedy, press conference, January 15, 1962. Author covered the press conference, held in the State Department auditorium, Washington, D.C., and asked the president what he thought of Eisenhower's comments a year earlier on the military-industrial-complex. Audio recording of the press conference available on YouTube at https://www.youtube.com/watch?v=ta9nNtVdePs&list=PL0 O5WNzrZqIOOpmfrurZtkYeYEL-onugx&index=20. To hear McCartney's question and JFK's answer, go to 28:59 on the time bar showing minutes and seconds.

43 defense community donated $27 million . . . first Senate campaign in 1978: Center for Responsive Politics, https://www.opensecrets.org/indus tries/indus.php?Ind=D.

44 Randy "Duke" Cunningham: Bill Chappell, "Former Rep. 'Duke' Cunningham Freed After Bribery Sentence," NPR, June 4, 2013, http://www .npr.org/sections/thetwo-way/2013/06/04/188667106/former-rep-duke -cunningham-freed-after-bribery-sentence. A list of some items that Cunningham admitted to taking in the bribery case are listed at the *San Diego Union-Tribune* Web site at http://www.utsandiego.com/news/2013/jun/04 /duke-cunningham-timeline-bribes-congress/.

44 "growing influence": Draft of Eisenhower speech described by Melvin A. Goodman, "Eisenhower's Neglected Warning," consortiumnews.com, January 16, 2011, http://www.consortiumnews.com/2011/011611b.html.

44 none of the twenty or so drafts: Author telephone interview with Valoise Armstrong, Eisenhower Presidential Library archivist, July 28, 2014.

45 "one of the drafts of the speech . . . Congress as well": Goodman, "Eisenhower's Neglected Warning."

45 "The fiftieth anniversary": Senator McCain, Senate floor statement on the "military-industrial-congressional" complex, December 15, 2011.

45 executive branch is also guilty: Author, interview April 19, 2012, with

Gordon Adams. He is the author of *Buying National Security* (2010) and *The Iron Triangle* (1981), which explores the bonds between the Pentagon, Congress, and the defense industry. This was the first of three interviews with Adams for this book.

45 Star Wars: For background on this program, see FitzGerald, *Way Out There in the Blue*.

45 Union of Concerned Scientists: Ibid., 246.

45 American Physical Society declared: Philip M. Boffey, "Physicists Express Star Wars' Doubt; Long Delays Seen," *New York Times*, April 23, 1987.

46 "Everyone knew it was loony": Author interview with Adams.

46 "impotent and obsolete": President Reagan, address to the nation on defense and national security, March 23, 1983, American Presidency Project, http://www.presidency.ucsb.edu/ws/?pid=41093. This is known as his Star Wars speech.

46 "didn't fit with their core missions": Author, interview with Adams.

46 Clinton kept Star Wars initiative: FitzGerald, *Way Out There in the Blue*, 490–99.

46 Pentagon asked Congress for $9.9 billion: Unsigned editorial, "Mr. Gates and the Pentagon Budget," *New York Times*, May 16, 2010.

46 United States has spent more than $200 billion: Stephen I. Schwartz, "The Real Price of Ballistic Missile Defense," *WMD Junction*, April 13, 2012, http://wmdjunction.com/120413_missile_defense_costs.htm.

46 "Every time the program": FitzGerald, 480.

46 "suggests that the support": Stephen M. Walt, "Rush to Failure: The Flawed Politics and Policies of Missile Defense," *Harvard Magazine*, May–June 2000.

47 Air Force requested a total of 5 C-130s: Walter Pincus, "Cargo Plane with Strings Attached; Congress Funds and Stations C-130s Unwanted by Pentagon," *Washington Post*, July 23, 1998; and Walter Pincus, "Congress Insists Air Force Buy Unwanted C-130s," *Sun-Sentinel*, July 24, 1998.

47 "We're purchasing equipment . . . in America": Senator McCain, quoted in Jim Mann, "Pentagon: A Game of Priorities," *Los Angeles Times*, January 31, 2001. Mann's story published on February 1, 2001, in *Sun-Sentinel*, "Other Priorities May Put Pinch on Star Wars."

47 lavish 1950s-style party . . . $60,000: William D. Hartung and Frida Berrigan, "Lockheed Martin and the GOP: Profiteering and Pork Barrel Politics with a Purpose," World Policy Institute, July 31, 2000, http://www.worldpolicy.org/projects/arms/reports/lockheedgop.htm.

47 "Congress has let me cancel . . . I don't need": Defense Secretary Dick Cheney, testimony before Senate Armed Services Committee, 1992, reported by Travis Sharp, "Cross Your Fingers: V-22 Ospreys Off to Iraq," Center for Arms Control and Non-Proliferation, September 28, 2007, http://archive.armscontrolcenter.org/issues/securityspending/articles/cross_your_fingers_ospreys_iraq/.

48 "You've directed me . . . in the district": Defense Secretary Dick Cheney, testimony before Senate Armed Services Committee, 1992, quoted in Goyette, *Red and Blue and Broke All Over*, 190.

48 Cheney tried to kill V-22 Osprey program: Mark Thompson, "V-22 Osprey: A Flying Shame," *Time*, September 26, 2007.

48 "It's unsafe": *Time*'s cover, October 8, 2007.

48 As *Time* reported: Mark Thompson, "Giving the Osprey More Firepower," *Time*, October 17, 2007.

48 "not performed": Michael J. Sullivan, testimony before House Committee on Oversight and Government Reform, June 23, 2009, http://www.gao.gov/products/GAO-09-692T. See section "Why GAO Did This Study."

49 "required level of versatility": Ibid., "Concluding Observations."

49 "It can't be used in hot weather": Representative Edolphus Towns, quoted in "Osprey Bound for Afghanistan, but Critics, Questions Persist," *San Diego Union-Tribune*, June 24, 2009. Representative Towns, then chairman of the House Committee on Oversight and Government Reform, made his critical remarks about V-22 Osprey at a hearing on June 23, 2009, according to the article.

49 Osprey crashed in southern Afghanistan: Bruce Rolfsen, "Generals Clash on Cause of April Osprey Crash," *Air Force Times*, January 22, 2011.

49 Campaign contributions have clearly played . . . "$132 million in 2012": "Defense: Background," Center for Responsive Politics, http://www.opensecrets.org/industries/background.php?ind=D.

49 Navy's initial plan: R. Jeffrey Smith and Ellen Nakashima, "Pentagon's Unwanted Projects in Earmarks," *Washington Post*, March 8, 2009.

50 "a ship you don't need": Ibid.

50 "costly and unnecessary": Secretary Gates, Department of Defense briefing with Secretary Gates and Adm. Mullen from the Pentagon, May 20, 2010, http://www.defense.gov/transcripts/transcript.aspx?transcriptid=4625.

50 "Every dollar additional to the budget": Donna Miles, American Forces Press Service, "Gates Explains Opposition to Alternate F-35 Engine," September 2, 2009, http://www.defense.gov/news/newsarticle.aspx?id=55711.

50 "Think about it: hundreds of millions of dollars": President Obama, remarks
at the Veterans of Foreign Wars convention, August 17, 2009, http://www
.whitehouse.gov/the-press-office/remarks-president-veterans-foreign-wars
-convention.

51 "This is the year": Craig Whitlock and Dana Hedgpeth, "Congress Pur-
sues F035 Engine that Defense Secretary Robert Gates Doesn't Want,"
Washington Post, May 28, 2010. The article quotes the Pratt & Whitney
ad that is part of a media campaign.

51 "It is important to the war fighter": Otto Kreisher, "Rolls-Royce Defends
Its F-35 Engine," *Government Executive,* July 7, 2010, http://www.gov
exec.com/defense/2010/07/rolls-royce-defends-its-f-35-engine/31873/.
Kreisher reports on a Rolls-Royce press briefing at the National Press
Club where Rolls-Royce officials argued for their alternate engine for
the F-35.

51 House, under Boehner's leadership: Roxana Tiron, "U.S. House Votes to
Kill GE Engine for F-35 Fighter," *Bloomberg,* February 16, 2011.

51 House reversed its approval: Ibid.

52 champion was John Murtha: R. Jeffrey Smith and Ellen Nakashima,
"Pentagon's Unwanted Projects in Earmarks," *Washington Post,* March 8,
2009.

52 top twenty contributors . . . to defense subcommittee members: Center
for Responsive Politics, OpenSecrets.org, https://www.opensecrets.org.

52 "Rather the money came from the organizations' PACs": Center for Responsive Politics, OpenSecrets.org, https://www.opensecrets.org.

53 "backyard" incentive: R. Jeffrey Smith and Ellen Nakashima, "Pentagon's
Unwanted Projects in Earmarks," *Washington Post,* March 8, 2009.

53 study on economics of federal spending: Robert Pollin and Heidi Garrett-
Peltier, *The U.S. Employment Effects of Military and Domestic Spending
Priorities: An Updated Analysis,* 2011 update, University of Massachusetts, http://www.peri.umass.edu/fileadmin/pdf/published_study/PERI
_military_spending_2011.pdf.

53 "more of the military dollar": William D. Hartung, quoted in Nick
Schwellenbach, "Study: Federal Spending on Defense Doesn't Create As
Many Jobs As Education Spending," *Time,* September 21, 2011, http://
nation.time.com/2011/09/21/study-federal-spending-on-defense-doesnt
-create-as-many-jobs-as-education-spending/.

54 "The days of Rosie": Mike Lofgren, "Goodbye to All That: Reflections
of a GOP Operative Who Left the Cult," *Truthout,* September 3, 2011.

54 "Take away the cash": Ibid.

54 "We don't need the tanks": Marjorie Censer, "The End of the Tank?," *Washington Post,* January 31, 2014.

55 "If someone could guarantee . . . security of this country": Drew Griffin and Kathleen Johnston, "Army to Congress: Thanks, but No Tanks," CNN, October 9, 2012.

55 Congress prevailed: Marjorie Cesner, "End of the Tank?"

4. Think-Tank Hawks and Interventionists

56 The term *think tank* is a misnomer: "View Source for Think Tanks," SourceWatch, Center for Media and Democracy, http://www.sourcewatch .org/index.php?title=Think_tanks&action=edit. The CMD's SourceWatch site quotes the late Jonathan Rowe, an editor at *Washington Monthly* and a staff writer at *The Christian Science Monitor.* According to Source-Watch, Rowe's comment "was directed at the conservative [Heritage Foundation], but it applies equally well to many other think tanks, regardless of ideology: 'They don't think; they justify.'"

56 "secure the interests of the U.S.": PNAC letter to President Clinton, January 26, 1998, https://web.archive.org/web/20130112203258/http://www .newamericancentury.org/iraqclintonletter.htm.

56 "It may be that the . . . the attack": PNAC letter to President George W. Bush, September 20, 2001, https://web.archive.org/web/20130112203252 /http://www.newamericancentury.org/Bushletter.htm.

57 premise that Iraq was prepared to use weapons: Powell speech to United Nations Security Council, "A Policy of Evasion and Deception," February 5, 2003, full text printed in *Washington Post*, http://www.washington post.com/wp-srv/nation/transcripts/powelltext_020503.html.

57 war would end in weeks and cost little: Vice President Dick Cheney, interview with CBS News chief Washington correspondent Bob Schieffer, March 16, 2003, http://www.cbsnews.com/news/ftn-3-16-03/. In the interview, Cheney said he expects the Iraq "operation" will go "weeks rather than months." Dan Murphy, "Iraq War: Predictions Made, and Results," *Christian Science Monitor,* December 22, 2011; and Kenneth T. Walsh, "10 Years Ago, the U.S. Invaded Iraq," *U.S. News,* March 19, 2013.

57 "universities without students": Tevi Troy, "Devaluing the Think Tank," *National Affairs,* Winter 2012.

57 America now is a beehive of 1,828 think tanks: James G. McGann, *2013 Global Go To Think Tank Index Report,* University of Pennsylvania, Think Tanks and Civil Societies Program, January 22, 2014, http://

repository.upenn.edu/cgi/viewcontent.cgi?article=1007&context=think
_tanks.

58 "Even if evidence": PNAC, letter to Bush.

58 "Cakewalk": Kenneth Adelman, opinion column, "'Cakewalk' in Iraq,"
Washington Post, February 13, 2002.

59 Adelman said President Bush was "responsible": Peter Baker, "Embittered
Insiders Turn Against Bush," *Washington Post*, November 19, 2006.

59 "America should seek": PNAC, *Rebuilding America's Defenses*, September 2000, iv.

59 "increase defense spending significantly": PNAC, "Statement of Principles," June 3, 1997.

59 "Of course, the United States must be prudent . . . they become dire":
PNAC, *Rebuilding America's Defenses*.

59 a detailed program of military spending: Ibid.

60 "We cannot defend America and our friends . . . pursuits of peace": President Bush, speech at the U.S. Military Academy at West Point, New York,
June 1, 2002, text printed in *New York Times,* http://www.nytimes.com
/2002/06/01/international/02PTEX-WEB.html.

61 Summary of what Baker reported . . . "right this minute?": Baker, *Days
of Fire,* 144.

61 "When the project started": Gary Schmitt, quoted in Paul Reynolds,
"End of the Neo-Con Dream," BBC News, December 21, 2006, http://
news.bbc.co.uk/2/hi/middle_east/6189793.stm.

62 "I've got to say": Richard Perle, NPR interview with Renee Montagne,
March 20, 2013, http://www.npr.org/2013/03/20/174812898/looking-back
-on-the-start-of-the-iraq-war.

62 "The principal reason": Paul Wolfowitz, opinion, "Iraq War Taught Tough
Lessons, but Better Off Without Saddam," Fox News, March 19, 2013,
http://www.foxnews.com/opinion/2013/03/19/iraq-war-taught-us-tough
-lessons-but-world-is-better-off-without-saddam.html.

62 Michael O'Hanlon of the Brookings: O'Hanlon, interview with O'Reilly,
Fox News, February 28, 2003. According to Wikipedia, O'Reilly asked
O'Hanlon during the interview, "Any doubt about going to war with Sad-
dam?" O'Hanlon replied, "Not much doubt," https://en.wikipedia.org/wiki
/Michael_E._O%27Hanlon#cite_ref-5. Glenn Greenwald, "The Really
Smart, Serious, Credible Iraq Experts O'Hanlon and Pollack," *Salon,* July
30, 2007, http://www.salon.com/2007/07/30/brookings/.

62 "surge": Mark Benjamin, "The Real Iraq Study Group," *Salon,* January 6,
2007.

62 "employed a variety of means . . . deploy such a system": Baker Spring, "The Heritage Foundation: Influencing the Debate on Missile Defense," *U.S. Foreign Policy* 7, no. 3 (November 2002) 32.

63 "they don't think, they justify": "View Source for Think Tanks," Source-Watch, Center for Media and Democracy, http://www.sourcewatch.org /index.php?title=Think_tanks&action=edit.

63 "way of generating self-serving scholarship . . . promote their ideas": Rampton and Stauber, *Trust Us, We're Experts,* 305–06.

63 "It's the noisiest": James McGann, "Development of Think Tanks and Their Role as Catalysts for Ideas and Actions in the U.S. Political System," Foreign Press Center briefing, U.S. State Department, February 28, 2006, http://2002-2009-fpc.state.gov/62388.htm. McGann is the director of the Think Tanks and Civil Societies Program, University of Pennsylvania.

63 Brookings played a role: Brookings Institution Web site, http://www .brookings.edu/about/history.

63 next model: McGann, "Development of Think Tanks and Their Role as Catalysts for Ideas and Actions in the U.S. Political System."

64 "a sort of conservative counter-revolution . . . right on policy": Ibid.

64 "The big development of the 1990s . . . James Q. Wilson": David Calla-han, "The Think Tank as Flack," *Washington Monthly,* November 1999.

64 Koch owners: Jane Mayer, "Covert Operations," *New Yorker,* August 30, 2010.

65 "the world's premier university source . . . interests of their funders": Ibid.

65 Paul Wolfowitz, the former: AEI Web site, July 2014, http://www.aei.org /scholar/paul-wolfowitz/.

65 "We try to get in the newspaper op-ed pages . . . three hundred corpo-rate donors": Christopher DeMuth, interview with Ben Wattenberg, "Thinking About Think Tanks, Part One of Two," PBS, October 13, 2005, http://www.pbs.org/thinktank/transcript1209.html.

66 $295 million . . . $75 million: David Teather, "Liberals Pledge Millions to Revive US Left," *Guardian,* August 7, 2005.

66 "During the last three decades a cottage industry . . . war in Iraq": Thomas Frank, "Thus Spake Zinsmeister," *New York Times,* August 25, 2006.

66 "The United States is supposed to be . . . anti-American governments": Ted Galen Carpenter, "Faulty Justifications for War with Iraq," *Orange County Register,* February 2, 2003.

67 Frederick and Kimberly Kagan: Rajiv Chandrasekaran, "Civilian Ana-

lysts Gained Petraeus's Ear While He Was Commander in Afghanistan," *Washington Post*, December 18, 2012.

5. Flawed Intelligence and Exaggerated Threats

68 "Bush wanted to remove Saddam Hussein": Note dated July 23, 2002, written by Matthew Rycroft, an aide to Prime Minister Tony Blair, reported in the *Boston Globe*, June 8, 2005. "Excerpts of the Downing Street Memo," June 8, 2005, http://www.boston.com/news/world/europe/articles/2005/06/08/excerpts_of_the_downing_street_memo/.

68 "My colleagues": Powell's speech to the United Nations National Security Council, February 5, 2003, full text printed in *Washington Post*, http://www.washingtonpost.com/wp-srv/nation/transcripts/powelltext_020503.html.

69 "independent source": "About CIA," Central Intelligence Agency, https://www.cia.gov/about-cia/faqs.

69 NSC-68: This top-secret report, "A Report to the National Security Council on United States Objectives and Programs for National Security," dated April 14, 1950, was declassified by National Security Adviser Henry Kissinger, February 27, 1975, http://www.trumanlibrary.org/whistlestop/study_collections/coldwar/documents/pdf/10-1.pdf.

70 Cheney was determined to start a war: Scott Shane and Mark Mazzetti, "Ex-C.I.A. Chief, in Book, Assails Cheney on Iraq," *New York Times*, April 27, 2007.

70 "It was all about finding a way": O'Neill, *Price of Loyalty*, 53.

70 "Simply stated, there is no doubt": Vice President Cheney, speech to Veterans of Foreign Wars, "Full Text: In Cheney's Words," *New York Times*, August 26, 2002.

71 "What have you got in terms of plans for Iraq?": Bob Woodward, "Woodward Shares War Secrets," *60 Minutes*, television interview with correspondent Mike Wallace, CBS News, April 15, 2004. Print version of the interview online at http://www.cbsnews.com/news/woodward-shares-war-secrets/. In reporting the Bush-Rumsfeld conversation in the prologue of his book *Plan of Attack*, Woodward used slightly different words. The prologue quotes the president telling Rumsfeld: "What kind of a war plan do you have for Iraq? How do you feel about the war plan for Iraq? Don't talk about what you are doing with others."

71 "Bush wanted to remove Saddam Hussein": July 23, 2002, note written by top aide to British prime minister Tony Blair.

71 He spent three days at the CIA headquarters: Bob Drogin and John

Goetz, "How U.S. Fell Under the Spell of Curveball," *Los Angeles Times*, November 20, 2005.

72 "I was being as careful as I possibly could": Ibid.

72 Wilkerson, Powell's chief of staff, remembers: Author interview, May 14, 2012.

72 "Throughout his years in Washington": Weiner, *Legacy of Ashes*, 487.

72 "slam dunk . . . ever said": Ibid., 496.

73 "highly doubtful": Joseph Wilson, opinion column, "What I Didn't Find in Africa," *New York Times*, July 6, 2003.

73 "The British government has learned": President Bush, State of the Union address, January 28, 2003, American Presidency Project, http://www.presidency.ucsb.edu/ws/index.php?pid=29645.

73 "little choice but to conclude": Wilson, "What I Didn't Find."

73 columnist Robert Novak disclosed: Robert D. Novak, "Mission to Niger," *Washington Post*, July 14, 2003.

74 "So why do you think he did it?": Baker, *Days of Fire*, 2.

74 "I think he still thinks he was protecting Cheney": Ibid.

74 "sickened . . . wrong decision": President Bush, interview with Matt Lauer, NBC News Special, "Decision Points," November 8, 2010.

75 "In Washington, the agency above all had to have the president's ear": Weiner, *Legacy of Ashes*, xv.

75 "Soviet societies": Authored by "X" (George Kennan), "The Sources of Soviet Conduct," *Foreign Affairs*, July 1947.

75 "wisely described Soviet communism . . . political problem": Robert Dallek, "The Tyranny of Metaphor," *Foreign Affairs*, October 12, 2010.

76 "the fulfillment or destruction": NSC-68, "A Report to the National Security Council on United States Objectives and Programs for National Security," April 14, 1950, http://www.trumanlibrary.org/whistlestop/study_collections/coldwar/documents/pdf/10-1.pdf.

76 Rhodes describes how: Rhodes, *Arsenals of Folly*.

76 "bludgeon the mass mind": Ibid., 104.

77 "animated by a new fanatic faith": NSC-68.

77 "sensible judgment": Raymond L. Garthoff, chapter 5, "Estimating Soviet Military Intentions and Capabilities," in *Essays on CIA's Analysis of the Soviet Union*, posted on CIA Web site, March 16, 2007, with foreword by Jack F. Matlock, Jr., former U.S. ambassador to the USSR, https://www.cia.gov/library/center-for-the-study-of-intelligence/csi-publications/books-and-monographs/watching-the-bear-essays-on-cias-analysis-of-the-soviet-union/Foreword.htm.

77 Truman "quadrupled the defense budget": Joseph Cirincione, "The Greatest Threat to Us All," *New York Review of Books*, March 6, 2008.

77 "Stalin never had a master plan . . . knew his weakness": Weiner, *Legacy of Ashes*, 73.

78 "savaged me": James Reston Papers, University of Illinois Library at Urbana-Champaign, http://archives.library.illinois.edu/coll/dl/reston /insider.htm.

78 "missile gap": "The Missile Gap Myth and Its Progeny," Arms Control Association, May 2011, https://www.armscontrol.org/act/2011_05/Thiel mann.

78 there was no gap: Jack Raymond, "White House Denies 'Missile Gap' Report," *New York Times*, February 9, 1961.

79 "nightmare for a good ten years . . . who was making it": Helms, *Look over My Shoulder*, 309–11.

79 "competitive analysis" of the Soviet threat: Christopher Preble, "The Uses of Threat Assessment in Historical Perspective," Cato Institute, Preble Papers, Princeton University.

79 "bizarre": Garthoff, *Journey through the Cold War*, 328.

79 Team A . . . Team B: Ibid, 328–30.

80 "It would have been impossible": Cirincione, "Greatest Threat."

80 "all of it was fantasy": Anne Hessing Cahm, quoted in Thom Hartmann, "Hyping Terror for Fun, Profit—and Power," commondreams.org, December 7, 2004.

80 "wildly off the mark": Fareed Zakaria, "Exaggerating the Threats," *Newsweek*, June 16, 2003.

80 "the impression of danger and a threat": Garthoff, *Journey through the Cold War*, 329.

80 "laying the foundation . . . time of war": Robert Gates, November 25, 1985, reported by William M. Welch, "Soviets Far Advanced on Defense, CIA Says," *Santa Cruz Sentinel*, November 26, 1986.

80 "failed to grasp the essence of Gorbachev's attempts . . . never be built": Hoffman, *Dead Hand*, 294.

82 "Our CIA was way, way behind the curve": Ibid., 319.

82 "domino theory": "Domino Theory," *History*, http://www.history.com /topics/cold-war/domino-theory.

83 "wittingly": James Clapper testimony before Congress, March 12, 2013, reported by Bill Chappell, "Clapper Apologizes for Answer on NSA's Data Collection," NPR, July 2, 2013, http://www.npr.org/sections/thetwo

-way/2013/07/02/198118060/clapper-apologizes-for-answer-on-nsas-data
-collection.

83 "deep emotional feeling": Michael Hayden, interview with Chris Wallace, *Fox News Sunday*, April 6, 2014.

83 "baseless smear": Ted Barrett, "Democrats Blast Hayden's 'Emotional' Comment About Feinstein," CNN, April 7, 2014, http://politicalticker .blogs.cnn.com/2014/04/07/democrats-blast-haydens-emotional-comment -about-feinstein/.

84 "I understand those involved": Dianne Feinstein, "Senate's Report on CIA Torture Was Comprehensive," Letters to the Editor, *Washington Post*, December 17, 2014.

6. The American Empire

85 "Once upon a time": Johnson, *Nemesis*, 138.

86 America spent $441 billion . . . $736 billion: Defense spending figures in this book are from the Green Book 2014 base budgets for the Department of Defense, adjusted for inflation. DOD base budgets, sometimes referred to as Pentagon budgets, represent only about half of all federal defense spending because the DOD base budgets do not include spending for nuclear, veterans affairs, Homeland Security, or other defense-related activities. Numbers assembled from Green Book FY 2014 by Todd Harrison, Center for Strategic and Budgetary Assessments.

86 "At the end of 1991": Mandelbaum, *Frugal Superpower*, 40–41.

87 33,686 American deaths: Staff Sgt. Kathleen T. Rheem, American Forces Press Service, "Korean War Death Stats Highlight Modern DOD Safety Record," June 8, 2000, http://www.defense.gov/news/newsarticle .aspx?id=45275.

88 killing 58,307 U.S. troops . . . 3.6 million war deaths: Wikipedia entry, "Vietnam War casualties," https://en.wikipedia.org/wiki/Vietnam_War _casualties#United_States_armed_forces.

88 "we would not exclude": President Jimmy Carter to Russian leader Leonid Brezhnev in 1979. Carter recalled the message in an interview on the *PBS NewsHour*, March 26, 2014, http://www.pbs.org/newshour/bb /jimmy-carter-ukraine-israel-addressing-injustices-faced-women -around-world/.

89 "that by 1987 our people": Friedman, *Spider's Web*, 38.

91 "Congress has no political incentive": John Yoo, opinion column, "Iraq and the Wobbly Congress," *Los Angeles Times*, April 3, 2007.

91 "aggression" in Kuwait: President George H. W. Bush, opening state-

ment at his news conference on the Persian Gulf Crisis, August 30, 1990, American Presidency Project, http://www.presidency.ucsb.edu/ws/?pid=18792.

92 "infidel" troops from America: Barry Lando, "Osama Bin Laden—Everyone's Missing the Point," *Huffington Post*, May 2, 2011, http://www.huffingtonpost.com/barry-lando/osama-bin-laden-dead_b_856251.html.

92 "outraged by U.S. support . . . crime in the world": Ibid.

92 "we have never once gotten it right": Robert Gates, speech at U.S. Military Academy at West Point, New York, February 25, 2011, http://www.defense.gov/speeches/speech.aspx?speechid=1539.

93 "a new form of empire . . . the military base": Johnson, *Sorrows of Empire*, 1.

93 basing his claim on a 2003 Pentagon report: Chalmers Johnson, "America's Empire of Bases," Global Policy Forum, January 2004, https://www.globalpolicy.org/component/content/article/153/26119.html.

93 "Once upon a time": Johnson, *Nemesis*, 138.

94 United States had eleven hundred overseas military bases: Sherwood Ross, "Pentagon Keeps Building Overseas Bases from Which It Can Menace the World," *Veterans Today*, April 13, 2012, http://www.veteranstoday.com/2012/04/13/pentagon-keeps-building-overseas-bases-from-which-it-can-menace-the-worls/.

94 "Most dangerously": David Vine, "Too Many Overseas Bases," *Foreign Policy in Focus*, February 25, 2009.

94 "No other military in world history": Timothy Kane, "Global U.S. Troop Deployment, 1950–2003," Heritage Foundation study, October 24, 2004, http://www.heritage.org/research/reports/2004/10/global-us-troop-deployment-1950-2003.

95 "The United States can, must, and will": Hillary Clinton, speech to the Council on Foreign Relations, September 8, 2010, http://www.cfr.org/world/conversation-us-secretary-state-hillary-rodham-clinton/p34808.

96 thirty-eight thousand troops in Afghanistan: CBS News.com, "How Many U.S. Troops Are Still in Afghanistan?" January 9, 2014, http://www.cbsnews.com/news/how-many-us-troops-are-still-in-afghanistan/.

96 6,839 U.S. troops in Afghanistan: Wikipedia entry, "United States military deployments," https://en.wikipedia.org/wiki/United_States_military_deployments.

96 "It is a dangerous . . . internal difficulties": Retired Army colonel Douglas Macgregor, panelist at Cato Institute forum, "Can the Pentagon Be

Fixed?," March 13, 2009, http://www.cato.org/events/can-pentagon-be
-fixed.

97 "The attacks of 9/11 opened a gusher": Gates, speech at the Eisenhower
Presidential Library, Abilene, Kansas, May 8, 2010, http://www.defense
.gov/speeches/speech.aspx?speechid=1467.

97 "we have fewer enemies": Dan Froomkin, "Deficit Group Formed by
Barney Frank Looks Where Others Dare Not—at Defense Budget,"
Huffington Post, June 23, 2010, http://www.huffingtonpost.com/2010/04
/23/the-barney-commission-def_n_550066.html.

97 "For the past few centuries": Walter Russell Mead, "Why We're in the
Gulf," *Wall Street Journal,* December 27, 2007.

98 "America's growing dependence": Priest, *Mission,* back-cover summary.

98 "fill a diplomatic void": Ibid., 45.

98 "new American militarism": Bacevich, *The New American Militarism,* xi.

98 "global interventionism": Bacevich, *Washington Rules,* 14.

98 "propelled the United States": Ibid., 16.

99 "has fostered an anxiety . . . never returned": Wills, *Bomb Power,* 1–2.

99 "The government has built a national security": Dana Priest and William M.
Arkin, "A Hidden World, Growing Beyond Control," *Washington Post,*
July 19, 2010, http://projects.washingtonpost.com/top-secret-america
/articles/a-hidden-world-growing-beyond-control/2.

100 summary of its findings: Ibid.

101 "The United States now runs": Kennedy, *Rise and Fall,* 515.

101 "Mounting domestic economic obligations": Mandelbaum, *Frugal Superpower,* 3.

102 detailed breakdown: Wessel, *Red Ink,* 73.

102 "the people for the regulation": Author interview with Christopher Preble at the Cato Institute, April 16, 2012.

103 "a burning fury": Branch, *Parting the Waters,* 269.

103 "These data, while technically accurate, are misused . . . during the
Reagan Administration": Winslow Wheeler, "Cooked Books Tell Tall
Tales," *Time* blog, July 15, 2013.

105 "How Mr. Romney Would Force-Feed": Carol Giacomo, "How Mr. Romney Would Force-Feed the Pentagon," *New York Times,* August 25,
2012.

7. The Vortex: The Middle East

106 "You know, some people never get the word": George H. W. Bush, remarks at a Republican fundraising breakfast in Des Moines, Iowa, Octo-

ber 16, 1990, American Presidency Project, http://www.presidency.ucsb
.edu/ws/?pid=18934.

106 "We are in the Mideast for three letters": Robert Dole, Senate floor, October 16, 1990, quoted in James McCartney, "Dole Right on O-I-L Issue,"
Pittsburgh Press, October 28, 1990.

106 "vital interests . . . including military force": President Carter, State of
the Union address, January 23, 1980, American Presidency Project, http://
www.presidency.ucsb.edu/ws/?pid=33079.

107 Eighty-five thousand American service members: This number was assembled from government reports, such as "Total Military Personnel
and Dependent End Strength," Office of the Secretary of Defense, December 31, 2012, and press reports, including the Associated Press.

108 Sitting knee to knee with Abdul Aziz: Eddy, *FDR Meets Ibn Saud,*
28–33.

108 peak in 2001: Chart titled "U.S. Imports from Persian Gulf Countries of
Crude Oil," U.S. Energy Information Administration, http://www.eia
.gov/dnav/pet/hist/LeafHandler.ashx?n=PET&s=MCRIMUSPG2&f=A.

109 Nixon stepped in: "Summary: Foreign Relations, 1969–1972, Volume
E-4, Iran and Iraq," U.S. State Department Archive, http://2001-2009
.state.gov/r/pa/ho/frus/nixon/e4/72108.htm.

109 "self-indulgence and consumption": President Carter, televised address,
"Crisis of Confidence" speech, July 15, 1979, Miller Center of Public
Affairs, University of Virginia, http://millercenter.org/president/speeches
/speech-3402.

110 "Let our position be absolutely clear . . . global peace and stability": President Carter, State of the Union address, January 23, 1980, American Presidency Project, http://www.presidency.ucsb.edu/ws/?pid=33079.

110 Centcom . . . directs U.S. military operations in twenty countries: U.S.
Centcom Web site, http://www.centcom.mil/en/about-centcom-en/area
-of-responsibility-countries-en.

110 "The ultimate in U.S. national interests . . . satisfy those new priorities":
Bacevich, *New American Militarism,* 176–77.

111 "I took this action to assist the Saudi Arabian government": George H. W.
Bush, address on Iraq's invasion of Kuwait, August 8, 1990, Miller Center
of Public Affairs, University of Virginia, http://millercenter.org/president
/bush/speeches/speech-5529.

112 "peace and stability . . . one man, Saddam Hussein": George H. W. Bush,
remarks to Department of Defense employees, August 15, 1990, American Presidency Project, http://www.presidency.ucsb.edu/ws/?pid=18768.

112 "aggression": George H. W. Bush, opening statement at his news conference on the Persian Gulf Crisis, August 30, 1990, American Presidency
Project, http://www.presidency.ucsb.edu/ws/?pid=18792.

112 "You know, some people never get the word": George H. W. Bush, remarks at a Republican fundraising breakfast in Des Moines, Iowa, October 16, 1990, American Presidency Project, http://www.presidency.ucsb
.edu/ws/?pid=18934.

112 he repeated this mantra in Vermont: George H. W. Bush, remarks at a
Republican fundraising breakfast in Burlington, Vermont, October 23,
1990, American Presidency Project, http://www.presidency.ucsb.edu/ws
/?pid=18954.

112 "We are in the Mideast for three letters—oil, O-I-L": Dole, quoted in
Pittsburgh Press.

112 "We are there because we do not want Saddam Hussein": James Mc-
Cartney, "Dole Right on O-I-L Issue," *Pittsburgh Press*, October 28,
1990.

113 ordered twenty-three cruise missiles: David Von Drehle and R. Jeffrey
Smith, "U.S. Strikes Iraq for Plot to Kill Bush," *Washington Post*, June 27,
1993.

114 "Using armed might to secure American preeminence": Bacevich, *New
American Militarism*, 201.

114 "The people of the United States and our friends and allies": George W.
Bush, radio address, March 22, 2003, American Presidency Project, http://
www.presidency.ucsb.edu/ws/?pid=25127.

114 "nothing to do with oil": Donald Rumsfeld, interview with Steve Croft,
Infinity CBS Radio Connect, November 15, 2002, http://www.defense.gov
/transcripts/transcript.aspx?transcriptid=3283.

114 "I am saddened that it is politically inconvenient": Peter Beaumont and
Joanna Walters, "Greenspan Admits Iraq Was About Oil," *Guardian*,
September 16, 2007, http://www.theguardian.com/world/2007/sep/16
/iraq.iraqtimeline.

114 "Of course it's about oil": Gerry Shih and Susana Montes, "Roundtable
Debates Energy Issues," *Stanford Daily*, October 15, 2007.

115 "People say we're not fighting for oil": Adil E. Shamoo and Bonnie Bricker,
"The Costs of War for Oil," *Foreign Policy in Focus*, October 19, 2007,
http://fpif.org/the_costs_of_war_for_oil/. The article quotes then Senator
Chuck Hagel's comments to law students at Catholic University in September 2006.

115 "If I thought for a minute": President Obama, addressing the troops in

Afghanistan, March 28, 2010, White House, Office of the Press Secretary, https://www.whitehouse.gov/the-press-office/remarks-president-troops.

115 United States spent $7.3 trillion: Dan Vergano, "Study: Middle East Oil Security Cost U.S. $7.3T Over Last Three Decades," *USA Today,* April 12, 2010.

115 cost $3 trillion: Joseph Stiglitz and Linda J. Bilmes, "The Iraq War Will Cost Us $3 Trillion, and Much More," *Washington Post,* March 9, 2008.

115 war's impact actually added at least $10 per barrel: Joseph E. Stiglitz and Linda J. Bilmes, "The True Cost of the Iraq War: $3 Trillion and Beyond," *Washington Post,* September 5, 2010.

116 cost for securing the free flow of oil was about $166 billion: Anita Dancs, *Global Research Newsletter,* May 23, 2010.

116 "It's insane that we have the Fifth Fleet": Benoit Faucon and Sarah Kent, "IEA Pegs U.S. as Top Oil Producer by 2020," *Wall Street Journal,* November 12, 2012. The article states that T. Boone Pickens made his remarks a week earlier in *Parade* magazine.

117 "stability": John F. Burns, "McChrystal Rejects Scaling Down Afghan Military Aims," *New York Times,* October 1, 2009. The article states that General McChrystal used a speech in London "to reject calls for the war effort to be scaled down" and that "stability" in Afghanistan was "vital to regional security" as well as to the United States.

117 "The answer is no . . . key": Ibid.

117 "You have to recognize . . . probably our kids' lives": Woodward, *Obama's Wars,* 332–33.

117 "nearing a decision to keep more troops in Afghanistan": Matthew Rosenberg and Mark Mazzetti, "More U.S. Troops Seen Staying in Afghanistan," *New York Times,* March 19, 2015.

117 "The United States of America does not quit": President Obama, addressing the troops in Afghanistan, March 28, 2010, White House, Office of the Press Secretary, https://www.whitehouse.gov/the-press-office/remarks -president-troops.

118 "succeeded far beyond anything Osama bin Laden": Ted Koppel, "Nine Years After 9/11, Let's Stop Playing into Bin Laden's Hands," *Washington Post,* September 12, 2010.

118 Koppel argued: Ibid.

118 "Most of our military spending . . . worth the cost": Benjamin Friedman and Christopher Preble, opinion column, "Defense Cuts: Start Overseas," *Los Angeles Times,* June 14, 2010.

119 "Over four generations the vocation of the Bushes": Phillips, *American Dynasty*, 123.

8. Nuclear Folly

120 "I see no compelling reason why": Paul H. Nitze, opinion column, "A Threat Mostly to Ourselves," *New York Times*, October 28, 1999.

121 total for the United States and Russia today is about 16,200: Ploughshares Fund, 2014.

121 "I see no compelling reason why": Paul H. Nitze, "A Threat Mostly to Ourselves," *New York Times*, October 28, 1999.

121 "So today, I state clearly and with conviction America's commitment": President Obama, remarks in Prague, April 5, 2009, White House, Office of the Press Secretary, https://www.whitehouse.gov/the-press-office /remarks-president-barack-obama-prague-delivered.

122 proposed cutting the U.S. nuclear arsenal: President Obama, remarks at the Brandenburg Gate, Berlin, Germany, June 19, 2013, White House, Office of the Press Secretary, https://www.whitehouse.gov/the-press -office/2013/06/19/remarks-president-obama-brandenburg-gate-berlin -germany.

122 "embraced the vision": President Obama, State of the Union address, January 27, 2010, American Presidency Project, http://www.presidency .ucsb.edu/ws/index.php?pid=87433.

122 Comprehensive Nuclear Test Ban Treaty: Arms Control Association report, March 2014, https://www.armscontrol.org/subject/45/date.

123 "My impression from what I have observed": Murrey Marder, "Summit Clouded by Watergate," *Washington Post*, July 4, 1974.

123 "One of the questions which we have to ask ourselves": Rhodes, *Arsenals of Folly*, 115.

123 "I'm proceeding from the assumption that both sides want to rid the world": Ibid., 239.

123 "Let me precisely, firmly, and clearly declare": Ibid., 241.

124 Strategic Defense Initiative (SDI): The best accounts of SDI are in Rhodes's *Arsenals of Folly* and FitzGerald's *Way Out There in the Blue*.

125 "The president first looked at Perle": Winik, quoted in Rhodes, *Arsenals of Folly*, 261.

125 "'Mr. President, we cannot conduct'": Ibid., 262.

125 "the best we have received in twenty-five years": Nitze, quoted in Rhodes, *Arsenals of Folly*, 248.

125 In a speech to the National Press Club . . . dangerous: George Lee Butler, National Press Club, December 4, 1996.

126 "As to those who believe nuclear weapons desirable . . . accepted as
commonplace": Ibid.

127 he told *Washington Post* reporter . . . "That's just wrong": R. Jeffrey Smith,
"The Dissenter," *Washington Post,* December 7, 1997.

127 "A World Free of Nuclear Weapons": *Wall Street Journal,* January 4,
2007.

127 "Nuclear weapons today present tremendous dangers . . . deterrence
obsolete": Ibid.

128 "extraordinary, with strong positive responses . . . increasingly hazardous":
George P. Schultz, William J. Perry, Henry A. Kissinger, and Sam Nunn,
"Toward a Nuclear-Free World," *Wall Street Journal,* January 15, 2008.

130 "With the monstrous weapons": General Omar Bradley, "An Armistice
Day Address," Boston, Massachusetts, November 10, 1948. Speech reprinted by OpinionBug.com, http://www.opinionbug.com/2109/armistice
-day-1948-address-general-omar-n-bradley/.

131 America's most contaminated nuclear site: Blaine Harden and Dan Mor-
gan, "Debate Intensifies on Nuclear Waste," *Washington Post,* June 2,
2004.

131 In a 2013 interview with National Public radio: Dick Gordon, interview
with Kathleen Flenniken, National Public Radio, July 11, 2013, http://
www.thestory.org/stories/2013-07/poetry-atomic-city.

9. Billions for Weapons Searching for Enemies

132 "Think hard about it": Jim Wolffe, "Powell: 'I'm Running Out of Demons,'" *Army Times,* April 15, 1991. The story stated that Powell made
his remarks during a ninety-minute interview with the *Army Times* on
April 2, 1991, in his Pentagon office.

132 "He just said, 'Laura, whatever you do, don't miss'": Laura Bush, remarks
at the christening of the USS *Texas,* July 31, 2004, press release, White
House, Office of the First Lady, http://georgewbush-whitehouse.archives
.gov/news/releases/2004/07/20040731-6.html.

132 $3 billion price tag: Dan Feldstein, "USS *Texas* Gladly Welcome Aboard,"
Houston Chronicle, September 10, 2006. The *Chronicle* article lists the
price as $2.7 billion, but analysis by the Center for Arms Control and
Non-Proliferation, "Analysis of the Fiscal Year 2010 Pentagon Spending
Request," May 8, 2009, includes a breakdown showing that Virginia-class

nuclear attack submarines like the USS *Texas* cost at about $3.1 billion per unit.

133 "I don't think any terrorist has ever been shot": Dan Froomkin, "Deficit Group Formed by Barney Frank Looks Where Others Dare Not—at Defense Budget," *Huffington Post*, May 25, 2011, http://www.huffington post.com/2010/04/23/the-barney-commission-def_n_550066.html.

133 "weapon looking for an enemy": quoted in Tom Curry, "Sub Makers Stress Economic Stimulus Mission," MSNBC, March 10, 2009.

133 "reform our defense budget": President Obama, address before a joint session of the Congress, February 24, 2009, American Presidency Project, http://www.presidency.ucsb.edu/ws/?pid=85753.

133 "We cannot take for granted that Congress . . . face as a nation today": quoted in Curry, "Sub Makers."

134 Navy plans to build thirty of these subs: Center for Arms Control, "Analysis." See also Secretary Gates, speech to Navy League, May 3, 2010.

134 Subcontractors producing parts are spread: Curry, "Sub Makers."

134 "require millions of parts": Jim Roberts, "Double Vision: Planning to Increase *Virginia*-Class Production," *Undersea Warfare*, Winter 2011.

134 created 31,500 direct and indirect jobs in 2005: Curry, "Sub Makers."

134 "fifty-seven nuclear-powered": Secretary Gates, speech to Navy League Sea-Air-Space Exposition, May 3, 2010, http://www.defense.gov/speeches /speech.aspx?speechid=1460.

134 $7 billion and $8 billion: Tom Colina and Jacob Marx, "A Better Way to Buy Nuclear Submarines," *Breaking Defense,* January 23, 2015, http:// breakingdefense.com/2015/01/a-better-way-to-buy-nuclear-submarines/.

135 "deprived us of an enemy . . . relaxed and dispirited": Robin, *Reactionary Mind*, 127.

135 "pivot": Hillary Clinton, "America's Pacific Century," *Foreign Policy*, October 11, 2011.

136 "The U.S. operates eleven large carriers . . . most world armies": Secretary Gates, speech to Navy League Sea-Air-Space Exposition, May 3, 2010.

137 "Does the number of warships": Secretary Gates, speech at Eisenhower Presidential Library in Abilene, Kansas, May 9, 2010, http://www.defense .gov/speeches/speech.aspx?speechid=1467.

137 "The major part of our weapons spending": Representative Barney Frank, television interview with Wolf Blitzer, *The Situation Room,* CNN, July 7, 2010.

138 "Think hard about it": Jim Wolffe, "Powell: 'I'm Running Out of Demons.'"

138 "peace dividend": Sanjeev Gupta, Benedict Clements, Rina Bhattacharya, and Shamit Chakravarti, "The Elusive Peace Dividend," *Finance & Development* (magazine of the International Monetary Fund), December 2002.

138 "impotent and obsolete": President Reagan, address to the nation on defense and national security, March 23, 1983, American Presidency Project, http://www.presidency.ucsb.edu/ws/?pid=41093.

138 Congress . . . $9 to $10 billion: Wade Boese, "Missile Defense Funding Request Tops $10 Billion," *Arms Control Association Journal*, March 1, 2004, http://www.armscontrol.org/act/2004_03/missiledefensefunding.

138 envisioned as a five-year program . . . $26 billion: William J. Broad, "The Secret Behind Star Wars," *New York Times*, August 11, 1985.

138 pumped more than $200 billion: Stephen I. Schwartz, "The Real Price of Ballistic Missile Defense," *WMD Junction*, April 13, 2012, http://wmdjunction.com/120413_missile_defense_costs.htm.

138 "Ronald Reagan's dream . . . enhancing it": David Wright and Lisbeth Gronlund, "Twenty-Five Years After Reagan's Star Wars Speech," *Bulletin of the Atomic Scientists*, April 1, 2008, http://thebulletin.org/twenty-five-years-after-reagans-star-wars-speech-0.

139 "vision of a shield": Gronlund's testimony before House Committee on Oversight and Government Reform, National Security and Foreign Affairs Subcommittee, April 16, 2008, U.S. Government Printing Office, http://www.gpo.gov/fdsys/pkg/CHRG-110hhrg48660/html/CHRG-110hhrg48660.htm.

139 tests have been rigged: Government Accounting Office, "Missile Defense: Actions Are Needed to Enhance Testing and Accountability," April 2004, http://www.gao.gov/new.items/d04409.pdf. In "Twenty-Five Years After Reagan's Star Wars Speech," Wright and Gronlund contend that the Missile Defense Agency (MDA), "to circumvent the rules," refers to "the ground-based missile defense components as fielded rather than deployed and has claimed that they are test assets used as part of the test program."

139 "The Pentagon has yet to demonstrate . . . a false warning": Gronlund's testimony before House Committee on Oversight and Government Reform, National Security and Foreign Affairs Subcommittee, April 16, 2008, https://fas.org/irp/congress/2008_hr/bmd-pt2.pdf.

140 "No such system yet operates . . . vastly destructive": Richard Rhodes, "Living with the Bomb," *National Geographic*, August 2005, 6.

141 "remains highly debatable": Richard Garwin, "Boost-Phase Intercept: A

Better Alternative," *Arms Control Today,* Arms Control Association, September 1, 2000, http://www.armscontrol.org/act/2000_09/bpisept00.

142 "to seal off and snatch back": *Pakistan Defence,* "Elite US Troops Ready to Combat Pakistani Nuclear Hijacks," January 17, 2010, http://defence.pk/threads/elite-us-troops-ready-to-combat-pakistani-nuclear-hijacks.44493/. Robert Windrem, "US Prepares for Worst-Case Scenario with Pakistan Nukes," NBC News, August 3, 2011, http://investigations.nbcnews.com/_news/2011/08/03/7189919-us-prepares-for-worst-case-scenario-with-pakistan-nukes, reports a "scenario of the U.S. attempting to 'snatch' Pakistan's 100-plus nuclear weapons if it feared they were about to fall into the wrong hands."

142 a missile fired from less than 120: David Ignatius, "The Real Missile Defense Gap," *Washington Post,* March 23, 2005.

142 "With technical expertise supplied by former Russian or Pakistani": Joseph Cirincione, "The Greatest Threat to Us All," *New York Review of Books,* March 6, 2008.

143 triad: "Arms Control and Proliferation Profile: The United States," Arms Control Association, April 2014, https://www.armscontrol.org/factsheets/unitedstatesprofile.

143 $30 billion per year: Amy F. Wolff, "U.S. Strategic Nuclear Forces: Background, Developments, and Issues," Congressional Research Service, March 18, 2015, p. 43, https://fas.org/sgp/crs/nuke/RL33640.pdf.

144 summary of America's nuclear strike force: Ibid.

144 450 Minuteman III missiles: Ibid., 9.

144 533 Trident missiles: Ibid., 21.

144 20 B-2 bombers, Ibid., 27.

144 76 B-52H bombers that can carry nuclear missiles: Ibid., 29.

145 nine nuclear-armed states: Federation of American Scientists, "Status of World Nuclear Forces," April 28, 2015, http://fas.org/issues/nuclear-weapons/status-world-nuclear-forces/.

145 U.S. commitment to triad: Micah Zenko, "Obama's Sensible Nuclear Posture Review," Council on Foreign Relations, April 6, 2010, http://www.cfr.org/proliferation/obamas-sensible-nuclear-posture-review/p21837.

146 United States spent at least $52.4 billion: Stephen I. Schwartz and Deepti Choubey, *Nuclear Security Spending,* Carnegie Endowment for International Peace, 2009, 6.

146 United States spent nearly $5.5 trillion: Stephen I. Schwartz, *The*

Hidden Costs of Our Nuclear Arsenal, Brookings Institution, June 30, 1998.

146 "In 1960 when the explosive power . . . overall program": Ibid.

147 "Effective oversight": Schwartz and Choubey, *Nuclear Security Spending*, 12.

147 Most expensive weapons: Douglas A. McIntyre and Michael B. Sauter, "The 10 Most Expensive Weapons in the World," *24/7WallSt*, January 9, 2012, http://247wallst.com/special-report/2012/01/09/the-10-most-expensive-weapons-in-the-world/.

10. Send in the Drones

149 "Targeted [drone] strikes": John Brennan, "The Efficacy and Ethics of U.S. Counterterrorism Strategy," speech at the Woodrow Wilson Center, April 30, 2012, http://www.wilsoncenter.org/event/the-efficacy-and-ethics-us-counterterrorism-strategy.

149 "You could see these little figures scurrying": former CIA officer, quoted in Jane Mayer, "The Predator War," *New Yorker*, October 26, 2009.

150 "the guy in the rear . . . ground that he died on": Brandon Bryant, NPR interview, May 10, 2013, http://www.npr.org/2013/05/10/182800293/former-air-force-pilot-shines-light-on-drone-program.

150 "Did that look like a child to you?" Matthew Power, "Confessions of a Drone Warrior," *GQ*, October 22, 2013.

150 credited with killing 1,626 "enemies": Jeremy Scahill and Glenn Greenwald, "The NSA's Secret Role in the U.S. Assassination Program," *The Intercept*, February 10, 2014, https://firstlook.org/theintercept/2014/02/10/the-nsas-secret-role/.

150 "stick monkey": Ibid.

151 "Yes, in full accordance with the law . . . beyond their intended target": Brennan, "Efficacy and Ethics."

152 killed some two thousand Al Qaeda . . . single civilian: Scott Shane, "CIA Is Disputed on Civilian Toll in Drone Strikes," *New York Times*, August 11, 2011.

152 Bureau of Investigative Journalism: Ongoing drone strike reports are posted on its Web site, http://www.thebureauinvestigates.com.

152 New America Foundation: www.newamerica.net; and Peter Bergen and Katherine Tiedemann, New America Foundation, "The Drone War," *New Republic*, June 3, 2009.

152 Department of Justice memo: Michael Isikoff, "Justice Department Memo

Reveals Legal Case for Drone Strikes on Americans," NBC News, February 4, 2013, http://investigations.nbcnews.com/_news/2013/02/04/16843014 -justice-department-memo-reveals-legal-case-for-drone-strikes-on -americans.

153 "For all the slick technology": "Reining in the Drones," Editorial Board, *New York Times,* July 6, 2014.

153 Government Accountability Office reported: "Nonproliferation: Agencies Could Improve Sharing and End-Use Monitoring on Unmanned Aerial Vehicle Exports," September 12, 2012, http://www.gao.gov/products /GAO-12-536.

153 "a higher degree of autonomy": Defense Department 2011 report "Un- manned Systems Integration Roadmap, FY2011–2036," vi.

154 Pentagon spends: Scott Shane and Thom Shanker, "Strike Reflects U.S. Shift to Drones in Terror Fight," *New York Times,* October 1, 2011; see also Mark Thompson, "Jobs Worth Keeping," *Time,* November 8, 2012.

154 "The United States government is very clearly on record": Ambassador Martin Indyk, July 2001, quoted in Jane Mayer, "The Predator War," *New Yorker,* October 26, 2009.

154 "terrible mistake . . . dead body": Benjamin and Simon, *Age of Sacred Terror,* 345.

155 Authorization for Use of Military Force: Public Law 107-40, 107th Con- gress, September 14, 2001; signed by President George W. Bush, Sep- tember 18, 2001.

155 seven thousand drones: Elisabeth Bumiller and Thom Shanker, "War Evolves with Drones, Some Tiny as Bugs," *New York Times,* June 19, 2011.

155 thirteen hundred drone pilots at thirteen bases: Elisabeth Bumiller, "A Day Job Waiting for a Kill Job a World Away," *New York Times,* July 29, 2012.

155 CIA conducted its first independent drone operation: John Sifton, "A Brief History of Drones," *Nation,* February 7, 2012.

156 "You could see these little figures scurrying": Mayer, "Predator War."

156 Bush administration conducted 52 reported strikes . . . next two years: Jack Serle, "Almost 2,500 Now Killed by Covert US Drone Strikes Since Obama Inauguration Six Years Ago," Bureau of Investigative Journalism, February 2, 2015, https://www.thebureauinvestigates.com/2015/02/02 /almost-2500-killed-covert-us-drone-strikes-obama-inauguration/.

156 "five or six people . . . total deaths": Leila Hudson, Colin S. Owens, and

Matt Flannes, "Drone Warfare: Blowback from the New American Way of War," *Middle East Policy,* Fall 2011, 125.

156 "would extend the spy service's": Greg Miller, "CIA Seeks to Expand Drone Fleet, Officials Say," *Washington Post,* October 18, 2012.

156 "A pilot operating this aircraft": Brennan, "Efficacy and Ethics."

157 kill list: Jo Becker and Scott Shane, "Secret 'Kill List' Proves a Test of Obama's Principles and Will," *New York Times,* May 29, 2012.

157 "Too much power": "Too Much Power for a President," editorial, *New York Times,* May 30, 2012.

157 "America's moral leadership is gone": Michael Brenner, "The (Very) Few Proud and Brave," *World Post,* Huffington Post–Berggruen Institute, February 18, 2013, http://www.huffingtonpost.com/michael-brenner/the -very-few-proud-and-br_b_2710413.html.

157 "building a second Air Force": Mazzetti, *Way of the Knife,* 228.

157 "The CIA gets what it wants": Ibid.

157 "warrior in chief . . . leaders in decades": Peter Bergen, "Warrior in Chief," *New York Times,* April 26, 2012.

158 "extraordinary assertion of the executive's powers": Dana Milbank, "John Brennan's 'Trust Me' Is Not Enough on Drone Warfare," *Washington Post,* February 8, 2013.

158 "It was not created by the Bush administration": Garry Wills, "Entan-gled Giant," *New York Review of Books,* October 8, 2009.

158 Bureau of Investigative . . . "The CIA declined to comment": Ishaan Tharoor, "The Debate on Drones: Away from the Politics, the Nameless Dead Remain," *Time,* February 8, 2013.

159 "Within the CIA . . . placed him under cover": Mayer, "Predator War."

159 "These are targeted international killings": quoted in ibid.

160 A 2010 report . . . "everything's fine": Philip Alston and Hina Shamsi, "A Killer above the Law," *Guardian,* August 2, 2010.

160 "The U.S. seems to be struggling": Lev Grossman, "Drone Home," *Time,* February 11, 2013.

160 drone strikes had been launched: Robert F. Worth, Mark Mazzetti, and Scott Shane, "Drone Strikes' Risks to Get Rare Moment in the Public Eye," *New York Times,* February 5, 2013.

160 "is how we are using a new military technology": Scott Shane, interview with Terry Gross on *Fresh Air,* "The Sticky Questions Surrounding Drones and Kill Lists," NPR, February 11, 2013, http://www.npr.org/templates /transcript/transcript.php?storyId=171719082.

160 "I don't think the president . . . what he once stood for": Rand Paul, Senate filibuster, March 5, 2013, quoted in "condensed version" of thirteen-hour filibuster in Conor Friedersoorf, "Cliff Notes for the Filibuster: Rand Paul in His Own Words," *The Atlantic,* March 7, 2013.

161 "lethal, targeted action . . . taken off the battlefields": President Obama, remarks by the president at the National Defense University, May 23, 2013, White House, Office of the Press Secretary, https://www.whitehouse.gov/the-press-office/2013/05/23/remarks-president-national-defense-university.

162 "Not all of these strikes that the U.S. carries out": *PBS NewsHour,* August 6, 2013, http://www.pbs.org/newshour/bb/terrorism-july-dec13-yemen2_08-06/.

162 more than four hundred: Craig Whitlock, "When Drones Fall from the Sky," *Washington Post,* June 20, 2014.

162 "A $3.8 million Predator carrying": Ibid.

163 In another case: Craig Whitlock, "Drone Crashes Mount at Civilian Airports Overseas," *Washington Post,* November 30, 2012.

163 Air Force lost control: Jeremy Hsu, "Air Force Shots Down Runaway Drone Over Afghanistan," *Popular Science,* September 14, 2009.

163 developed in an estimated seventy-five countries: Government Accountability Office report, "Nonproliferation—Agencies Could Improve Information Sharing and End-Use Monitoring on Unmanned Aerial Vehicle Exports," July 2012, http://www.gao.gov/assets/600/593131.pdf.

163 "It can't be a small group": Matthew Power, "Confessions of a Drone Warrior," *GQ,* October 22, 2013.

11. The Media: Cheerleaders for War

164 "I couldn't believe it": Goulden, *Truth Is the First Casualty,* 158.

165 President Kennedy was so unhappy: "One on 1: Pulitzer Prize-Winning Author David Halberstam," interview with David Halberstam, by Budd Mishkin, Time Warner Cable News, March 25, 2007, http://nycxml.twcnews.com/content/shows/one_on_1_archives_hp/68013/one-on-1--pulitzer-prize-winning-author-david-halberstam/.

165 *Times* refused: Ibid.

165 "Katie Graham": Graham, *Personal History,* 465.

165 Obama's Justice Department secretly seized: Mark Sherman, "Gov't Obtains Wide AP Phone Records in Probe," Associated Press, May 13, 2013, http://www.ap.org/Content/AP-In-The-News/2013/Govt-obtains-wide-AP-phone-records-in-probe.

165 department seized e-mail . . . "co-conspirator": Judson Berger, "DOJ Invoked Espionage Act in Calling Fox News Reporter Criminal 'Co-conspirator,'" Fox News, May 22, 2013, http://www.foxnews.com/politics/2013/05/22/doj-invoked-espionage-act-in-calling-fox-news-reporter-criminal-co-conspirator/.

165 government has been trying to force: Jonathan Mahler, "Reporters Case Poses Dilemma for Justice Dept.," New York Times, June 27, 2014.

166 withdrew its subpoena: Mark Apuzzo, "Times Reporter Will Not Be Called to Testify in Leak Case," New York Times, January 12, 2015.

166 U.S. spy plane photographed Soviet missile bases under construction in Cuba: "The Cuban Missile Crisis," George Washington University National Security Archive, http://nsarchive.gwu.edu/nsa/cuba_mis_cri/photos.htm.

166 Kennedy had arranged a secret compromise with Khrushchev: James McCartney, "Rallying Around the Flag," American Journalism Review, September 1994; and Leslie H. Gelb, "The Myth That Screwed Up 50 Years of U.S. Foreign Policy," Foreign Policy, October 8, 2012.

167 6.5 million: Author interview with Jeff Nelson, historian, Saturday Evening Post, July 27, 2015.

167 "We were eyeball to eyeball": Stewart Alsop and Charles Bartlett, "Time of Crisis: Two Top Reporters Combine Forces to Reveal the Drama and Struggle Out of Which Emerged a Turning Point in the Cold War," Saturday Evening Post, December 18, 1962.

167 "Once or twice the president lost his temper . . . eyeball to eyeball": Ibid.

168 "wanted a Munich . . . military action": Ibid.

168 "was in no way, shape, or form": Risse-Kappen, Cooperation among Democracies, 175–76.

168 "That is correct, sir": Ibid.

168 "Absolutely not . . . to discuss it": Nash, Other Missiles of October, 157.

168 Kennedy's declaration: President Kennedy, radio and television report to the American people on the Soviet arms buildup in Cuba, October 22, 1962, Kennedy Presidential Library, http://www.jfklibrary.org/Asset-Viewer/sUVmCh-sB0moLfrBcaHaSg.aspx.

169 "first strike": John Finney, "U.S. Atomic Edge Believed in Peril: Loss of Nuclear Deterrent Feared in Soviet Build-Up of Cuban Arsenal," New York Times, October 27, 1962.

169 "The press approached the missile crisis": William LeoGrande, "Uneasy Allies: The Press and the Government During the Cuban Missile Crisis," paper for the Center for War, Peace, and the News Media, New York University, 1987.

170 "To the whole world it displayed the ripening . . . dazzled the world": Schlesinger, *Thousand Days*, 840.

170 Sorensen edited that scene out: Jim Hershberg, "Anatomy of a Controversy," *Cold War International History Project Bulletin*, Spring 1995, in the National Security Archive, George Washington University, http://nsarchive.gwu.edu/nsa/cuba_mis_cri/moment.htm; and Allyn, Blight, and Welch, *Back to the Brink*, 92–93.

170 Schlesinger discovered the secret deal: In Schlesinger's foreword to *Thirteen Days*, he wrote, "The [missile exchange] deal remained secret until I came across the relevant documents in Robert Kennedy's papers and published them in *Robert Kennedy and His Times* in 1978."

170 files on the Cuban missile crisis . . . declassified: "The Pentagon during the Cuban Missile Crisis," National Security Archive, http://nsarchive.gwu.edu/NSAEBB/NSAEBB397/.

170 Dobrynin's cable: Hershberg, "Anatomy of a Controversy."

171 "The introduction of strategic missiles into Cuba": Arnold Horelick and Myron Rush, *Strategic Power and Soviet Foreign Policy* (report for RAND Corporation, 1965), 154.

171 "solution to a whole set of problems": Hilsman, *Cuban Missile Crisis*, 201.

171 "the purpose of these bases can be none other": President Kennedy, radio and television report to the American people on the Soviet arms buildup in Cuba, October 22, 1962, Kennedy Presidential Library, http://www.jfklibrary.org/Asset-Viewer/sUVmCh-sB0moLfrBcaHaSg.aspx.

172 Operation Mongoose: This was the action arm of Robert Kennedy's interdepartmental Special Group, which had been created at the end of 1961. The goal of Operation Mongoose was to "help the people of Cuba overthrow the Communist regime from within Cuba." Reeves, *President Kennedy*, 335–36.

172 "The U.S. will make use of indigenous resources": Ibid., 336.

172 Mongoose had a budget of $100 million and four hundred U.S. employees and two thousand Cubans: Hilty, *Robert Kennedy*, 423.

172 overstated the threat: Hersh, *The Dark Side of Camelot*, 343. The Soviet Union had 250 nuclear warheads and 24 to 44 ICBMs compared to U.S. possession of 3,000 warheads and nearly 300 missile launchers.

172 "As I suggested, I don't believe": McNamara, EXCOM meeting, October 16, 1962, http://wps.prenhall.com/wps/media/objects/173/177562/27_excom.HTM.

172 "The United States might not be in mortal danger": Benjamin Schwarz, "The Real Cuban Missile Crisis," *Atlantic*, January 2, 2013.

172 250 nuclear warheads: Hersh, *The Dark Side of Camelot*, 343.

172 "communism's first Caribbean base": John F. Kennedy, Democratic dinner speech, Cincinnati, Ohio, October 6, 1960, American Presidency Project, http://www.presidency.ucsb.edu/ws/index.php?pid=25660.

173 "You have to remember that, right from the beginning": McNamara, interview with James G. Blight, May 21, 1987, quoted by Lebow and Stein, *We All Lost the Cold War*, 97.

173 Robert Kennedy offered the Soviet diplomat a simple deal: Details of the offer are in the cable that Dobrynin sent Moscow, in Hershberg, "Anatomy of a Controversy."

174 Gulf of Tonkin: Sources include Goulden's classic *Truth Is the First Casualty*; the *Pentagon Papers*, published in 1971; Wells, *War Within*; and Hallin, *"Uncensored War."*

175 "activity in 34-A Operations has increased": Goulden, *Truth Is the First Casualty*, 125.

176 "pull together": Ibid., 136.

177 "numerous thunderstorms": Ibid., 142.

177 "Our destroyers were just shooting at phantom targets": Jeff Cohen and Norman Solomon, "30-Year Anniversary: Tonkin Gulf Lie Launched Vietnam War," Fairness and Accuracy in Reporting, July 27, 1994, http://fair.org/media-beat-column/30-year-anniversary-tonkin-gulf-lie-launched-vietnam-war/. A year after the Tonkin incident, Stockdale, a Medal of Honor winner, was shot down in a mission over Vietnam; he was held prisoner for more than seven years.

177 "If I had fired, it would have blown it": Goulden, *Truth Is the First Casualty*, 147.

178 Johnson ordered the drafting of a target list for retaliatory raids: "LBJ Tapes on Gulf of Tonkin Incident," National Security Archive, http://www2.gwu.edu/~nsarchiv/NSAEBB/NSAEBB132/tapes.htm.

178 "Review of action makes many reported contacts and torpedoes fired appear doubtful": Goulden, *Truth Is the First Casualty*, 152.

178 "I wish the hell we had more information": Ibid., 151.

178 "The latest dope . . . what went on": McNamara, *In Retrospect*, 134.

178 "It may be just as well": Porter, *Perils of Dominance*, 199.

178 At 4:49 P.M. Washington time: Sheehan, Smith, Kenworthy, and Butterfield, *Pentagon Papers*, 262.

178 "A second deliberate attack . . . two others were damaged": *New York Times,* "Statement by Pentagon," August 4, 1964.

179 "The night glowed eerily": *Time,* "Nation: Action in Tonkin Gulf," August 14, 1964.

179 "I couldn't believe it, the way they blew that story out of proportion": Goulden, *Truth Is the First Casualty,* 158.

179 "unprovoked attack": Pentagon press statement, August 2, 1964; Goulden, *Truth Is the First Casualty,* 23.

179 "attacks were unprovoked": President Johnson, remarks at Syracuse University on the communist challenge in Southeast Asia, August 5, 1964, American Presidency Project, http://www.presidency.ucsb.edu /ws/?pid=26419.

179 "deliberate attack": Arnold H. Lubasch, "Reds Driven Off: Two Torpedo Vessels Believed Sunk in Gulf of Tonkin," *New York Times,* August 5, 1964. The other two front-page stories about Tonkin in the *Times* that day were Tom Wicker, "Stevenson to Appeal for Action by U.N. on 'Open Aggression,'" and Jack Raymond, "2 Carriers Used: McNamara Reports on Aerial Strikes and Reinforcements."

179 "American Planes Hit North Vietnam": Murrey Marder, "American Planes Hit North Vietnam After 2nd Attack on Our Destroyers; Move Taken to Halt New Aggression," *Washington Post,* August 5, 1964.

180 August 8 analysis by . . . *Le Monde*: Jean Planchais, "Les Circonstances du Second Combat Naval Demeurent Impecises," *Le Monde,* August 8, 1964, quoted in Hallin, *The "Uncensored War."*

180 "classic John Wayne image for American behavior": Moïse, *Tonkin Gulf,* 233.

180 "The *Maddox* was operating in international waters": Goulden, *Truth Is the First Casualty,* 59.

180 the *Maddox* was a spy ship: Senator Wayne Morse, Senate Foreign Relations Committee, reported in "Morse Disputes McNamara Testimony on Tonkin Issue," *Rome (Ga.) News-Tribune,* February 23, 1968.

181 interviewed them: Goulden, *Truth Is the First Casualty,* 201.

181 none of the nation's big, influential newspapers . . . did appear in the **Arkansas** Gazette: Ibid., 202.

181 faithful readers included: Ibid.

181 called the hearings: Fulbright reopened the inquiry to demand why the Congress and the people had been "so grossly misled in August 1964": Goulden, *Truth Is the First Casualty,* 210.

181 "appears probable but not certain": McNamara, *In Retrospect,* 128.

181 "I am absolutely positive the second attack": Keith B. Richburg, "Mission to Hanoi: McNamara Asks Ex-Foes to Join in Search for War's Lessons," *Washington Post,* November 11, 1995.

181 "Four years ago this spring the Bush administration": "Buying the War," *Bill Moyers Journal,* PBS, April 25, 2007.

182 at least six faulty stories: Franklin Foer, "The Source of the Trouble," *New York Magazine,* May 21, 2005. Another source: Michael Massing, "Now They Tell Us," *New York Review of Books,* February 26, 2004.

182 Safire wrote twenty-seven: "Buying the War," *Bill Moyers Journal,* PBS, April 25, 2007.

182 "the form of a nearly encyclopedic catalog": Steven Weisman, "Powell, in U.N. Speech, Presents Case to Show Iraq Has Not Disarmed" Threats and Responses: Security Council, *New York Times,* February 6, 2003.

182 "intelligence breakthrough . . . many had expected": Patrick Tyler, "Intelligence Break Led U.S. to Tie Envoy Killing to Iraq Qaeda Cell," Threats and Responses: Terror Network, *New York Times,* February 6, 2003.

183 "vigorously argued": Michael Gordon, "Powell's Trademark: Overwhelm Them," Threats and Responses: News Analysis, *New York Times,* February 6, 2003.

183 *Post* headline: Peter Selvin, "Data on Efforts to Hide Arms Called 'Strong Suit' of Speech" *Washington Post,* February 6, 2003.

183 "It is hard to imagine": *Washington Post,* "Irrefutable," February 6, 2003.

183 "An Old Trooper's Smoking Gun": Peter Hoagland, *Washington Post,* February 6, 2003.

183 "I'm Persuaded": Mary McGrory, *Washington Post,* February 6, 2003.

183 some doubts: Walter Pincus, "U.S. Lacks Specifics on Banned Arms," *Washington Post,* March 16, 2003.

183 "You could see that it was all inferential": Exoo, *Pen and the Sword,* 89.

183 "Despite the Bush administration's claims": Pincus, "U.S. Lacks Specifics on Banned Arms."

183 "The front pages of *The New York Times* . . . make a difference": Massing, "Now They Tell Us."

184 "There was a lot of skepticism . . . stories instead": "Buying the War," *Bill Moyers Journal.*

184 "That was so different from what we were hearing": Ibid.

184 "we now know that Saddam has resumed his efforts": Vice President Cheney, remarks to the Veterans of Foreign Wars 103rd national convention, Nashville, Tennessee, August 26, 2002, White House, Office of the

Press Secretary, http://georgewbush-whitehouse.archives.gov/news/releases
/2002/08/20020826.html.

184 "Quest for A-Bomb Parts": Michael R. Gordon and Judith Miller, "U.S.
Says Hussein Intensifies Quest for A-Bomb Parts," *New York Times,*
September 8, 2002.

184 story to *The New York Times*: Vice President Dick Cheney, interview
with Tim Russert on *Meet the Press,* NBC News, September 8, 2002.

184 "These officials charge that administration hawks": Warren P. Strobel and
Jonathan S. Landay, "Some Administration Officials Expressing Misgiv-
ings on Iraq," *Houston Chronicle,* October 8, 2002.

185 4,486 U.S. soldiers: Paul Post, "Taking Up 4,486 Flags for Slain Soldiers,"
New York Times, May 28, 2012.

185 More than one hundred thousand: Wikipedia entry, "Iraq War," compiled from news reports, NGO, and other reports, https://en.wikipedia
.org/wiki/Iraq_War#Casualty_estimates.

185 war would cost up to $60 billion: Elisabeth Bumiller, "White House Cuts
Estimate of Cost of War with Iraq," Threats and Responses: The Cost,
New York Times, December 31, 2002.

185 U.S. budget figures . . . $567 billion: Anthony H. Cordesman, "The Un-
certain Cost of the Global War on Terror," Center for Strategic and International Studies, August 2007, p. 7, http://csis.org/files/media/csis/pubs
/080907_thecostsofwar.pdf.

185 overall costs . . . to reach $4 trillion to $6 trillion: Ernesto London: "Study:
Iraq, Afghan War Costs to Top $4 Trillion," *Washington Post,* March 28,
2013. The story is based on a study by Harvard public-policy professor
Linda J. Bilmes.

185 "added substantially to the federal debt": Joseph E. Stiglitz and Linda J.
Bilmes, "The True Cost of the Iraq War: $3 Trillion and Beyond," *Wash-
ington Post,* September 5, 2010.

12. The Reckoning

187 "Every gun that is made, every warship launched": President Eisenhower,
"The Chance for Peace" speech, delivered before the American Society
of Newspaper Editors, April 16, 1953, American Presidency Project, http://
www.presidency.ucsb.edu/ws/?pid=9819.

187 "What a deformed monster": Quincy, *Memoir of the Life of Josiah
Quincy,* 412.

187 "A standing Army, however necessary": Samuel Adams letter to James

Warren, January 7, 1776, https://www.milestonedocuments.com/documents/view/samuel-adamss-letter-to-james-warren/explanation.

187 "A standing military force, with an overgrown Executive": James Madison, speech to Constitutional Convention, June 29, 1787, quoted in Steve Coffman, *Words of the Founding Fathers* (Jefferson, N.C.: McFarland & Company), 163.

188 "It was no demobilization, it was a rout": Cray, *General of the Army*, 628.

188 military had peaked at 3.6 million . . . 1.4 million: Department of Defense.

188 United States spends about as much: Winslow Wheeler, "The Military Imbalance: How the U.S. Outspends the World," *Breaking Defense*, March 16, 2012.

188 United States now spends more on its armed forces than during the Cold War: See Department of Defense Budgets for 1948–2015, p. 23–25.

188 most expensive Cold War year was 1985: Ibid.

188 $604.2 billion for 2013: Ibid.

188 "With the Iraq war over and troops coming home": "Reality Sets In," Editorial Board, *New York Times*, November 9, 2013.

189 Hagel revealed plans to shrink: Thom Cooper and Helene Shanker, "Pentagon Plans to Shrink Army to Pre–World War II Level," *New York Times*, February 23, 2014.

189 "You have to always keep your institutions prepared": Ibid.

189 "It's dead on arrival": Susan Ferrechio, "Senate Republican Vow to Block Chuck Hagel's Military Cuts," *Washington Examiner*, February 26, 2014.

189 "A force built to fight the Cold War is now battling changes": Mark Thompson, "The War Within the Army," *Time*, November 4, 2013.

190 Buck McKeon's family was also involved in the "defense lobbying game": Austin Wright and Byron Lau, "Buck McKeon Kin Join Defense Lobbying Game," *Politico*, May 24, 2013.

191 "There are some in government . . . driver of the debt": Representative McKeon, opening statement, House Armed Services Committee, October 13, 2011, http://www.gpo.gov/fdsys/pkg/CHRG-112hhrg71447/html/CHRG-112hhrg71447.htm.

191 "the driver of the debt is . . . killing this country": Jill Lepore, "The Force," *New Yorker*, January 28, 2013.

191 United States could save about $50 billion: Stimson Center, *Strategic Agility: Strong National Defense for Today's Global and Fiscal Realities*,

September 2013, http://www.stimson.org/images/uploads/Strategic
_Agility_Report.pdf.

192 "Iraq and Afghanistan have cost us well over a trillion dollars . . . costs of going to war," Senator Al Franken, Senate floor, April 6, 2011, https:// www.franken.senate.gov/?p=news&id=1430.

192 "By tying military action": R. Russell Rumbaugh, "A Tax to Pay for War," *New York Times*, February 10, 2013.

193 Costs of War Project report: http://watson.brown.edu/costsofwar/.

193 Brown University team's recommendations: "Recommendations," *Costs of War*, Brown University–Watson Institute for International Studies, http://costsofwar.org/article/recommendations.

194 "taxing the hell out of everybody": Author interview with Gordon Adams, September 30, 2013.

194 between 5 and 10 percent: Author interview with Adams. Also, David E. Rosenbaum, "Tax Cuts and War Have Seldom Mixed," *New York Times*, March 9, 2003.

194 $686 billion: "Iraq War's Price Tag Nears Vietnam's," Associated Press report on CBS News, July 25, 2008, http://www.cbsnews.com/news/iraq -wars-price-tag-nears-vietnams/. CBS based its report on a Congressional Research Service report.

194 $859 billion: Julian E. Barnes, "Obama Requests $83.4 Billion More for War Spending," *Los Angeles Times*, April 10, 2009.

195 "That bitch of a war is killing the woman I love": Julian E. Zelizer, "The Nation: Guns and Butter; Government Can Run More Than a War," *New York Times*, December 30, 2001.

195 "Historically, the government has built . . . into the war budget": Author interview with Adams.

195 became part of the federal deficit: Joseph E. Stiglitz and Linda J. Bilmes, "The True Cost of the Iraq War," *Washington Post*, September 5, 2010.

195 Iraq and Afghanistan Wars . . . are the most expensive: Linda J. Bilmes, *The Financial Legacy of Iraq and Afghanistan: How Wartime Spending Decisions Will Constrain Future National Security Budgets*, Harvard Kennedy School of Government Faculty Research Working Paper Series 13-006, March 2013, p. 1.

195 "The largest portion of that bill is yet to be paid . . . far into the future": Ibid., p.1.

196 "Every gun that is made, every warship launched . . . housed more than eight thousand people": President Eisenhower, "The Chance for Peace" speech, delivered before the American Society of Newspaper Editors,

April 16, 1953, American Presidency Project, http://www.presidency.ucsb
.edu/ws/?pid=9819.

197 1.3 million troops to help: Brazinsky, *Nation Building in South Korea,* 26.

197 "guard against the acquisition": President Eisenhower, Farewell Address,
January 17, 1961, Eisenhower Presidential Library, http://www.eisenhower
.archives.gov/research/online_documents/farewell_address/1961
_01_17_Press_Release.pdf .

197 "the conjunction of a large and permanent military establishment": President Eisenhower, draft of Farewell Address, Eisenhower Presidential
Library, http://www.eisenhower.archives.gov/research/online_documents
/farewell_address/Typescript_Speech_Draft.pdf.

197 "As early as 1959, he began working": "Fifty Years Later, We're Still Ignoring Ike's Warning," *Washington Post,* January 16, 2011.

197 "old soldier": Peter Lisagor, "Ike Ready to Give Up Reins: Packs Mementoes, Leaves Warning," *Chicago Daily News,* January 18, 1961.

199 "staggeringly in excess of those required . . . central to the American
identity": Bacevich, *Washington Rules,* 13.

199 "I didn't become the chairman of the Joint Chiefs to oversee": Martin
Dempsey, testimony before the House Armed Services Committee,
October 13, 2011, http://www.defense.gov/transcripts/transcript.aspx
?transcriptid=4905.

199 "from a dollar-and-cents perspective": Peter Pace, testimony before the
House Armed Services Committee, September 8, 2011, http://www.gpo
.gov/fdsys/pkg/CPRT-112HPRT71102/html/CPRT-112HPRT71102.htm.

199 "Only an alert and knowledgeable citizenry": President Eisenhower,
Farewell Address, January 17, 1961.

201 as much as $6 trillion: Bilmes, *The Financial Legacy of Iraq and Afghanistan.*

201 "All of the costs of these wars": "Recommendations," *Costs of War,* Brown
University–Watson Institute for International Studies, http://costsofwar
.org/article/recommendations.

201 "the U.S. government's arguments": Ibid.

Epilogue

202 "Naturally, the common people don't want war": Gilbert, *Nuremberg
Diary,* 278.

204 "Naturally, the common people don't want war . . . works the same way
in any country": Ibid.

206 rate at which wounded soldiers die has reached a wartime low: C. J.

Chivers, "In Wider War in Afghanistan, Survival Rate of Wounded Rises," *New York Times,* January 7, 2011.

206 fatality rate among servicemen and servicewomen in Iraq and Afghanistan: Brad Knickerbocker, "In Iraq, Fewer Killed, More Are Wounded," *Christian Science Monitor,* August 29, 2006.

207 "ration of combat-zone deaths": Ibid.

207 deaths of forty veterans: Scott Bronstein and Drew Griffin, "A Fatal Wait: Veterans Languish and Die on a VA Hospital's Secret List," CNN, April 23, 2014, http://www.cnn.com/2014/04/23/health/veterans-dying-health -care-delays/.

207 "I think we ought to have a draft . . . unrepresentative of the population": Josh Rogin, "McChrystal: Time to Bring Back the Draft," *Foreign Policy,* July 3, 2012, quoting General Stanley McChrystal at the Aspen Ideas Festival, June 29, 2012, http://foreignpolicy.com/2012/07/03/mcchrystal-time -to-bring-back-the-draft/.

208 "best way to reconnect . . . we could turn our backs": Thomas E. Ricks, "It's Time to Toss the All-Volunteer Military," *Washington Post,* April 19, 2012.

208 Ricks wrote that a retired general . . . had been a draft: Ibid.

208 Ricks has suggested . . . no mortgage guarantees: Thomas E. Ricks, "Let's Draft Our Kids," *New York Times,* July 9, 2012.

208 "Those who want minimal government can have it": Ibid.

208 "Relying on a small number of volunteers": Bacevich, *Limits of Power,* 155.

209 "Let's do away with the secret military": Rachel Maddow, *Drift,* 249.

210 "The United States should not conduct a long-term killing program": Stimson Center, *Recommendations and Report of the Task Force on US Drone Policy,* April 2015, second edition, p. 43, http://www.stimson.org /images/uploads/research-pdfs/recommendations_and_report_of_the _task_force_on_us_drone_policy_second_edition.pdf.

210 nine countries had 17,300 nuclear weapons . . . 16,200: Estimates by the Ploughshares Fund. See table on p. 125 for a breakdown, based on 2014 reports. As of mid-2015, the total for the world had decreased to about 16,000, Ploughshares said.

210 "Unless urgent new actions are taken": George P. Schultz, William J. Perry, Henry A. Kissinger, and Sam Nunn, "A World Free of Nuclear Weapons," *Wall Street Journal,* January 4, 2007.

211 "We've got to spend time in the shadows": Vice President Dick Cheney,

interview with Tim Russert on *Meet the Press,* NBC News, September 16, 2001.

212 "the military simply filled a vacuum": Priest, *Mission,* 14.

213 "revelation of widespread secret surveillance": *The 2014 Pulitzer Prize Winners: Public Service,* http://www.pulitzer.org/citation/2014-Public-Service.

214 "Auditing the Pentagon is critically important": Senator Tom Coburn, "Why We Must Audit the Pentagon," *Washington Examiner,* August 18, 2012.

214 "rent-a-general": Bryan Bender, "From the Pentagon to the Private Sector," *Boston Globe,* December 26, 2010.

214 "It is a dangerous deluding statement": Retired Army colonel Douglas Macgregor, panelist at Cato Institute forum, "Can the Pentagon Be Fixed?," March 13, 2009, http://www.cato.org/events/can-pentagon -be-fixed.

BIBLIOGRAPHY

Abramoff, Jack. *Capitol Punishment: The Hard Truth About Washington Corruption from America's Most Notorious Lobbyist.* Washington, D.C.: WND Books, 2011.

Adams, Gordon. *The Iron Triangle: The Politics of Defense Contracting.* New York: Council on Economic Priorities, 1981.

Adams, Gordon, and Cindy Williams. *Buying National Security: How America Plans and Pays for Its Global Role and Safety at Home.* New York: Routledge, 2010.

Allyn, Bruce J., James G. Blight, and David A. Welch, eds. *Back to the Brink: Proceedings of the Moscow Conference on the Cuban Missile Crisis, January 27–28, 1989.* Lanham, Md.: University Press of America, 1992.

Alter, Jonathan. *The Promise: President Obama, Year One.* New York: Simon & Schuster, 2010.

Alterman, Eric. *When Presidents Lie.* New York: Penguin, 2004.

Bacevich, Andrew J. *The Limits of Power: The End of American Exceptionalism.* New York: Henry Holt, 2008.

———. *The New American Militarism: How Americans Are Seduced by War.* New York: Oxford University Press, 2005.

———. *Washington Rules: America's Path to Permanent War.* New York: Henry Holt, 2010.

Baker, Peter. *Days of Fire: Bush and Cheney in the White House.* Garden City, N.Y.: Doubleday, 2013.

Benjamin, Daniel, and Steven Simon. *The Age of Sacred Terror.* Edinburgh, Scotland: Floris Books, 2002.

Bird, Kai. *The Color of Truth: McGeorge Bundy and William Bundy, Brothers in Arms.* New York: Simon & Schuster, 1998.

Branch, Taylor. *Parting the Waters.* New York: Simon & Schuster, 1988.

Brazinsky, Gregg. *Nation Building* in *South Korea.* Chapel Hill: University of North Carolina Press, 2007.

Bush, George W. *Decision Points.* New York: Crown, 2010.

Butler, Smedley D. *War Is a Racket.* London: Aziloth Books, 2011.

Cray, Ed. *General of the Army: George C. Marshall, Soldier and Statesman.* New York: Cooper Square Press, 2010.

Eddy, William. *FDR Meets Ibn Saud.* New York: American Friends of the Middle East, 1954.

Exoo, Calvin F. *The Pen and the Sword: Press, War, and Terror in the 21st Century.* Thousand Oaks, Calif.: Sage Publications, 2010.

FitzGerald, Frances. *Way Out There in the Blue: Reagan, Star Wars and the End of the Cold War.* New York: Simon & Schuster, 2000.

Flenniken, Kathleen. *Plume.* Seattle: University of Washington Press, 2012.

Friedman, Alan. *The Spider's Web: The Secret History of How the White House Illegally Armed Iraq.* New York: Bantam Books, 1993.

Garthoff, Raymond. *A Journey through the Cold War.* Washington, D.C.: Brookings Institution Press, 2001.

Gilbert, G. M. *Nuremberg Diary.* New York: Farrar, Straus, 1947.

Goulden, Joseph C. *Truth Is the First Casualty: The Gulf of Tonkin Affair— Illusion and Reality.* New York: Rand McNally, 1969.

Goyette, Charles. *Red and Blue and Broke All Over: Restoring America's Free Economy.* New York: Penguin Group, 2012.

Graham, Katharine. *Personal History.* New York: Alfred A. Knopf, 1997.

Hallin, Daniel. *The "Uncensored War": The Media and Vietnam.* Oakland: University of California Press, 1989.

Helms, Richard. *A Look over My Shoulder: A Life in the Central Intelligence Agency.* New York: Presidio Press, 2004.

Hersh, Seymour M. *The Dark Side of Camelot.* Boston: Little, Brown, 1997.

Hilsman, Roger. *The Cuban Missile Crisis: The Struggle over Policy.* Santa Barbara, Calif.: Praeger, 1996.

Hilty, James. *Robert Kennedy: Brother Protector.* Philadelphia: Temple University Press, 2000.

Hoffman, David E. *The Dead Hand: The Untold Story of the Cold War Arms Race and Its Dangerous Legacy.* New York: Doubleday, 2009.

Johnson, Chalmers. *Nemesis: The Last Days of the American Republic.* New York: Henry Holt, 2007.

———. *The Sorrows of Empire: Militarism, Secrecy and the End of the Republic.* New York: Henry Holt, 2004.

Kennedy, Paul. *The Rise and Fall of the Great Powers.* New York: Random House, 1987.

Kennedy, Robert F. *Thirteen Days.* Foreword by Arthur Schlesinger, Jr. New York: Norton, 1999.

Lebow, Richard Ned, and Janice Gross Stein. *We All Lost the Cold War.* Princeton, N.J.: Princeton University Press, 1994.

MacArthur, John R. *Second Front: Censorship and Propaganda in the Gulf War.* Berkeley: University of California Press, 1992.

Maddow, Rachel. *Drift: The Unmooring of American Military Power.* New York: Crown Publishing, 2012.

Mandelbaum, Michael. *The Frugal Superpower: America's Global Leadership in a Cash-Strapped Era.* New York: PublicAffairs, 2010.

Mann, James. *Rise of the Vulcans: The History of Bush's War Cabinet.* New York: Penguin Books, 2004.

Mazzetti, Mark. *The Way of the Knife: The CIA, a Secret Army and a War at the Ends of the Earth.* New York: Penguin Books, 2013.

McNamara, Robert. *In Retrospect: The Tragedy and Lessons of Vietnam.* New York: Random House, 1995.

Moïse, Edwin E. *Tonkin Gulf and the Escalation of the Vietnam War.* Chapel Hill: University of North Carolina Press, 1996.

Nash, Philip. *The Other Missiles of October: Eisenhower, Kennedy, and the Jupiters, 1957–1963.* Chapel Hill: University of North Carolina Press, 1997.

Oberdorfer, Don. *Tet: The Story of a Battle and Its Historic Aftermath.* New York: Doubleday, 1971.

O'Neill, Paul. *The Price of Loyalty.* New York: Simon & Schuster, 2004.

Perret, Geoffrey. *Eisenhower.* New York: Random House, 1999.

Phillips, Kevin. *American Dynasty: Aristocracy, Fortune, and the Politics of Deceit in the House of Bush.* New York: Penguin Group, 2004.

Porter, Gareth. *Perils of Dominance: Imbalance of Power and the Road to War in Vietnam.* Berkeley: University of California Press, 2005.

Preble, Christopher A. *The Power Problem: How American Military Dominance Makes Us Less Safe, Less Prosperous, and Less Free.* New York: Cornell University Press, 2009.

Priest, Dana. *The Mission: Waging War and Keeping Peace with America's Military*. New York: W. W. Norton, 2004.

Quincy, Josiah. *Memoir of the Life of Josiah Quincy*. Charleston, S.C.: Biblio-Life, 2009.

Rampton, Sheldon, and John Stauber. *Trust Us, We're Experts*. New York: Penguin, 2000.

Reeves, Richard. *President Kennedy: Profile of Power*. New York: Simon & Schuster, 1993.

Rhodes, Richard. *Arsenals of Folly: The Making of the Nuclear Arms Race*. New York: Alfred A. Knopf, 2007.

Risse-Kappen, Thomas. *Cooperation among Democracies*. Princeton, N.J.: Princeton University Press, 1995.

Robin, Corey. *The Reactionary Mind: Conservatism from Edmund Burke to Sarah Palin*. Oxford: Oxford University Press, 2012.

Sanger, David E. *The Inheritance: The World Obama Confronts and the Challenges to American Power*. New York: Harmony Books, 2009.

Schlesinger, Arthur, Jr. *A Thousand Days: John F. Kennedy in the White House*. Houghton-Mifflin, 1965.

———. Foreword to *Thirteen Days: A Memoir of the Cuban Missile Crisis*, by Robert F. Kennedy. New York: W. W. Norton, 1999.

Schram, Martin. *The Great American Video Game*. New York: William Morrow, 1987.

Sheehan, Neil, and Hedrick Smith, E. W. Kenworthy, and Fox Butterfield. *The Pentagon Papers*. New York: Bantam, 1971.

Smith, Hedrick. *The Power Game: How Washington Works*. New York: Random House, 1988.

Smith, Jean Edward. *Eisenhower: In War and Peace*. New York: Random House, 2012.

Solomon, Norman. *War Made Easy: How Presidents and Pundits Keep Spinning Us to Death*. Hoboken, N.J.: John Wiley & Sons, 2005.

Suskind, Ron. *The Price of Loyalty: George W. Bush, the White House, and the Education of Paul O'Neill*. New York: Simon & Schuster, 2004.

Thomas, Evan. *The Very Best Men: The Daring Early Years of the CIA*. New York: Simon & Schuster, 1995.

Weiner, Tim. *Legacy of Ashes: The History of the CIA*. New York: Doubleday, 2007.

Wells, Tom. *The War Within: America's Battle over Vietnam*. Berkeley: University of California Press, 1994.

Wessel, David. *Red Ink: Inside the High-Stakes Politics of the Federal Budget*. New York: Crown, 2012.

Wheeler, Winslow T. *The Pentagon Labyrinth: 10 Short Essays to Help You Through It*. Washington, D.C.: Center for Defense Information, 2011.

Wills, Garry. *Bomb Power: The Modern Presidency and the National Security State*. New York: Penguin Group, 2010.

Woodward, Bob: *The Commanders: The Pentagon and the First Gulf War, 1989–1991*. New York: Simon & Schuster, 1991.

———. *Obama's Wars*. New York: Simon & Schuster, 2010.

———. *Plan of Attack: The Definitive Account of the Decision to Invade Iraq*. New York: Simon & Schuster, 2004.

———. *State of Denial: Bush at War*. New York: Simon & Schuster, 2007.

Yant, Martin. *Desert Mirage: The True Story of the Gulf War*. New York: Prometheus Books, 1991.